Trackside in East

WITH THE PLANT FAMILY

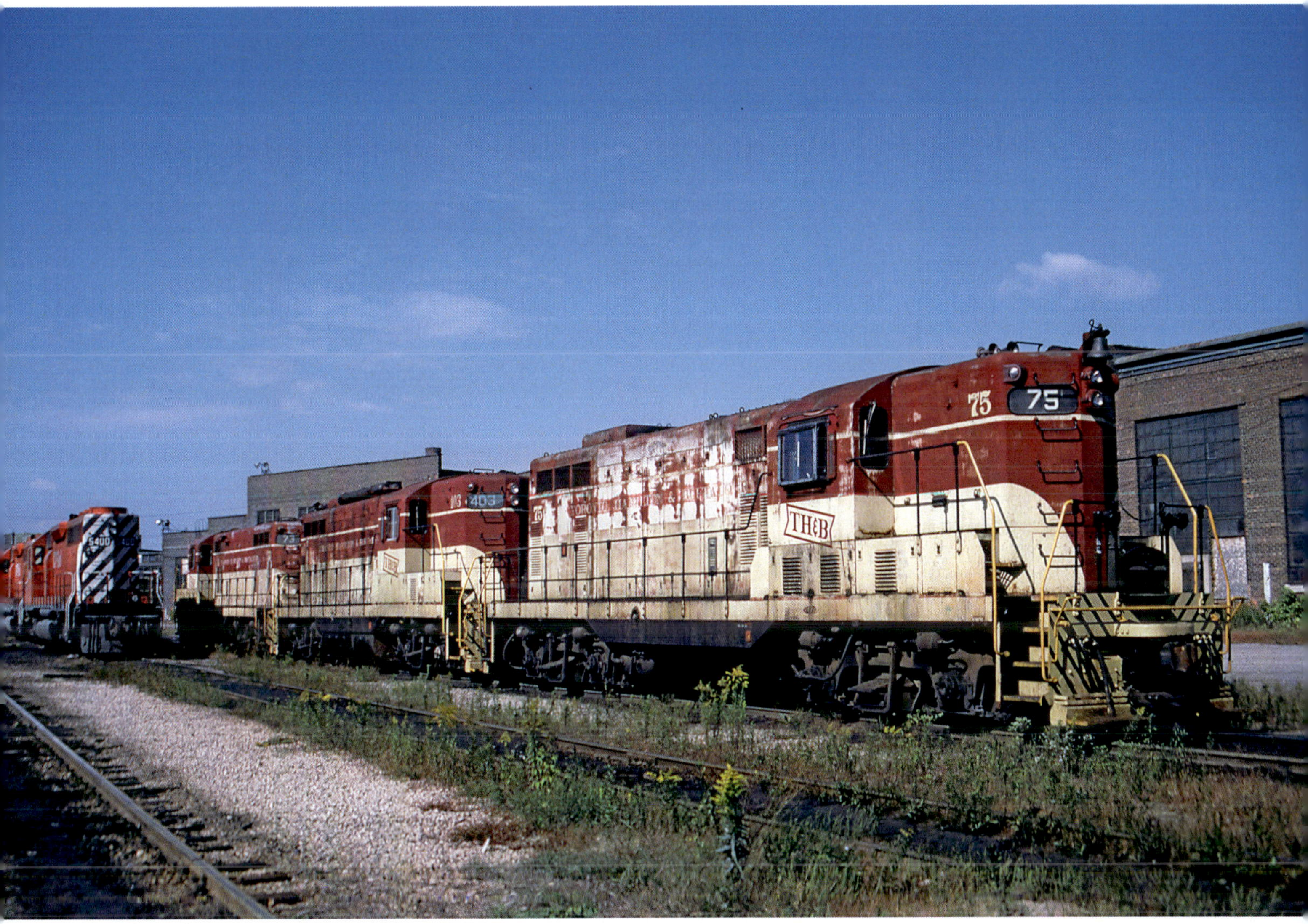

JEREMY F. PLANT, JEFFREY G. PLANT, AND BRIAN D. PLANT

The GARBELY PUBLISHING Company
EST. 2012

FRONT COVER, TOP LEFT: See page 39. *(JC)*

FRONT COVER, TOP RIGHT: See page 18. *(JGP)*

FRONT COVER, MIDDLE: See page 71. *(JGP)*

FRONT COVER, BOTTOM LEFT: See page 22. *(JC)*

FRONT COVER, BOTTOM RIGHT: See page 26. *(BDP)*

TITLE PAGE: See page 64. *(JGP)*

REAR COVER: See page 30. *(BDP)*

The Garbely Publishing Company's books may be purchased for educational, business, or sales promotional use. For information, address The Garbely Publishing Company, 146 Hillside Drive, Dingmans Ferry, PA 18328 or email info@garbelypublishing.com.

Visit The Garbely Publishing Company's website at www.garbelypublishing.com.

First edition, published June 2026.

Designed by The Garbely Publishing Company.
Printed in Totowa, New Jersey by Lightning Press.

ISBN: 979-8-9946504-0-0

Contents

Introduction

Eastern Canada: The Maritimes, Quebec, and Ontario. A vast and varied expanse, from the Maritime provinces to western Ontario and from the densely populated southern regions of Ontario and Quebec to the lakes and forests and mining regions of the Canadian Shield to the north. Growing up in upstate New York, Canada was near enough to beckon the Plant family rail photographers (brothers Jeffrey and Jeremy, and Jeremy's son Brian) to explore over five decades, from 1970 to the 2020s. The lure of Canada was also in their heritage, with Quebecois ancestors on both the paternal and maternal sides of the brothers and reinforced by Brian's maternal ties to Nova Scotia.

For a rail photographer in 1970, eastern Canada offered a wide range of attractions. Alco cab units, nearing extinction in the U.S., were still operating on both the Canadian National and Canadian Pacific lines. A variety of Alco switchers and road-switchers could be found on both major Canadian railways and on smaller regional lines. The most heavily trafficked main lines of both CN and CP were close to the U.S., making long weekend trips possible from the Plant family homes in upstate New York. Since the CN and CP competed in most of the major markets, it was easy to plan trips to photograph both roads in many locations.

Eastern Canada also was home to many interesting regional and short line railways that required longer and more distant travel. The vast Canadian Shield (also called the Laurentian Plateau) to the north of the more populated south was being tapped for its wealth of minerals and forest products. Railways such as the Cartier, Roberval & Saguenay, Chemin de Fer Arnaud, and Quebec, North Shore & Labrador in northeast Quebec, as well as Ontario Northland and Algoma Central in north-central Ontario, offered a wide range of scenery, operations, and motive power. The Maritimes provided interesting railway operations in the distinct coastal setting of Nova Scotia and New Brunswick and an opportunity to mix rail photography with family vacations.

Beginning in 1970 and continuing into the 1980s, one of the Plant brothers' favorite trips was to a triangle of locations in eastern Ontario: Brockville and Gananoque on the Canadian National and Smiths Falls on the Canadian Pacific. Other favored locations close to the U.S. included the bridges over the Ottawa River at Vaudreuil-Dorion, Quebec and the CP line from Montreal to the border with Maine in the Eastern Townships of Quebec.

In June 1976, Jeffrey and Jeremy made a more ambitious trip to the Ontario Northland and Algoma Central, including chasing some CP trains around North Bay, ON and Sault Sainte Marie, ON.

Jeffrey explored the northern parts of the Ontario Northland and Algoma Central in the late 1970s and 1980s. In the summer of 1987, Jeremy joined him and fellow photographer Glen Perry to visit the northern Quebec railways: Cartier Railway, Arnaud Railway, and the Quebec, North Shore & Labrador. On the way back to New York State, they were able to also photograph operations on the Roberval & Saguenay and the CP between Farnham and Megantic, Quebec.

Again accompanied by Glen Perry, Jeffrey, a fan of Alco locomotives, documented the operations of the Cape Breton & Central Nova Scotia in the summer of 1995. This was a year when operations on the former CN line were busy and entirely run with Alco units, at a time when Alcos were becoming extremely rare finds in regular rail service. While the CB&CNS was the major focus of the trip, it yielded additional valuable coverage of the Windsor & Hantsport, CP, and CN in the Maritimes.

The trip to Nova Scotia also provided a curious incident. When Jeff Plant tried to check in to a hotel in Sydney, he was told all the rooms were taken by a Plant Family Reunion – of which he was unaware!

Brian's first exposure to Canadian railroading came in June 2000, when he traveled to northern Quebec along with railfans Doug Koontz and Dave Patch to chronicle operations on the Cartier Railway. They photographed trains on the entire line between the iron mine at the northern end of the line and the southern terminus at Port Cartier at a time when the Cartier was still all-Alco.

Looking back over three decades of photographing trains in the eastern provinces of Canada, we are struck once again by the variety of rail operations, motive power, and scenery we experienced. We hope you enjoy this trip back in time. In this volume, we move from east to west, beginning with the Maritime provinces and moving first to Quebec and then finishing with lines in Ontario.

Abbreviations

AC	Algoma Central Railway
ARND	Arnaud Railway
CBNS	Cape Breton & Central Nova Scotia Railway
CNR	Canadian National Railway
CPR	Canadian Pacific Railway/CP Rail
DAR	Dominion Atlantic Railway
GMDD	General Motors Diesel Division
MLW	Montreal Locomotive Works
MP	Milepost Marker
ONR	Ontario Northland Railway
QNSL	Quebec, North Shore & Labrador Railway
RS	Roberval Saguenay Railway
WHRC	Windsor & Hantsport Railway

Caption Credits

BDP	Brian Plant
JC	Joint Credit, Jeffrey & Jeremy Plant
JFP	Jeremy Plant
JGP	Jeffrey Plant

Acknowledgements

Thanks to the friendly folks who provided valuable information and hospitality at many of the locations covered in this book. We are indebted to the many fine books on Canadian railways that have proved invaluable in researching train operations and equipment. A particular thanks goes to Bill Linley, for his informative books on the Maritimes and eastern Canada. Thanks to friends on Facebook who helped identify locations and train movements. Thanks go out also to Rapido Trains, whose amazing HO models have enabled fans of Canadian railways to replicate many of the scenes in this book. As always, thanks to Rudy Garbely for his support of our work and his wonderful work of layout and production.

About the Authors

Jeremy F. Plant is the author of numerous articles and author or co-author of over 60 illustrated books on railroad subjects.

He began his railroad photography in 1967, and in the ensuing years, he photographed trains in settings across North America, often in the company of his brother Jeffrey and son Brian. Jeremy's photographic career spanned years of great change in the railroad landscape, with first-generation diesels giving way to newer types of locomotives, and mergers leaving many formerly independent roads as "Fallen Flags." He still occasionally ventures trackside, but he ceased active rail photography in 2016.

Jeremy is an Army veteran and retired from a career in academia in 2016. He lives in Hershey, Pennsylvania with his wife of 49 years, Susan Brown Plant, and two orange cats, Henna and Soleil.

Jeffrey G. Plant is the co-author of several books of railroad photography with brother Jeremy. His photography has appeared in numerous other books and articles.

At three years old, his parents took him to Union Station in Troy, New York, then a bustling center of steam passenger activity, which sparked his interest in railroading. Jeffrey began his photographic career in 1967, when he finished law school and moved back to New York's Capital District. This also began a "love affair" with the Delaware & Hudson, his favorite railroad. While working as a labor lawyer in Albany, Jeffrey was able to travel widely in search of trains, including a two-month cross-country trip while on leave from his job.

Jeffrey is retired and living in Colonie, New York.

Brian D. Plant was born on March 3, 1981 in Fairfax County Virginia. A lifelong love of trains was instilled in him from an early age, beginning with trips to Manassas, VA on the Norfolk Southern Railway and CSXT in the Brunswick, Maryland area.

Brian's first trip to Canada was with his father and Uncle Jeff in the Summer of 1991, but was cut short by an unfortunate case of food poisoning. His next trip across the border wouldn't happen again until the Spring of 2000, when he was a freshman at Ithaca College studying cinema and photography.

A career in photography didn't materialize for Brian, but it didn't dampen his pursuit of photography. He has been in the railroad industry for the past fifteen years and is currently a locomotive engineer, as well as a union officer.

Nova Scotia

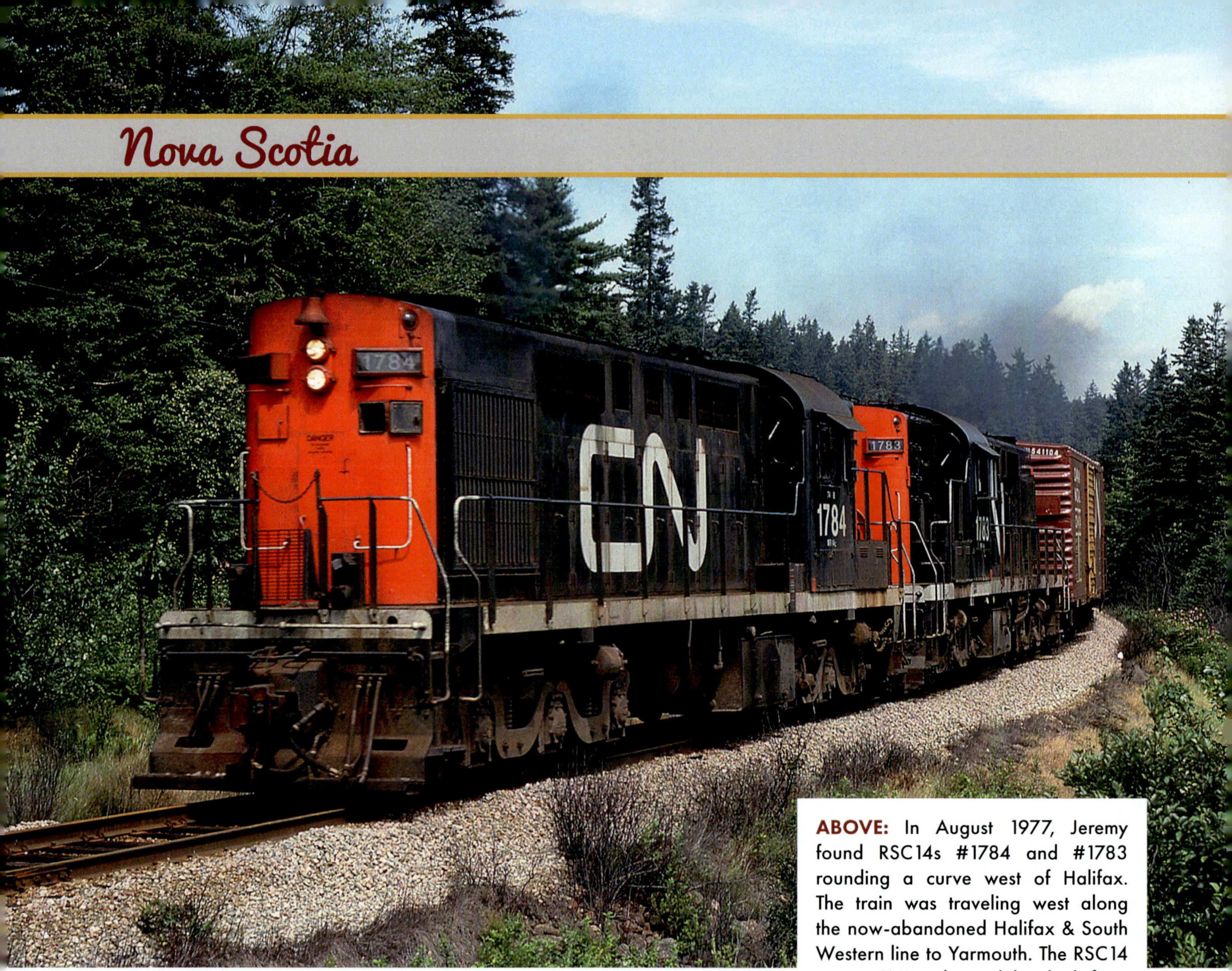

ABOVE: In August 1977, Jeremy found RSC14s #1784 and #1783 rounding a curve west of Halifax. The train was traveling west along the now-abandoned Halifax & South Western line to Yarmouth. The RSC14 was a CNR-only model, rebuilt from RS18s with A-1-A trucks from retired RS13 and RS23 units replacing the RS18's original B-B trucks. The units were also downgraded from 1,800 horsepower to 1,400 horsepower, hence the designation as RSC14. The 38 RSC14s were used almost exclusively in the Maritimes, where the A-1-A trucks enabled them to operate on the light rail of branch lines in Nova Scotia. *(JFP)*

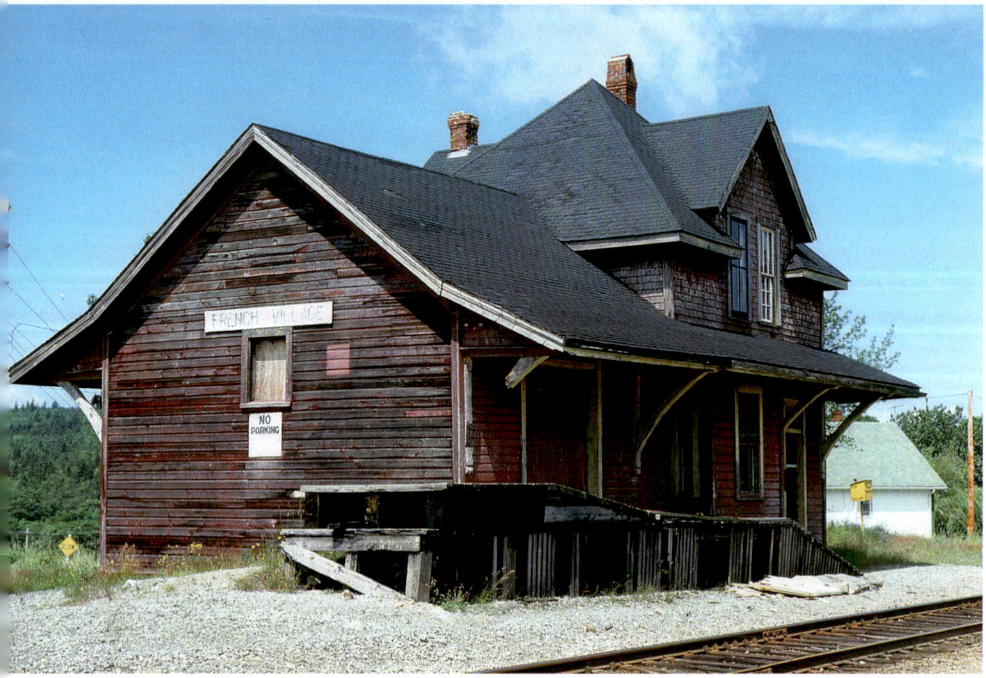

LEFT: The station at French Village, NS was a popular spot for photographers along the CNR's former Halifax & South Western line in southwestern Nova Scotia. Despite its rickety appearance, the station survived to become a café along the bike and hiking trail after the tracks were abandoned. *(JFP)*

Dominion Atlantic Railway

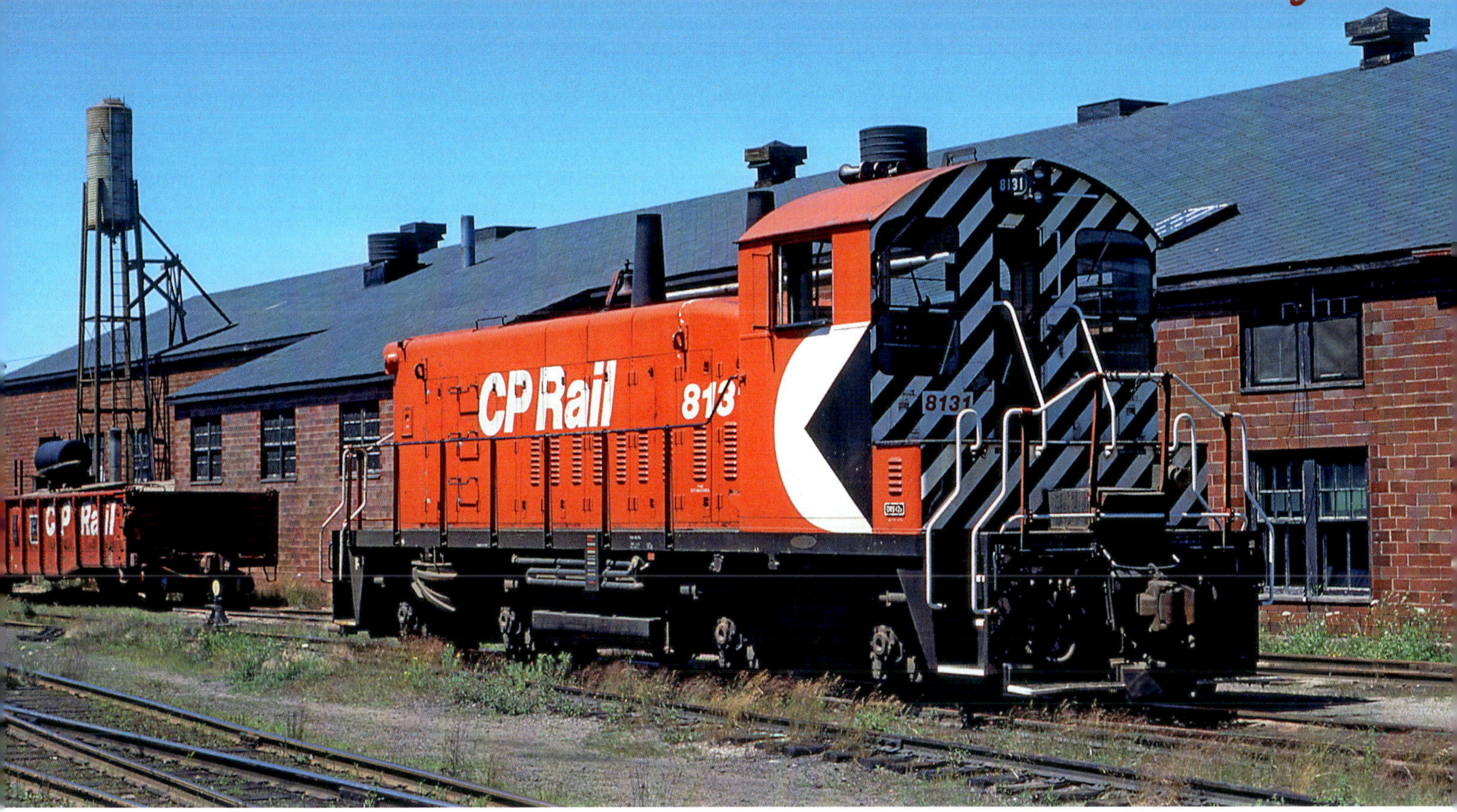

ABOVE: The Dominion Atlantic (reporting marks DAR) was a CPR subsidiary operating in western Nova Scotia. It used CPR-lettered equipment such as SW1200 #8131, resting alongside the facilities at its operational center of Kentville, NS in August 1977. *(JFP)*

BELOW: Eastbound train #2, the *Evangeline*, passed Kentville on its way to Halifax from Yarmouth in August 1977. From Windsor Junction to Halifax, it will finish its trip on CNR tracks. Budd cars like this provided passenger service on the DAR. *(JFP)*

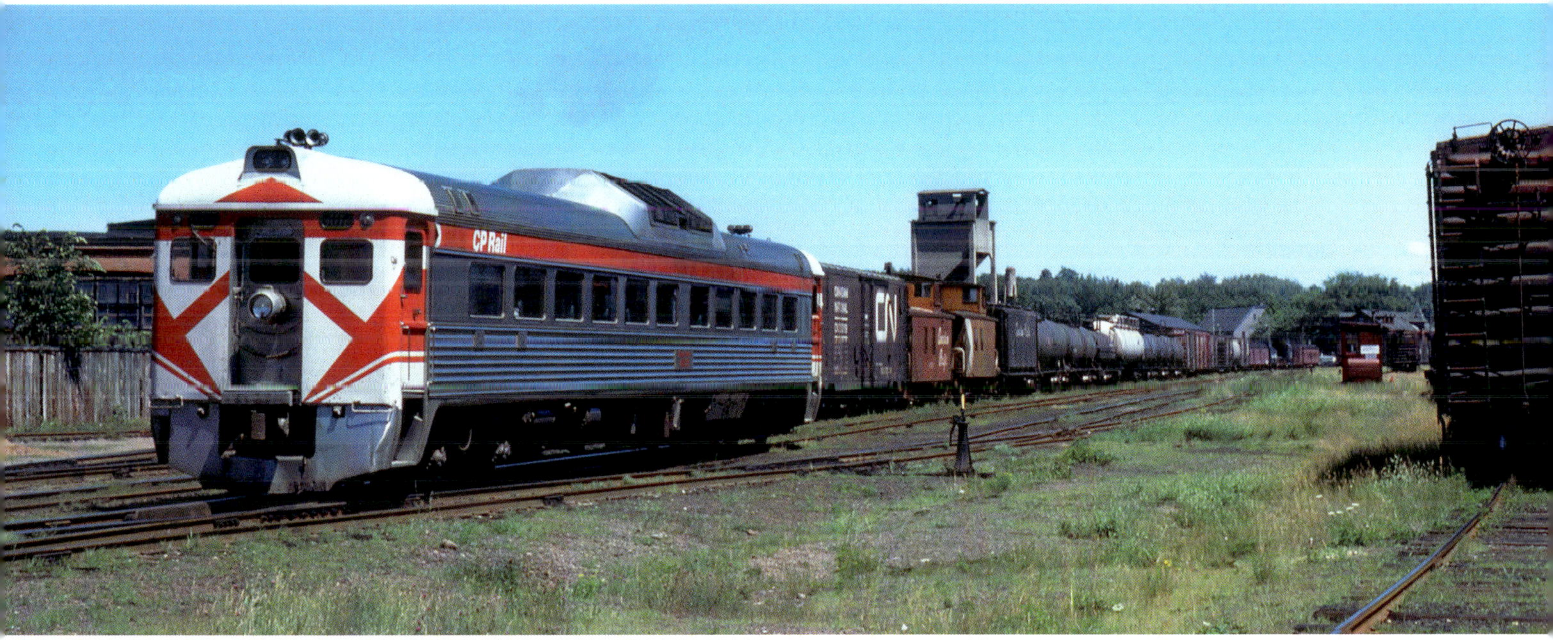

Windsor & Hantsport Railway

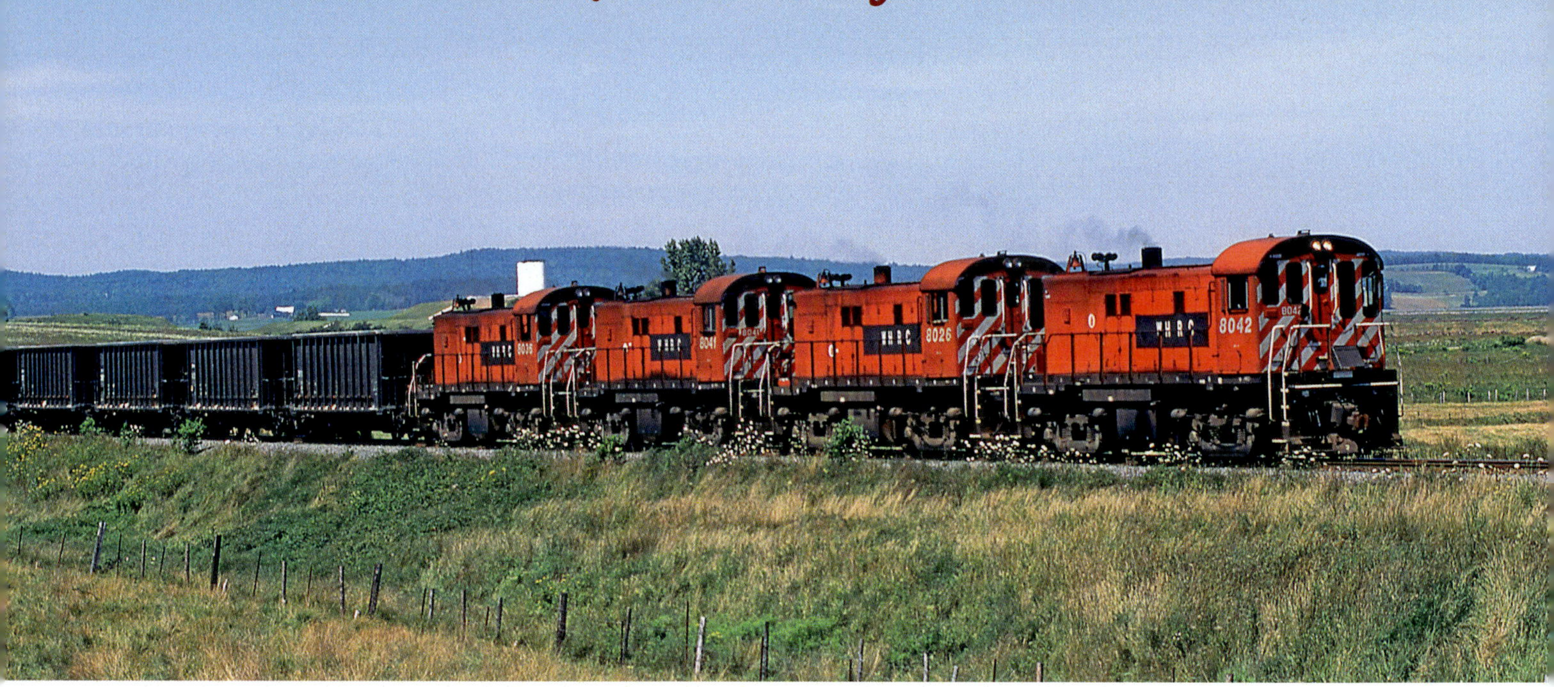

ABOVE & BELOW: The Windsor & Hantsport Railway operated a stretch of former Dominion Atlantic trackage between its namesake communities. It assumed operations in October 1994. It served mostly one purpose: to move loads of gypsum from mines near Windsor to the port of Hantsport on the Avon River estuary, where the mineral was loaded onto ships for movement to manufacturers of wall board. The Windsor & Hantsport operated a fleet of former CPR RS23 locomotives, four of which were moving empty gypsum cars south near Windsor in August 1995. *(JGP)*

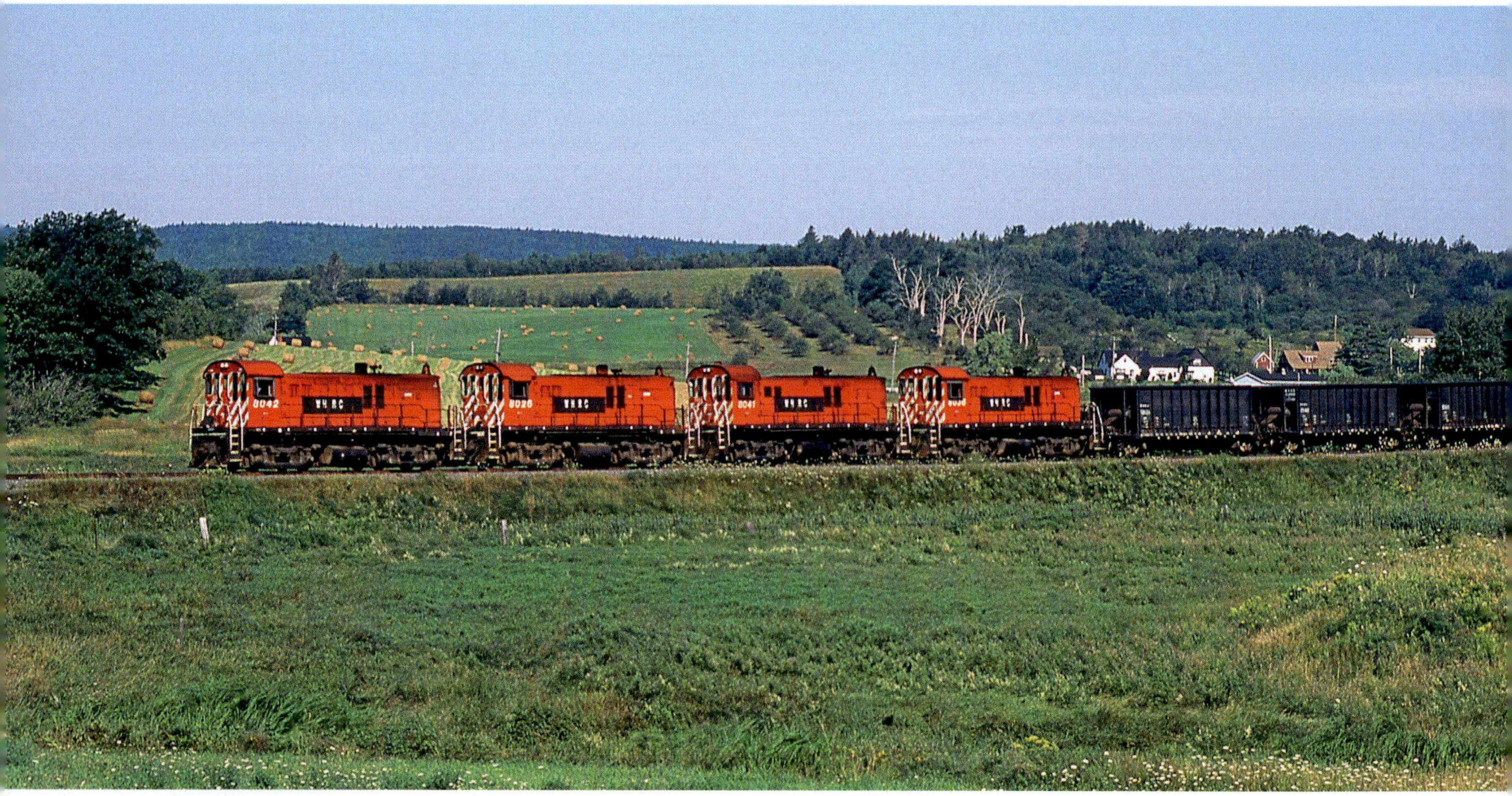

RIGHT: A quartet of RS23s passed through the village of Hantsport on their way back to the gypsum mines in August 1995. Four units was the normal set of power for these trains, with cabs facing eastward. *(JGP)*

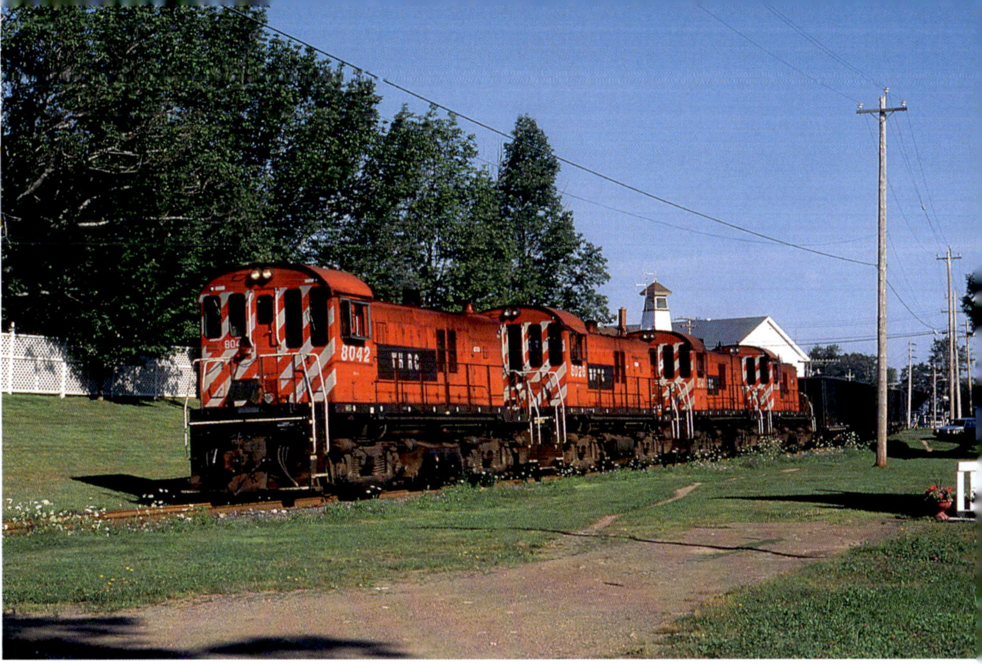

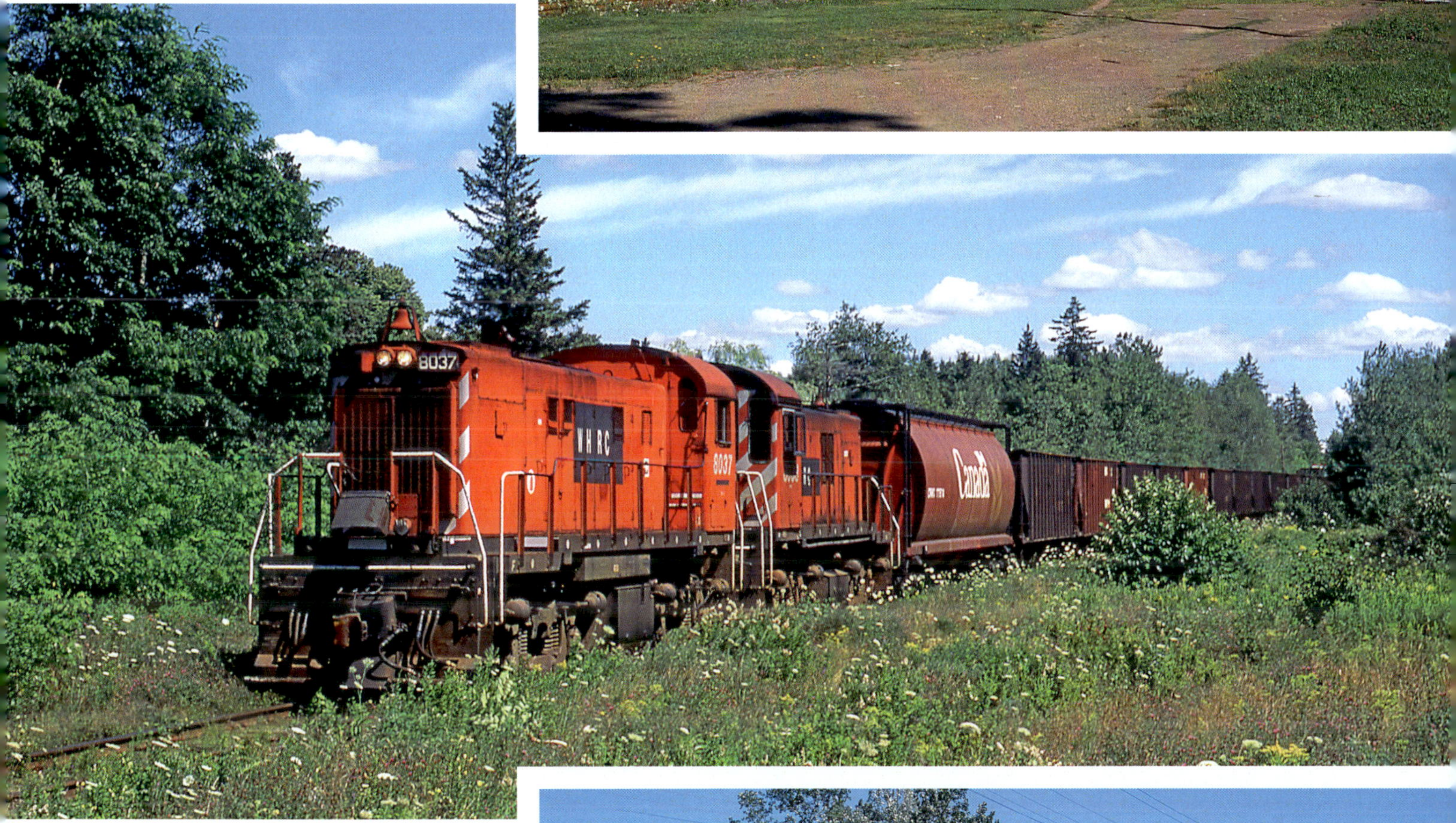

ABOVE: In addition to the gypsum traffic, the WHRC also had a modest business in general freight traffic. A westbound train was heading to Windsor from the CNR connection at Windsor Junction in August 1995 behind a pair of RS23s. The signs of late summer – goldenrod and Queen Anne's Lace – announce the impending change of seasons on this warm and sunny late summer day. *(JGP)*

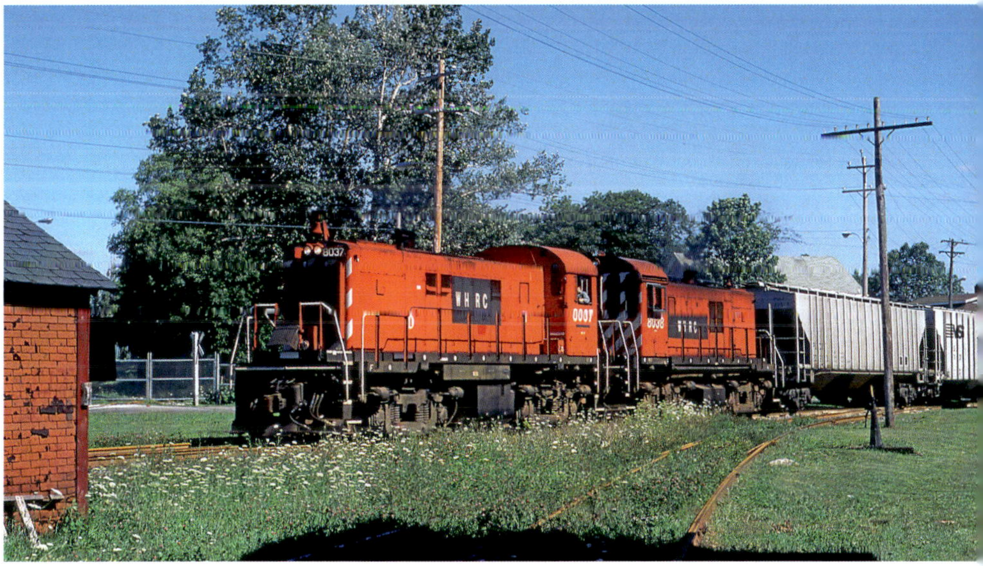

LEFT: A pair of RS23s brought some mixed freight into Hantsport from Windsor in August 1995. *(JGP)*

Bedford

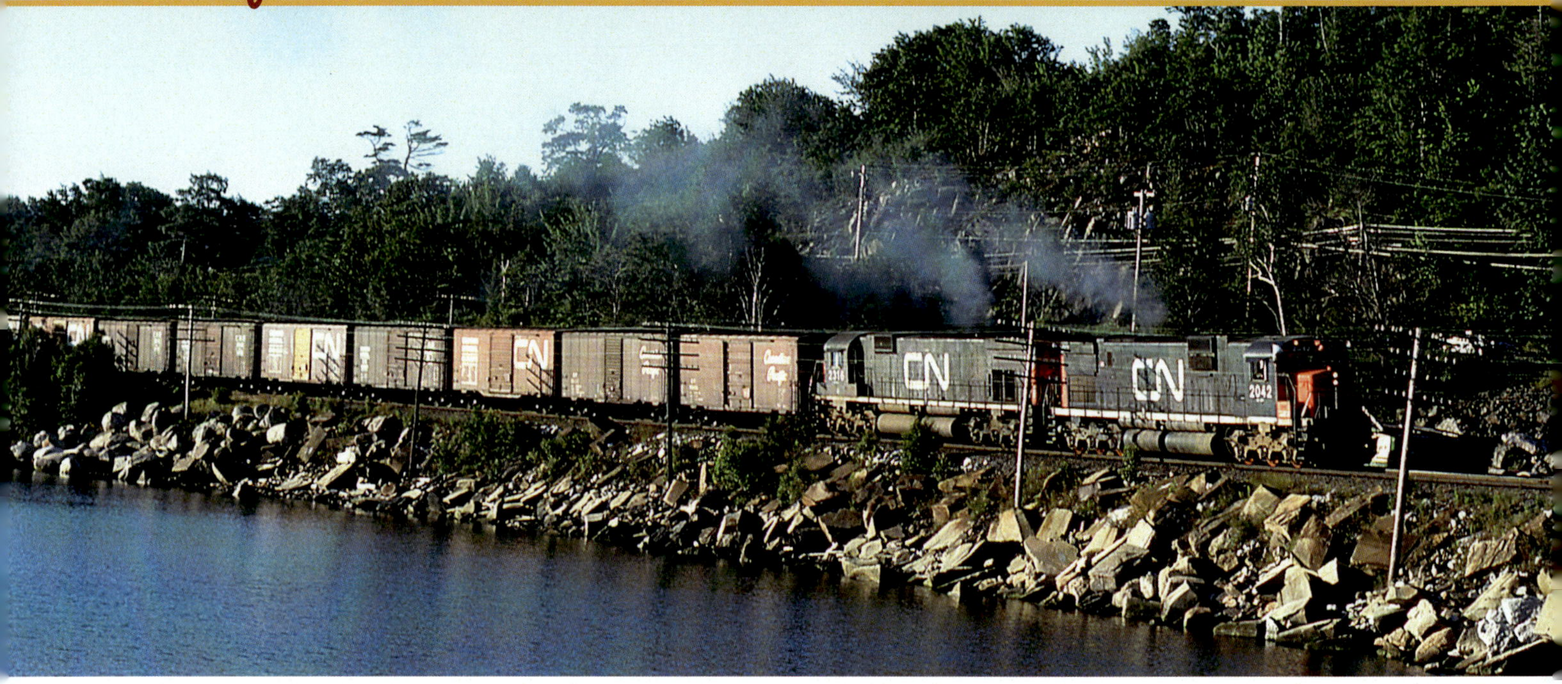

ABOVE: Jeremy picked a Chinese restaurant in Bedford for dinner on an August evening in 1977, partly for the excellent food and partly in hopes of seeing a train along Bedford Basin adjacent to the restaurant parking lot. Sure enough, a westbound CNR freight hugged the blue waters behind a pair of six-axle MLW units, catching the low light as the delightful odors of Chinese cooking filled the evening air. *(JFP)*

BELOW: An eastbound CNR freight with six units waited for clearance into Halifax in August 1977. At this point in time, six-axle MLW units dominated the through freights into and out of Nova Scotia. Nova Scotia was an exception to the usual pattern of both CNR and CPR serving most major markets in Canada. Nova Scotia was primarily CNR territory, with CPR's subsidiary Dominion Atlantic a minor player compared to CNR. *(JFP)*

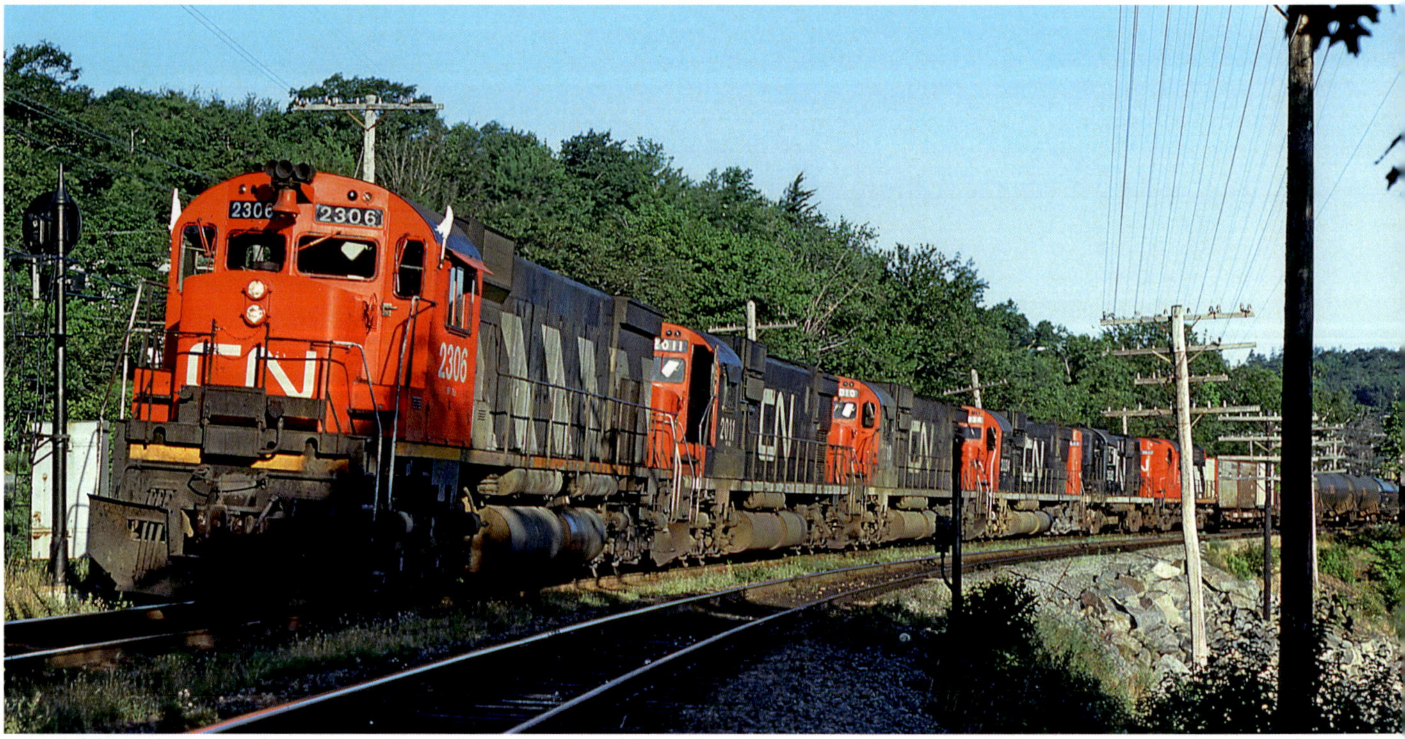

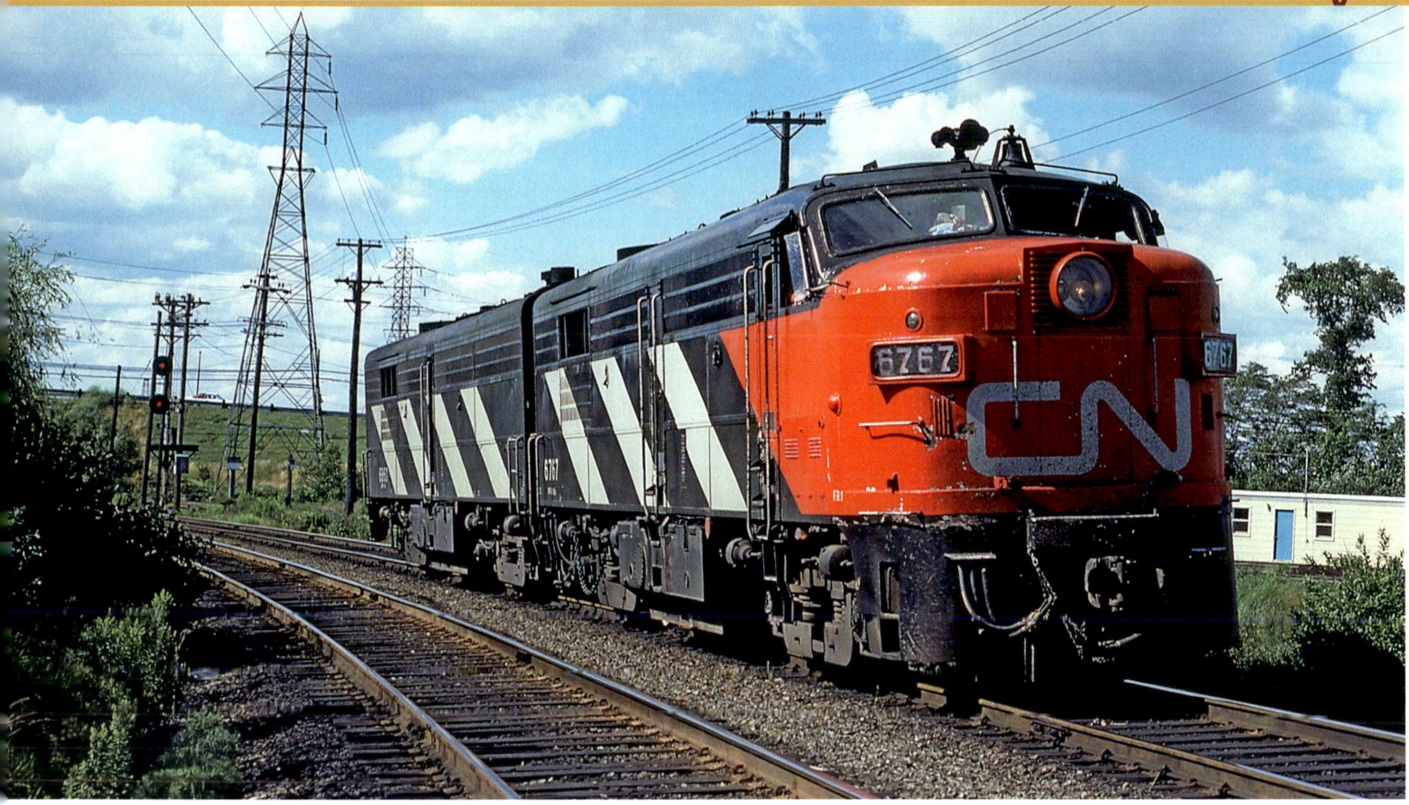

ABOVE: Between 1958 and 1959, CNR acquired 34 FPA-4 and 12 FPB-4 units from Montreal Locomotive Works. These were the last Alco cab units built, only purchased by CNR. Unlike earlier Alco cab units, the FPA-4s were powered by the more modern 251 prime movers and were rated at 1,800 horsepower. An A/B pair arrived at Halifax on the *Ocean* in August 1977 and was backing light to the Fairview engine terminal, showing off their boxy lines and CN markings. *(JFP)*

BELOW: C630m #2001 rested at the Fairview engine terminal outside Halifax in August 1977. The CNR rostered 44 of these 3,000 horsepower units built in 1967 and 1968. They were a common sight on trains to the Maritimes and in gypsum service in Nova Scotia. *(JFP)*

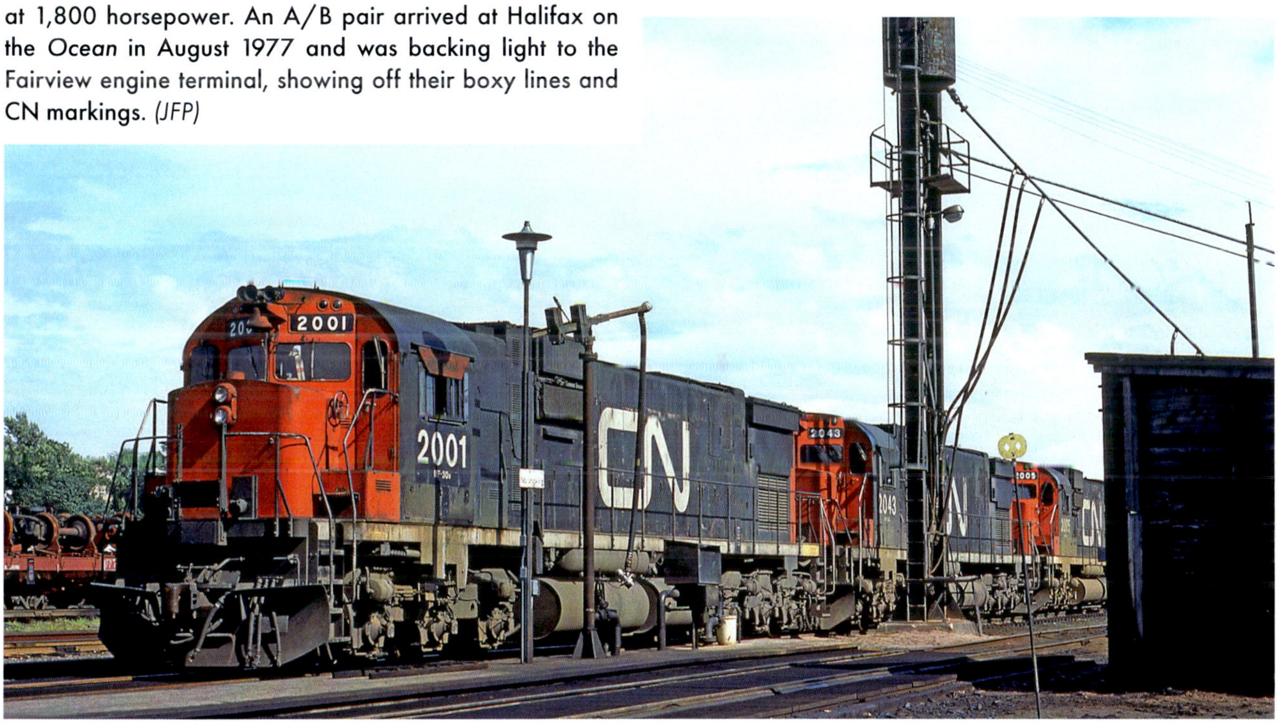

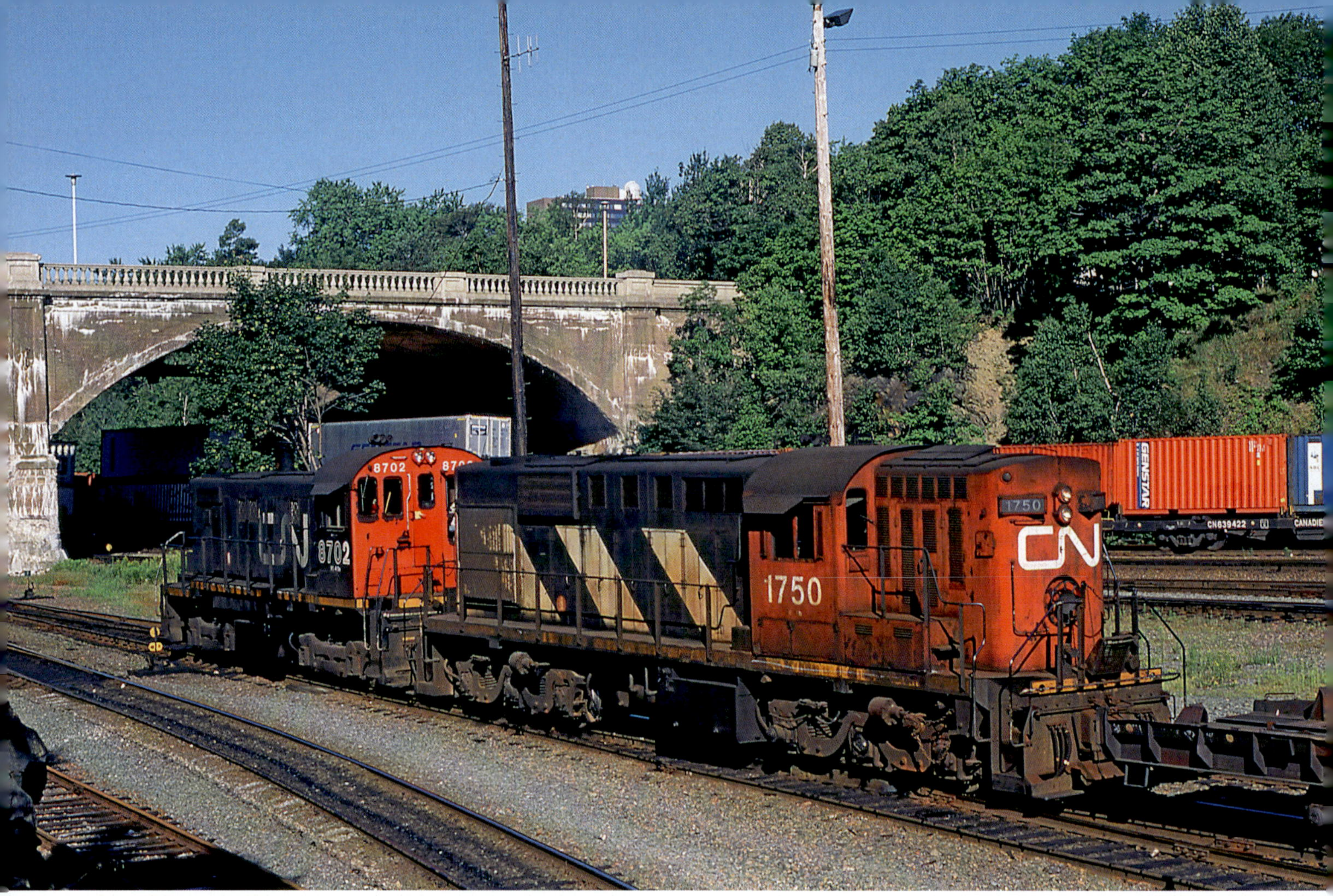

ABOVE AND BELOW: Halifax, the capital of Nova Scotia and its largest city, is one of Canada's major Atlantic Ocean ports (along with its sister city, Dartmouth). RSC14 #1750 and S13u #8702 worked the Ocean Terminal yard at Halifax in August 1995. The #8702 was one of 12 of its type rebuilt in the mid-1980s; all were gone from the CNR roster by 1997. Note the outlined numerals on the cab of #8702. *(JGP)*

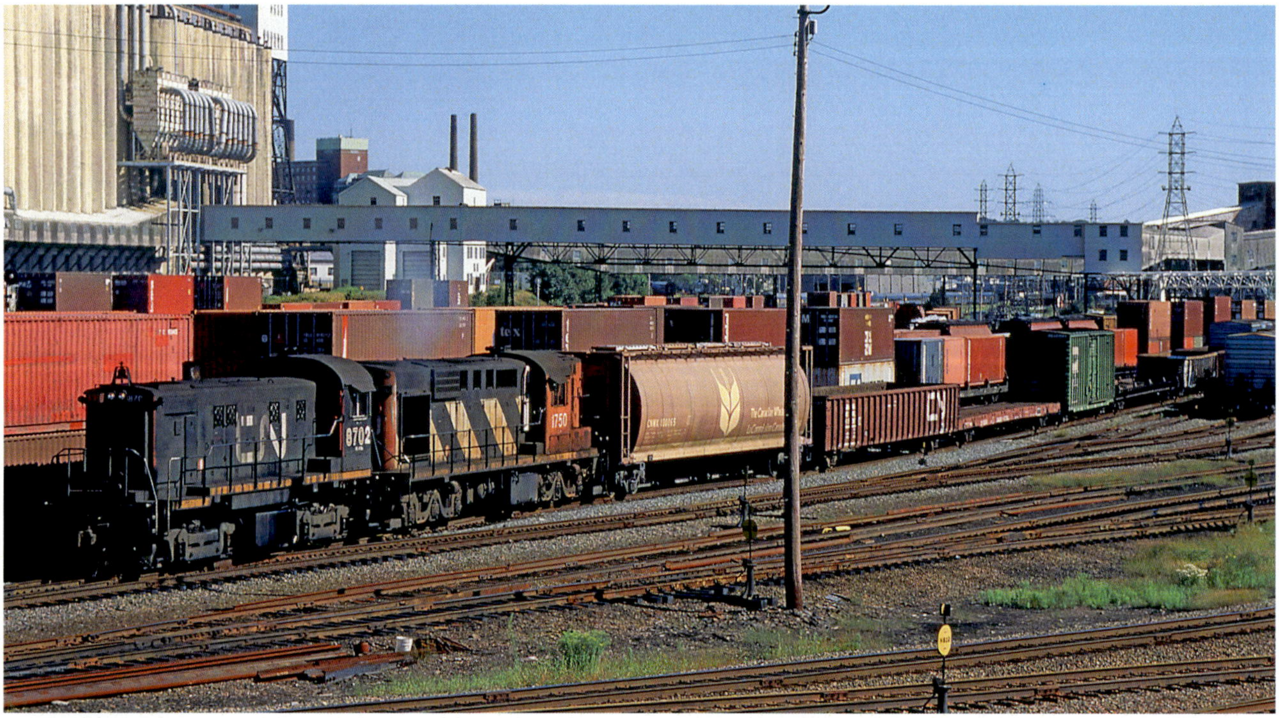

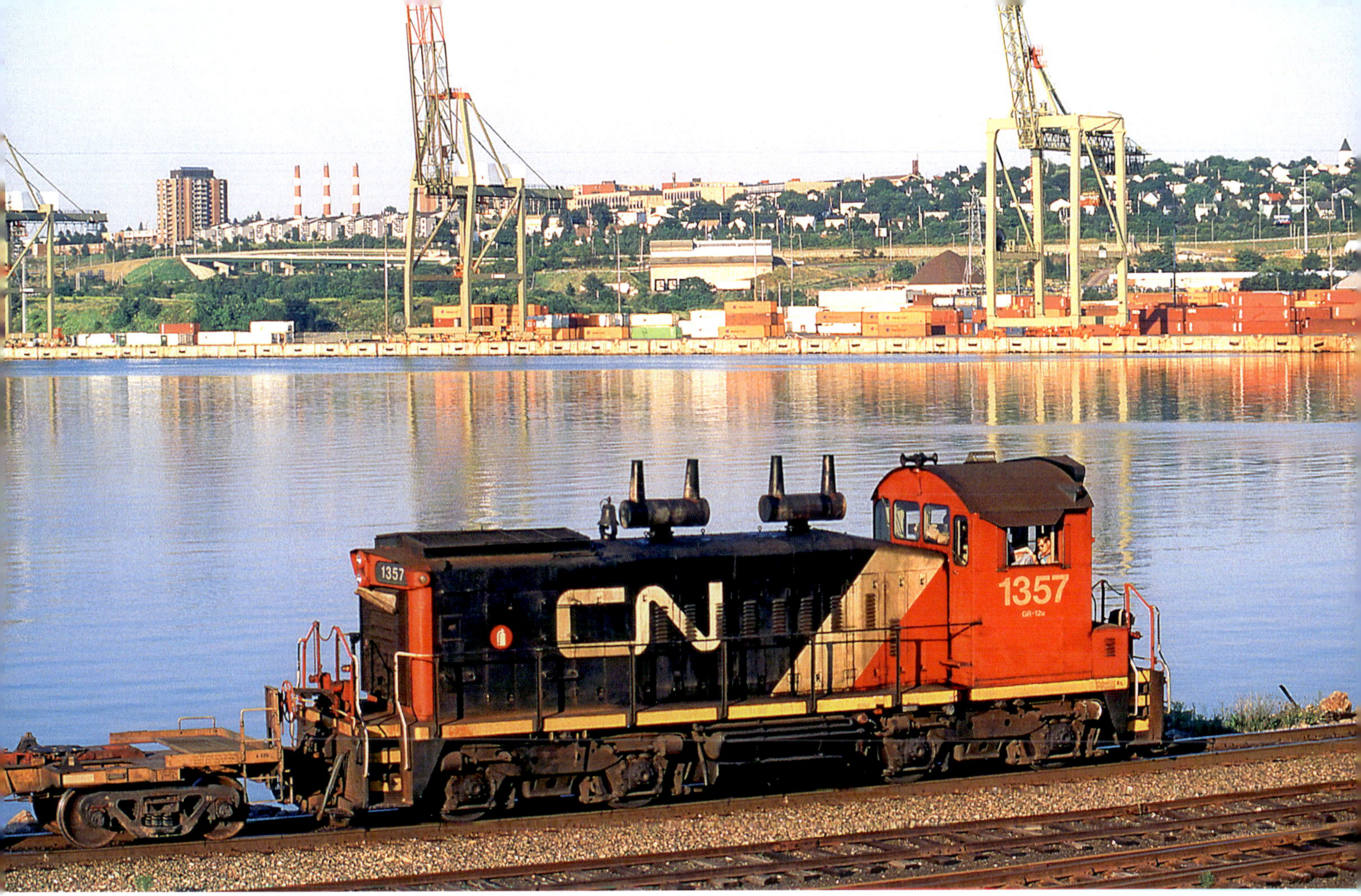

LEFT: Rockingham Yard is adjacent to Halifax Harbor, where CNR SW1200RS #1357 was working in August 1995. The 1,200-horsepower unit was one of 208 of its type employed by CNR. The port and city of Dartmouth are in the background. *(JGP)*

BELOW: In Dartmouth, NS, across the harbor from Halifax, a pair of S13us handled a transfer run in August 1995. The CNR roster included 12 of the type, #8700-#8711, rebuilt by CNR in 1984 from as-delivered S13s. *(JGP)*

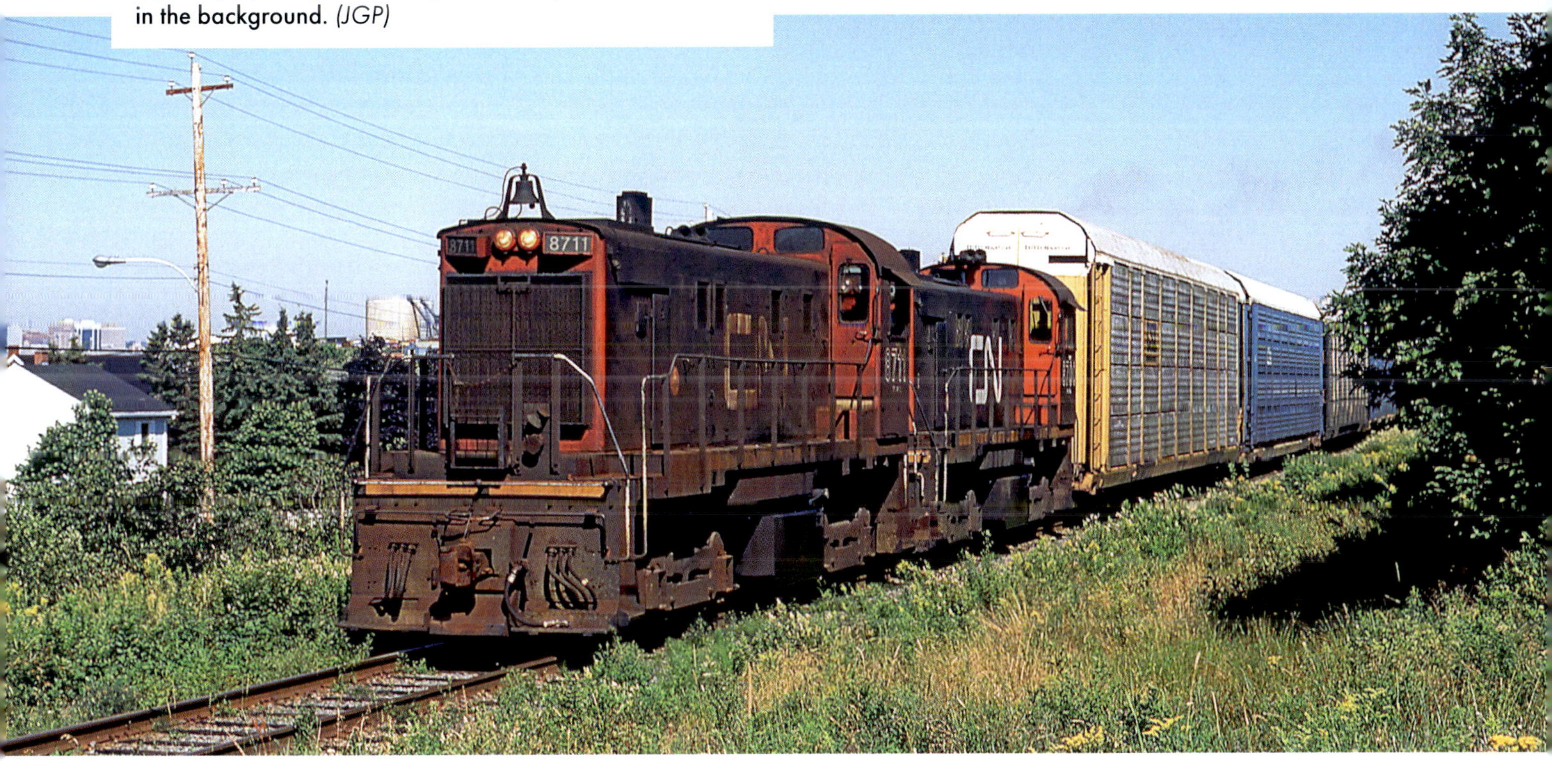

Cape Breton & Central Nova Scotia Railway

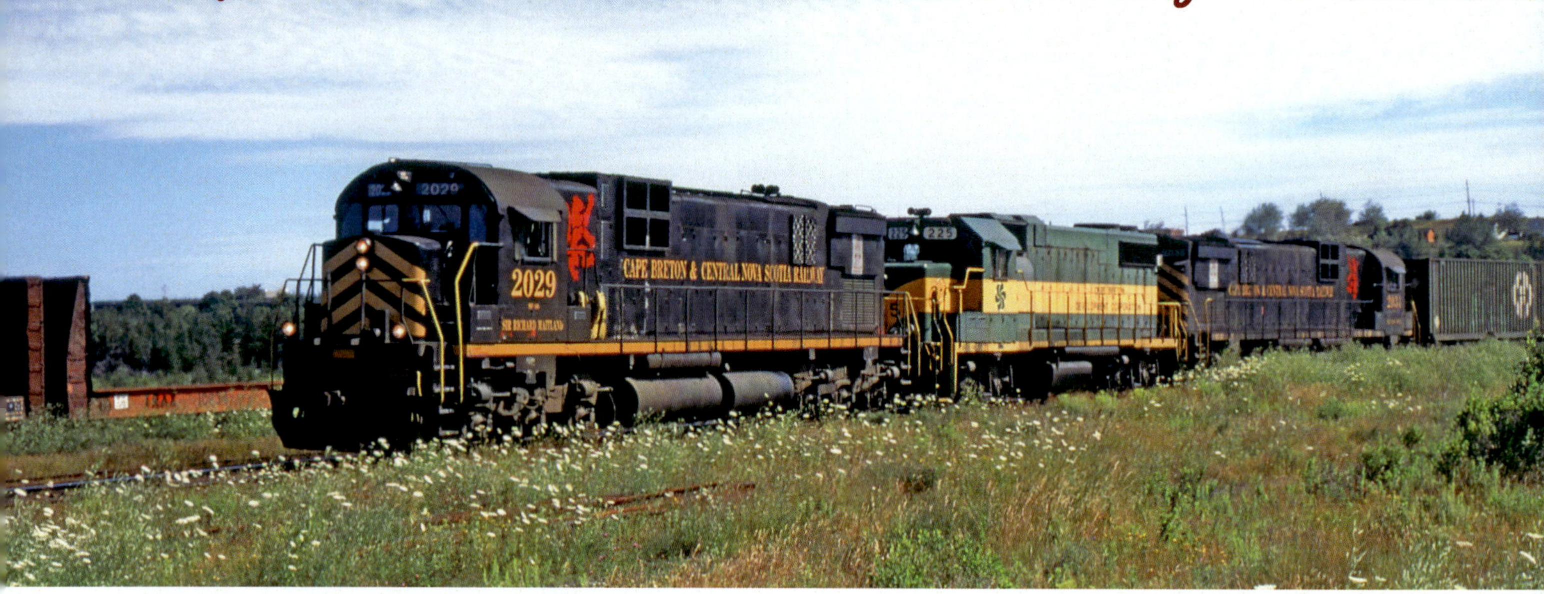

ABOVE: The railfan community was excited to hear about the formation of the Cape Breton & Central Nova Scotia Railway (CBNS) in 1994 and its acquisition of a fleet of former CNR Alco power to operate 245 miles of former CNR trackage from Sydney to Truro in northern Nova Scotia. Jeff Plant and Glen Perry made the wise decision to visit the CBNS in the late summer of 1995, when traffic was still at a high level before the gradual decline and sale of the line to RailAmerica in 2000. Seven C630ms and one M636 provided the road power for the railway, painted in a black and gold scheme with a red lion emblem on the flanks. A pair of C630ms spliced a Devco GP38 on eastbound train #306 at North Sydney, NS in August 1995. The train is moving intermodal cargo to be delivered by ship to Newfoundland, passing a meadow filled with Queen Anne's Lace, a sign of late summer. *(JGP)*

BELOW: Switching was handled by RS18s, like #3842 moving a cut of coal hoppers at Sydney, NS in August 1995. The CBNS named their locomotives for famous individuals; in this case, the #3842 was named after Sir Robert Laird Borden, Canadian Prime Minister during World War I and a native Nova Scotian. *(JGP)*

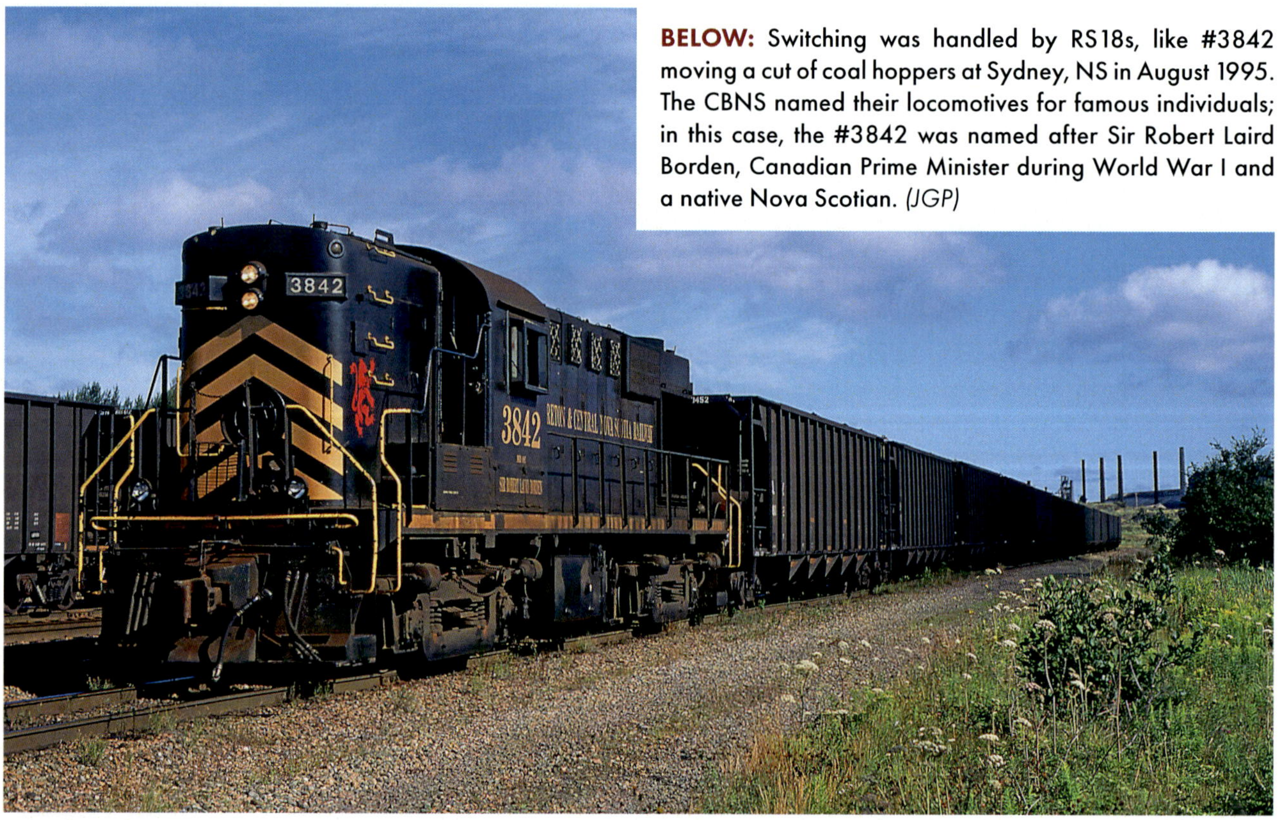

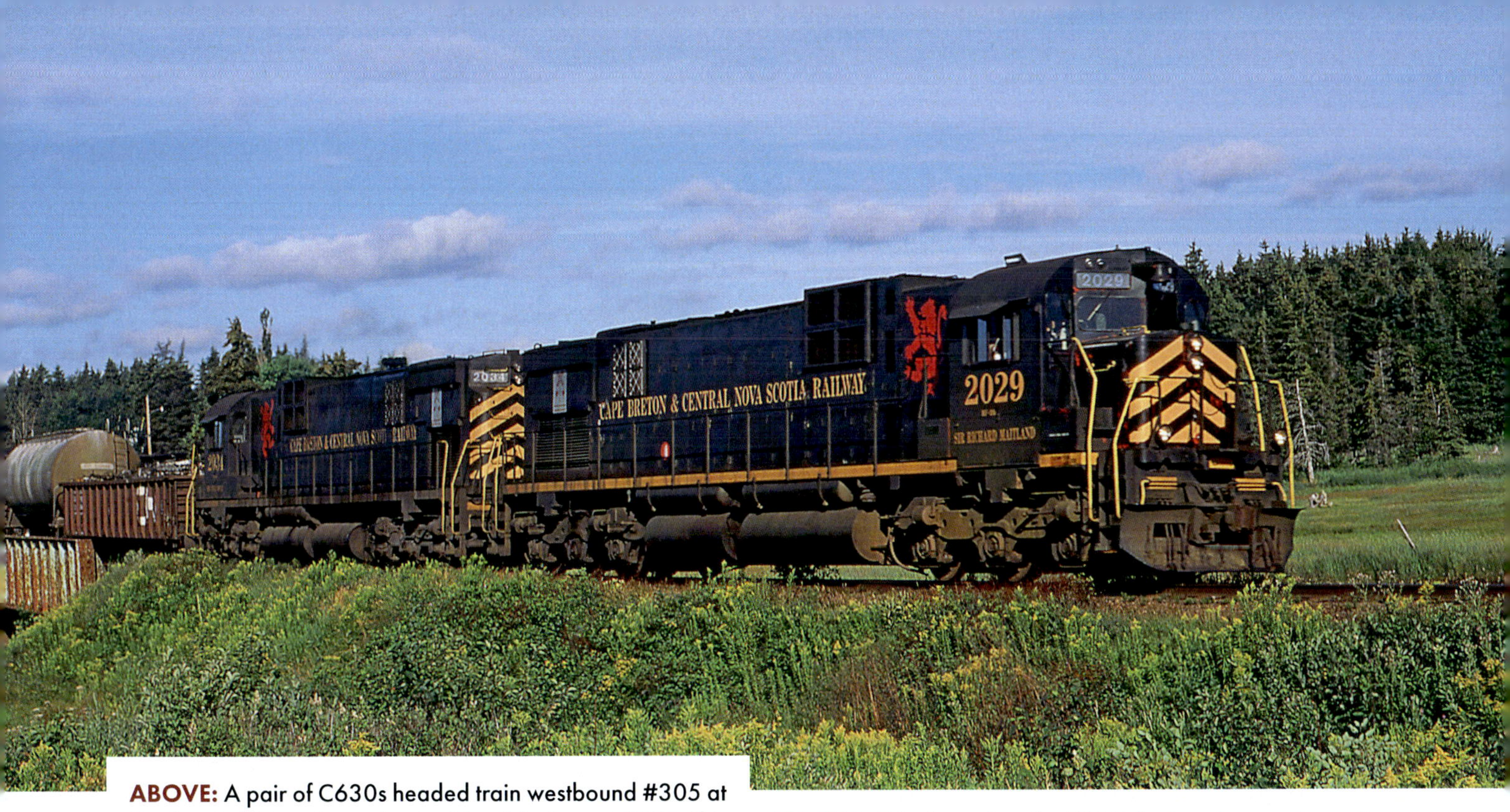

ABOVE: A pair of C630s headed train westbound #305 at Coxheath, NS on Cape Breton Island in August 1995. This train left Sydney in the morning for its all-day trip westward. Lead unit #2029 is named for Sir Richard Maitland, Lord Lethington, a Scottish poet and statesman of the 16th century. Scottish heritage runs deep in Nova Scotia! *(JGP)*

BELOW: Westbound train #305 had a long string of loaded coal cars as it skirted the blue waters of Lake Bras d'Or in August 1995. This huge lake largely bisects Cape Breton Island. It is not a typical fresh-water lake, but rather an estuary with a degree of salinity. *(JGP)*

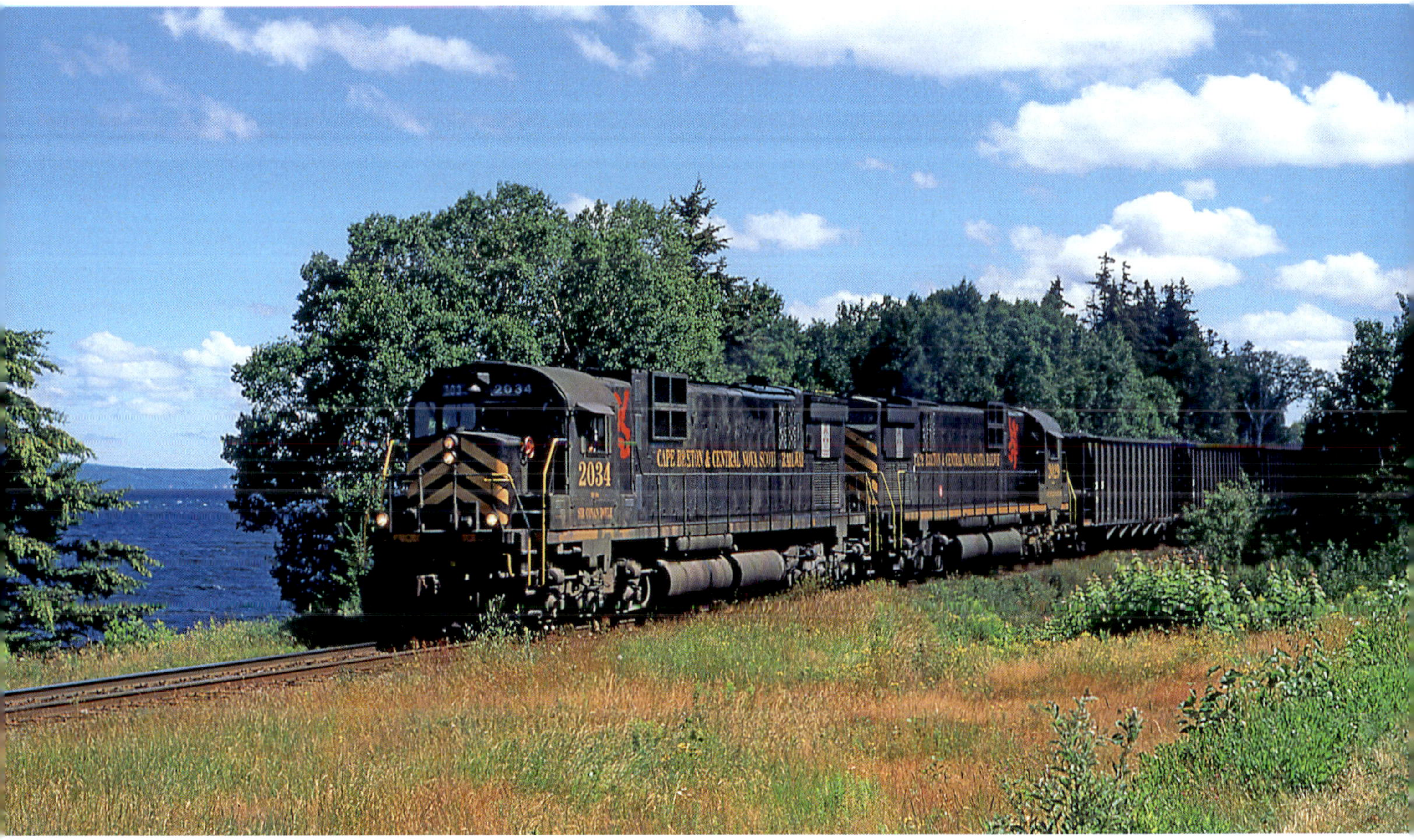

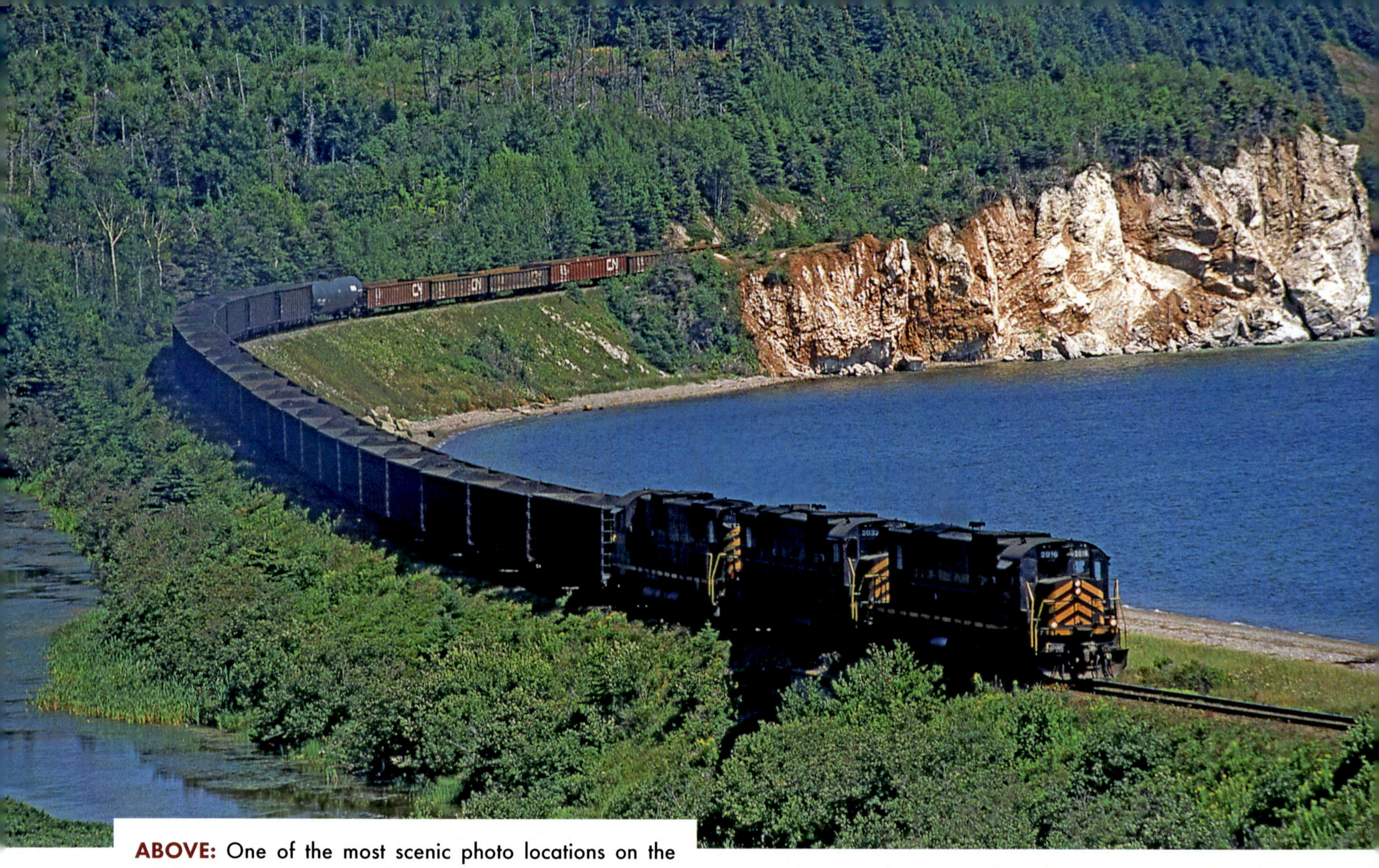

ABOVE: One of the most scenic photo locations on the CBNS is at Iona, on Cape Breton Island, where the railway crosses the Barra Strait. A trio of C630ms led westbound train #305 toward the crossing in August 1995. *(JGP)*

BELOW: Train #305 soared high above the marshland near Estmere, NS, near the western end of Cape Breton Island, in August 1995. *(JGP)*

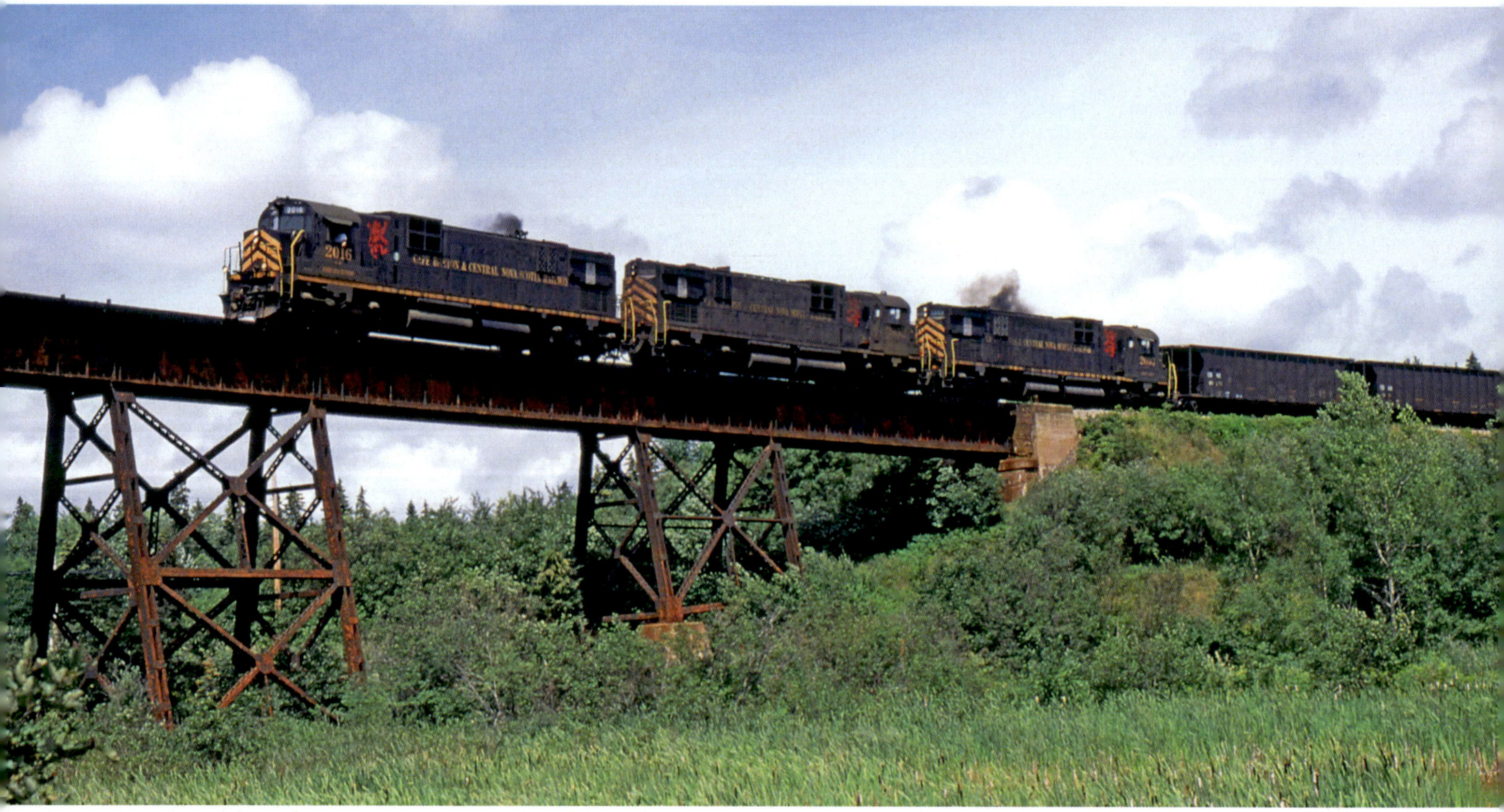

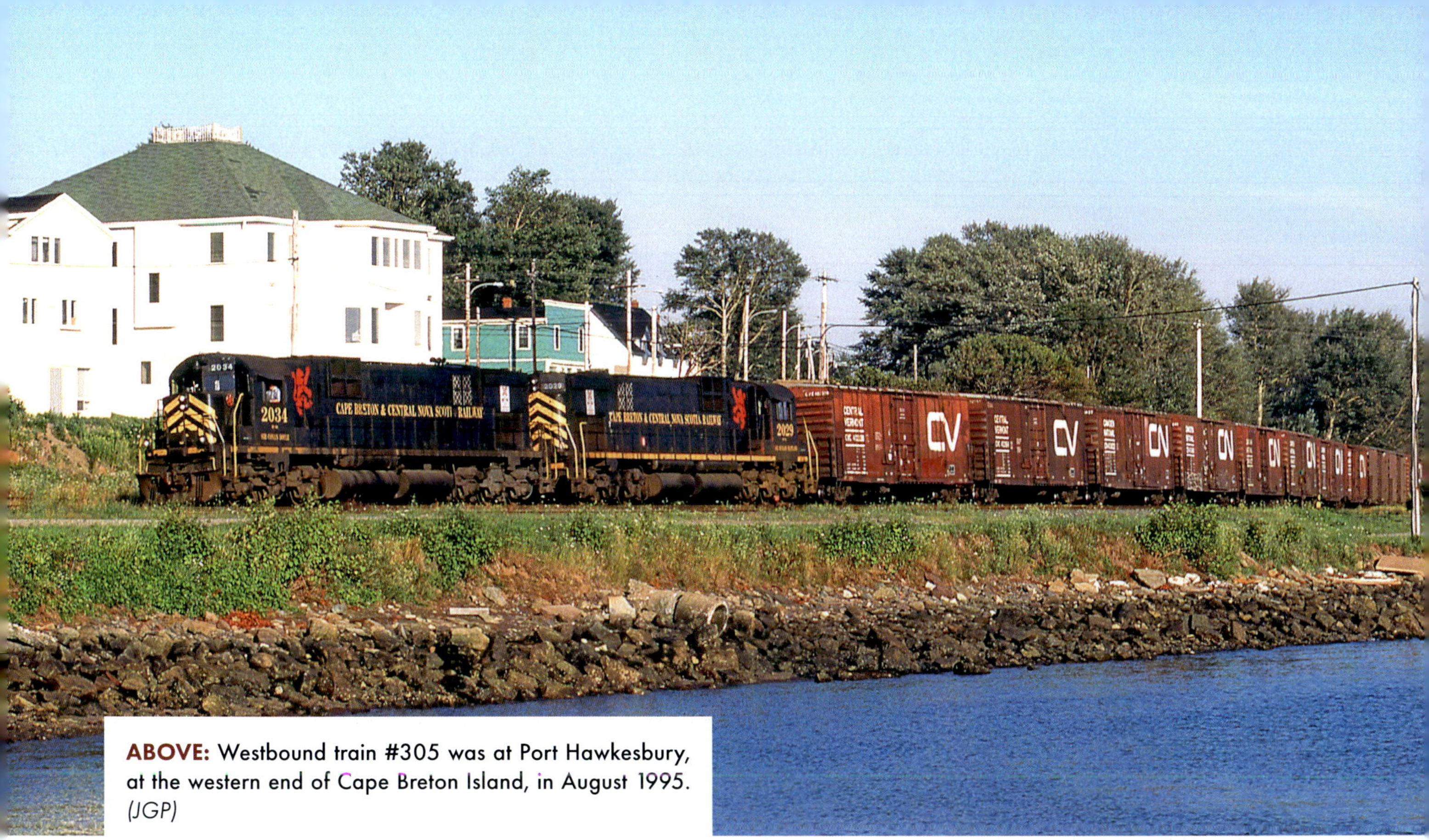

ABOVE: Westbound train #305 was at Port Hawkesbury, at the western end of Cape Breton Island, in August 1995. *(JGP)*

BELOW: The Port Tupper Generating Station at Point Tupper (on the Strait of Canso) burned coal from the Sydney Coal Field transported to the facility by the CBNS. The CBNS moved the coal westward on train #305 to Port Hawkesbury, where a 1.2-mile-long spur led to the generating plant. The power for train #305 detached at Port Hawkesbury and was bringing coal loads southward to Point Tupper in August 1995. *(JGP)*

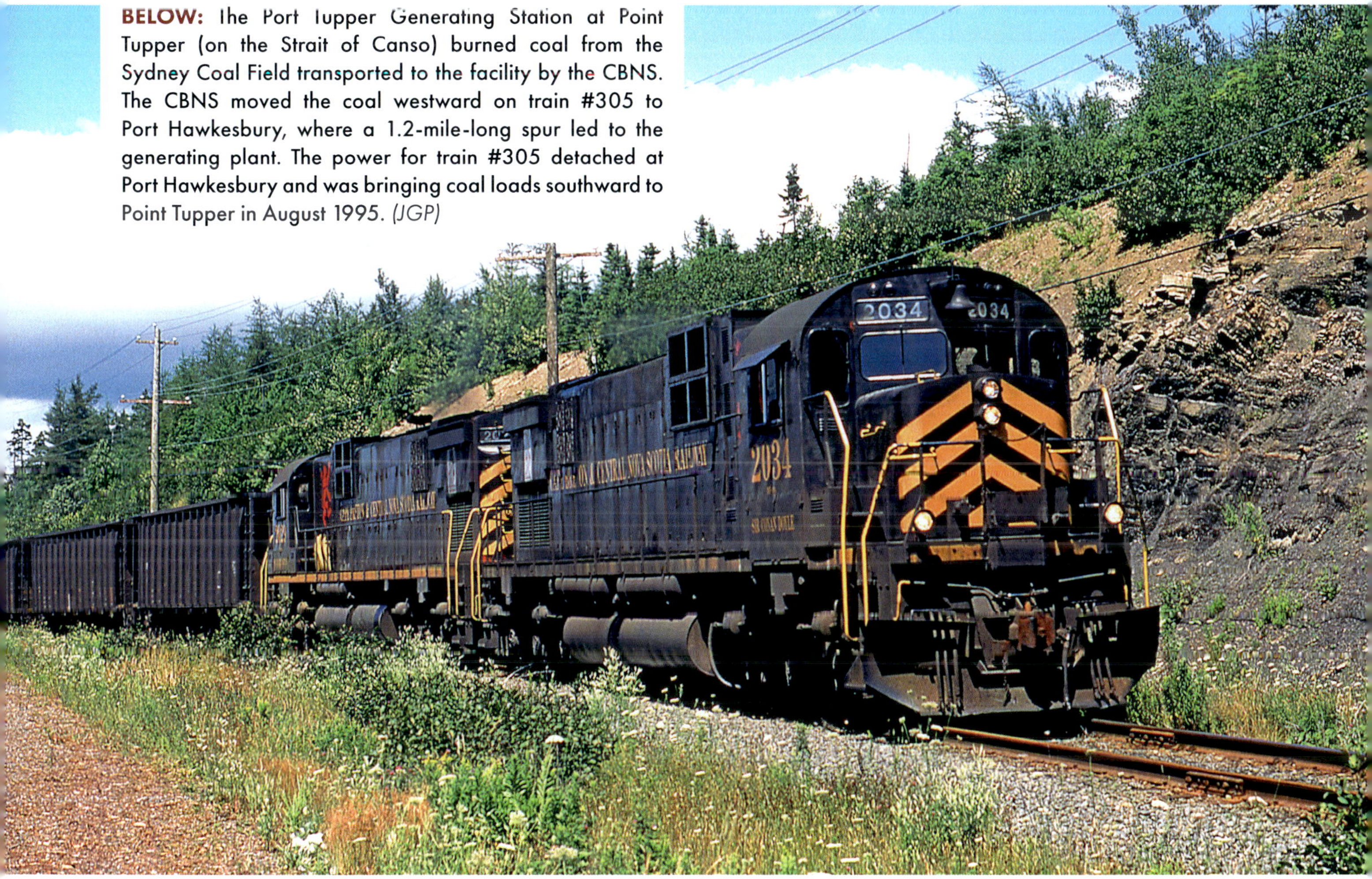

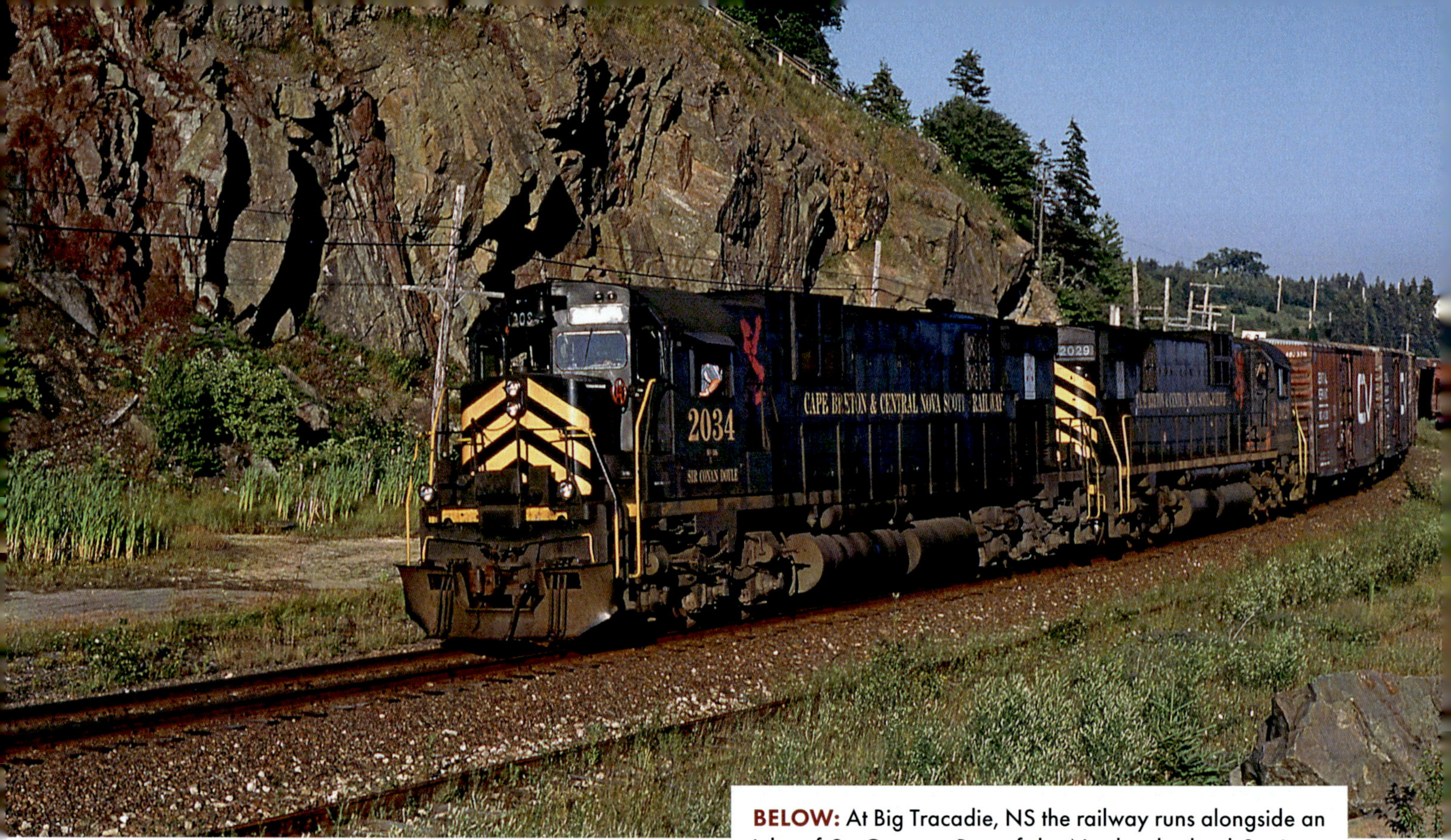

ABOVE: Train #305 passed a rock cut at Port Hastings, NS in August 1995. Just ahead, the train will cross from Cape Breton Island to the Nova Scotia mainland on the Canso Causeway, a combination highway and rail crossing of the Strait of Canso. *(JGP)*

BELOW: At Big Tracadie, NS the railway runs alongside an inlet of St. Georges Bay of the Northumberland Strait on the Nova Scotia mainland. On an August evening in 1995, C630m #2016 led westbound train #305 through the marshy area near the inlet. Big Tracadie was largely settled by Black former slaves liberated during the American Revolution and re-settled in Nova Scotia. *(JGP)*

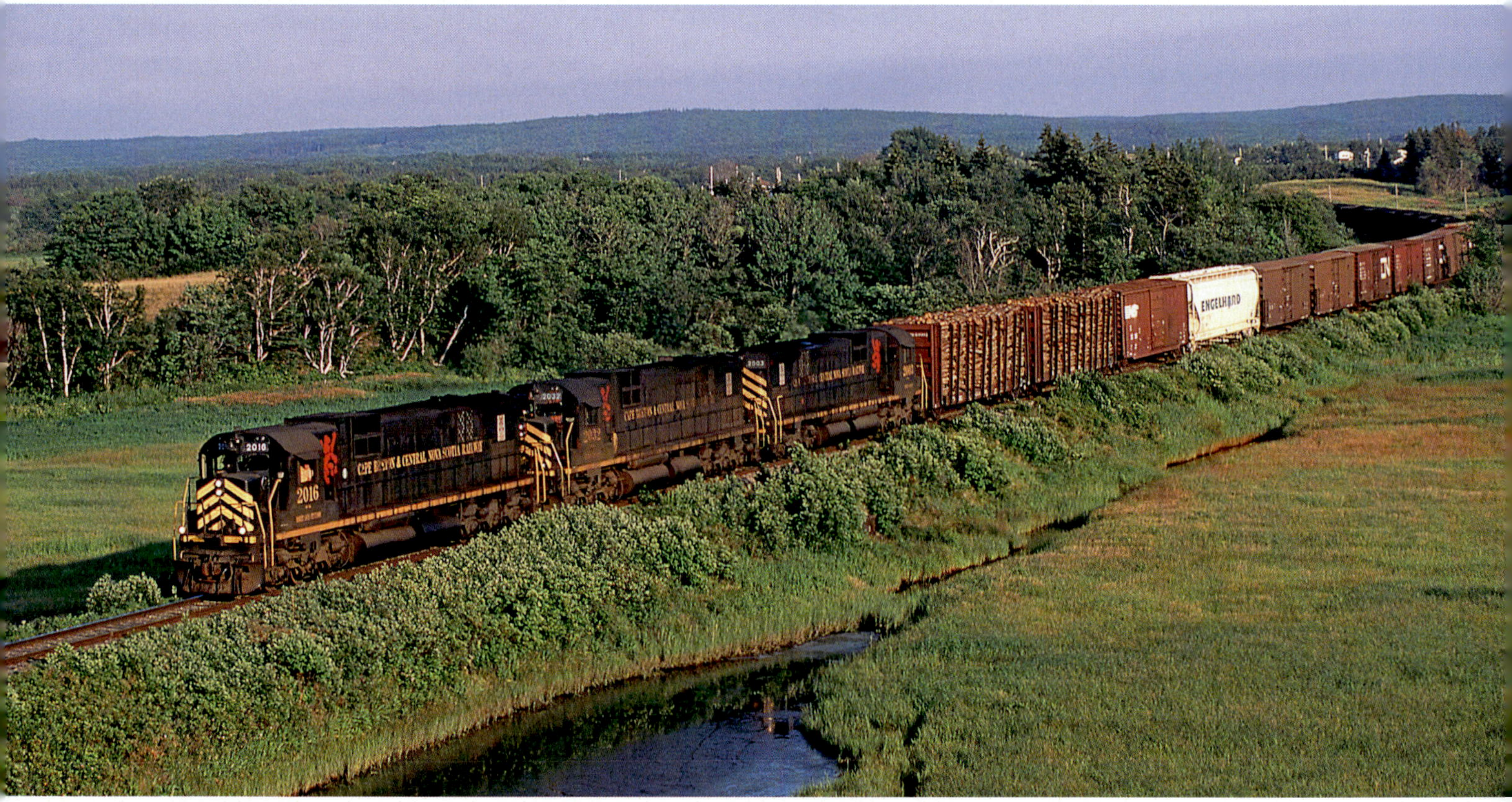

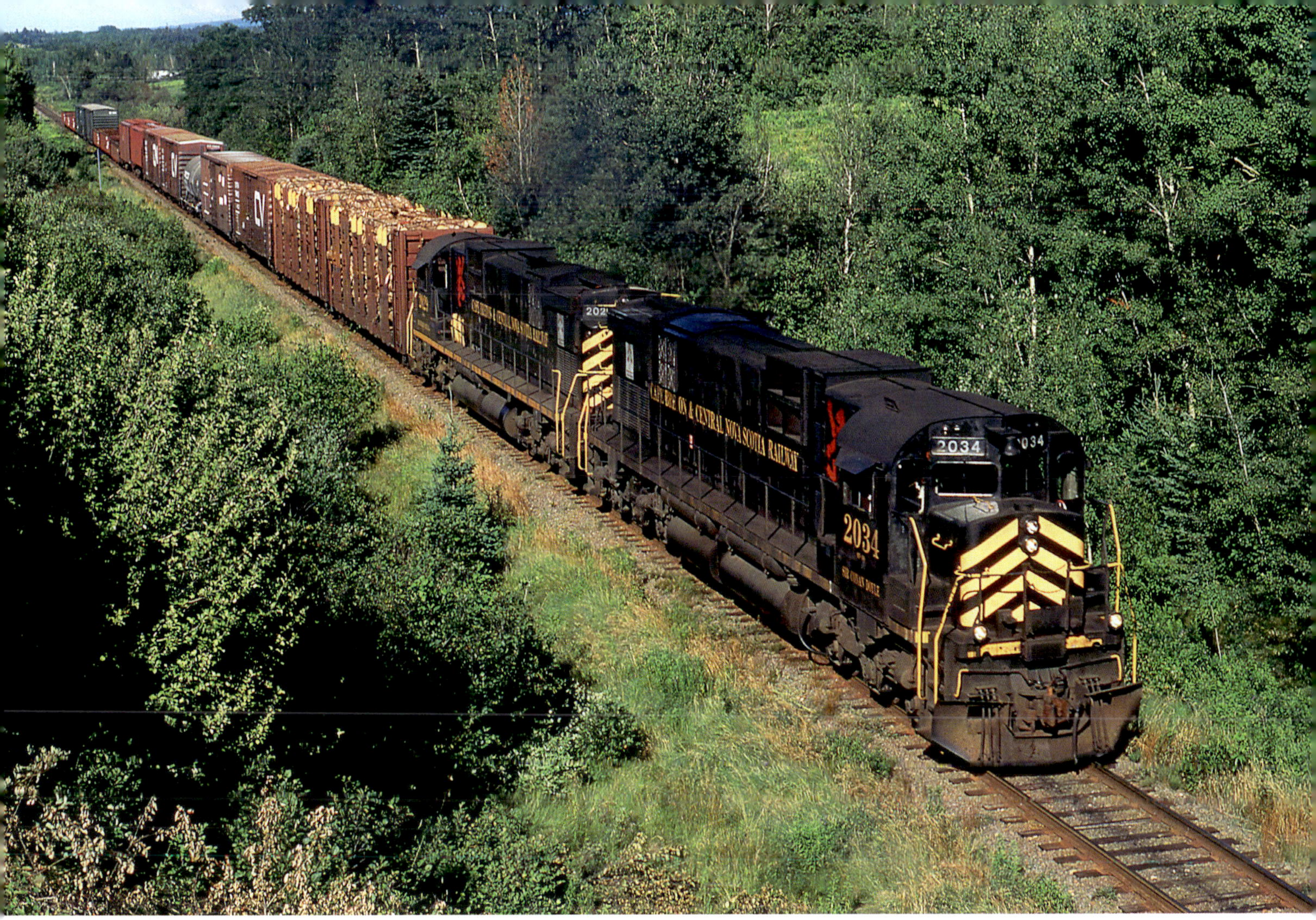

ABOVE: A short train #305 headed toward Truro at Egerton, NS in August 1995. Lead unit #2034 was named for Sir Arthur Conan Doyle, author of the Sherlock Holmes tales. *(JGP)*

BELOW: Former CN RS18s #3716 and #3627 switched the yard at Stellarton, NS in August 1995. Stellarton was the headquarters for the CBNS. Lead unit #3716 bears the name of Joseph Howe, a Nova Scotia journalist, politician, and poet of the 19th century. *(JGP)*

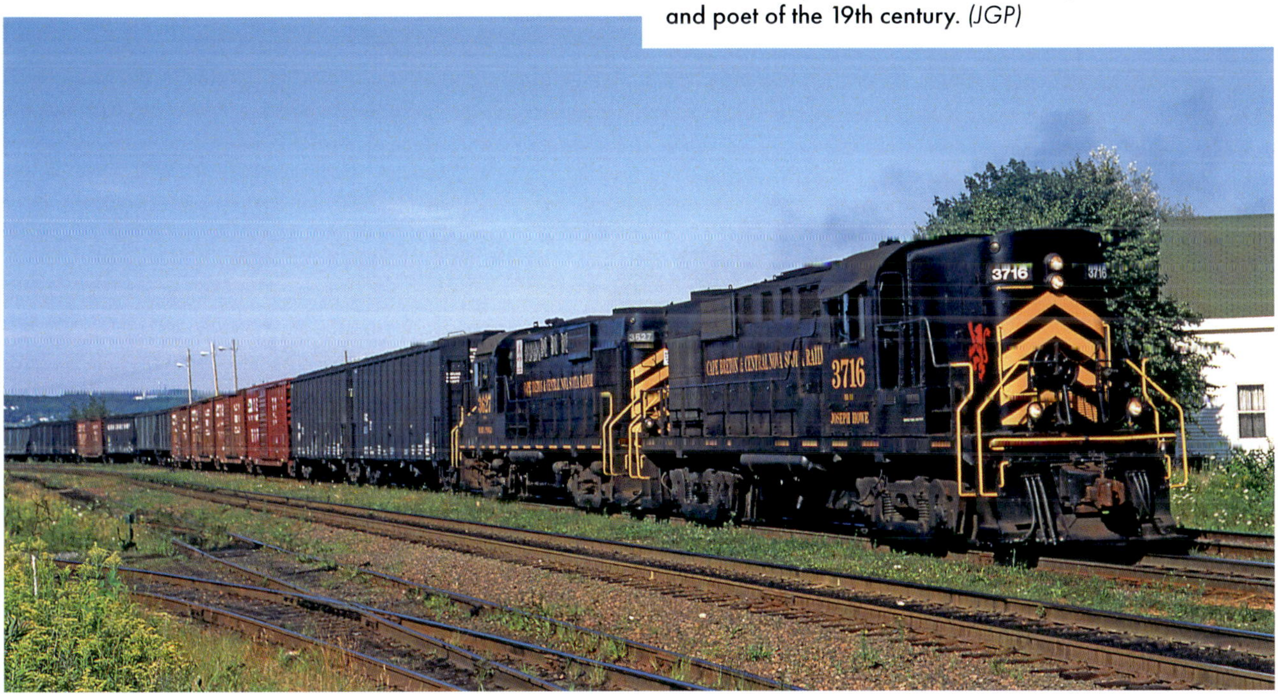

New Brunswick

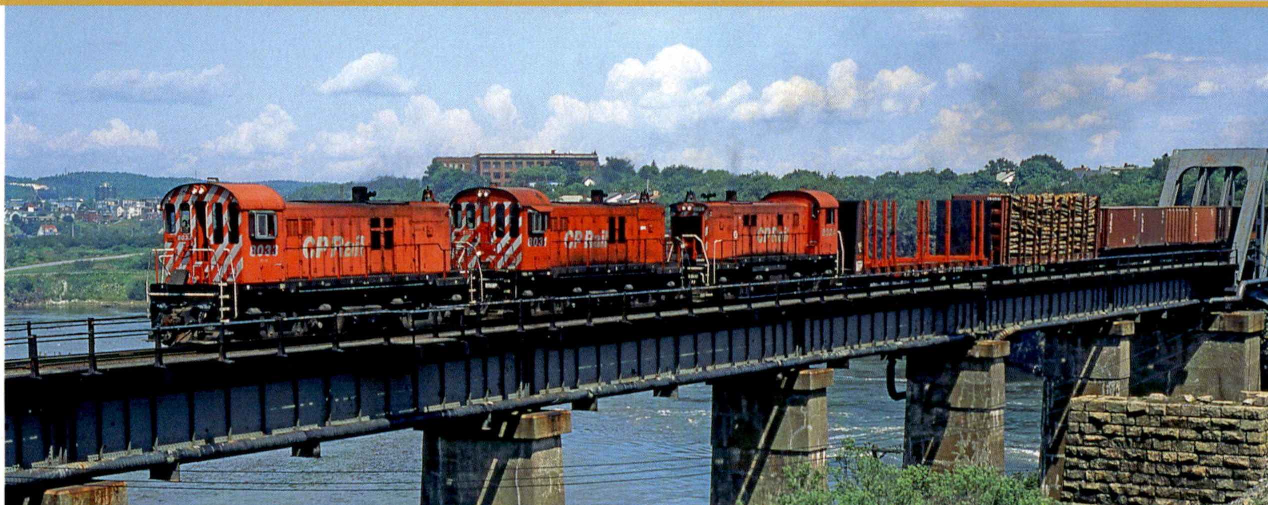

BELOW: From the Maritimes, we head north to the lines in northeastern Quebec. In August 1987, Jeffrey, Jeremy, and fellow photographer Glen Perry visited northern Quebec railroads not connected to the broader North American rail system: the Cartier Railway, the Arnaud Railway, and the Quebec, North Shore & Labrador Railway. They had contacted both the QNSL and Cartier before the trip to arrange for visits to the railroad facilities at Port Cartier and Sept-Ile. None of the three railfans spoke French, but the railroads generously arranged for English-speaking guides for the visits. On the day of the visit to the QNSL, August 13, 1987, a heavy fog lay over the St. Lawrence Valley, making the gray engines of the QNSL almost fade into the gray of the sky. At this time, SD40s and SD40-2s were the prime power on the QNSL. *(JC)*

ABOVE: Three RS23s led a CPR transfer run from the CNR yard over the St. John River in St. John, NB in August 1995. In the background is the famous Reversing Rapids of the St. John River, caused by the river waters colliding with the tides of the Bay of Fundy. *(JGP)*

Quebec, North Shore & Labrador Railway

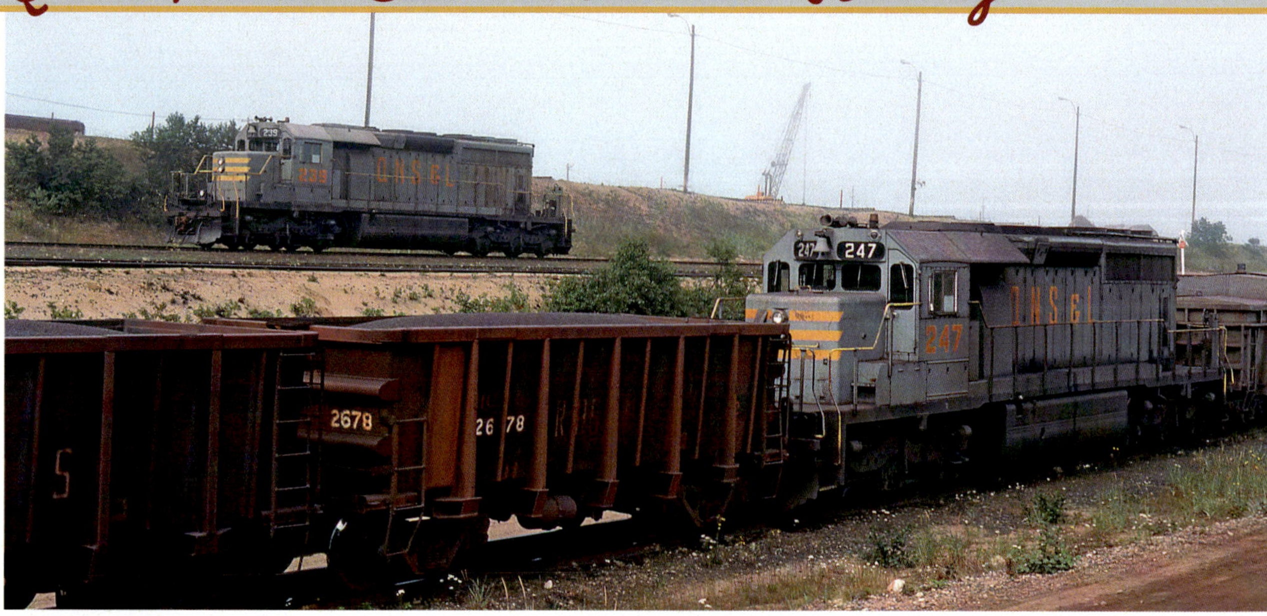

RIGHT: The modern engine terminal at Sept-Ile was servicing several of the SD40s while others rested outside in August 1987. At this date the iron ore operations were booming; as a result, shipments of iron ore made Sept-Ile in tonnage shipped the second busiest port in Canada, behind only Vancouver. *(JC)*

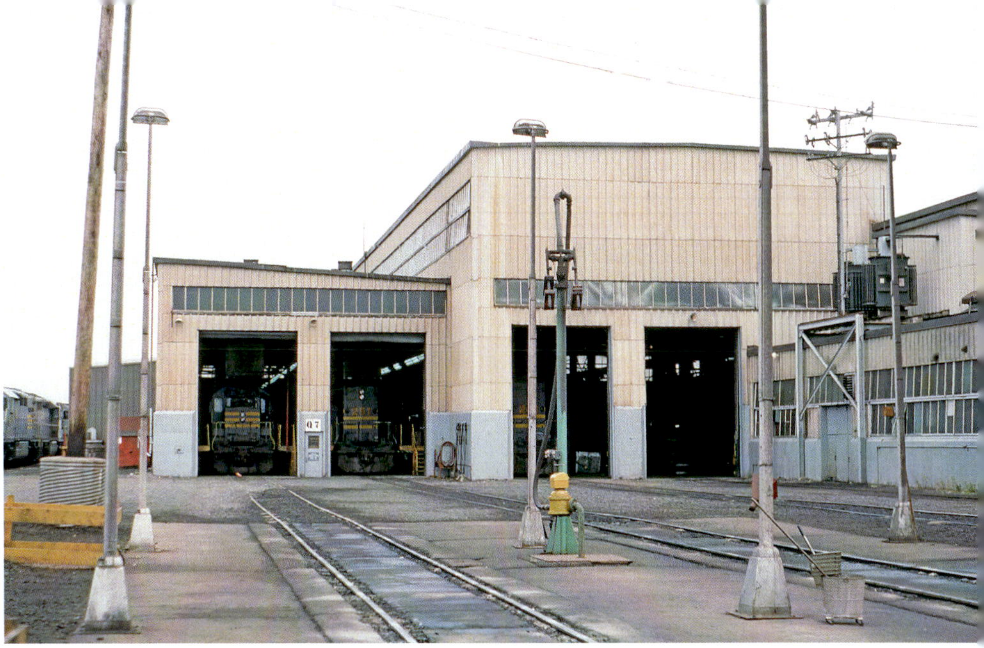

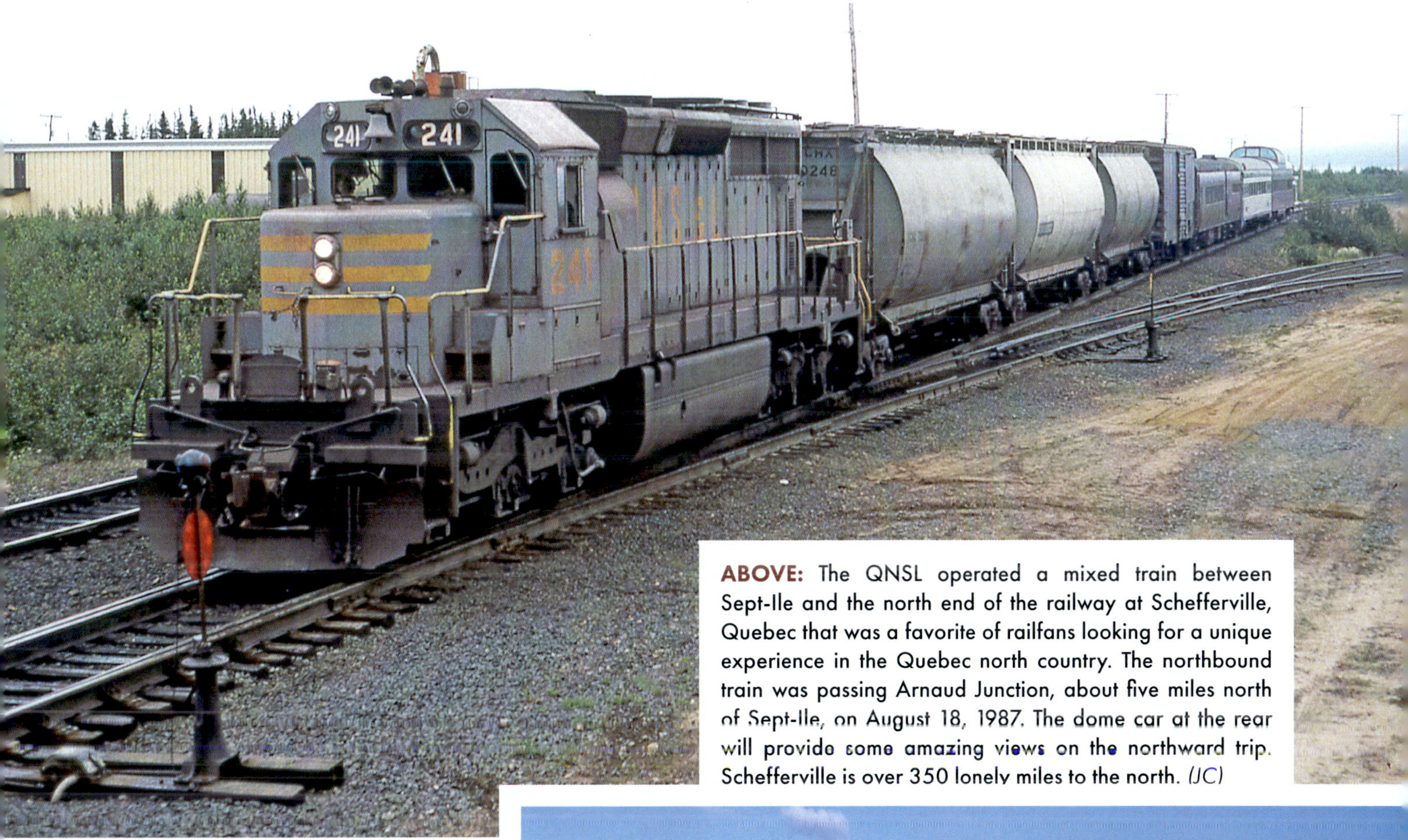

ABOVE: The QNSL operated a mixed train between Sept-Ile and the north end of the railway at Schefferville, Quebec that was a favorite of railfans looking for a unique experience in the Quebec north country. The northbound train was passing Arnaud Junction, about five miles north of Sept-Ile, on August 18, 1987. The dome car at the rear will provide some amazing views on the northward trip. Schefferville is over 350 lonely miles to the north. *(JC)*

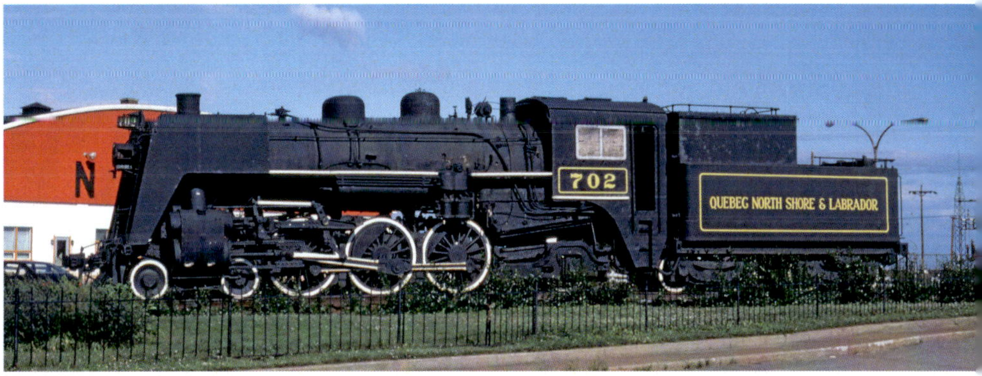

RIGHT: On display outside the QNSL headquarters in Sept-Ile was 4-6-2 #702, a former Temiskaming & Northern Ontario engine that the QNSL used in the construction of the railroad in the late 1950s. The stubby Pacific has a distinct Canadian look, with its large all-weather cab and smoke lifters. It was built in 1921 and is still in the same location today. *(JC)*

Arnaud Railway

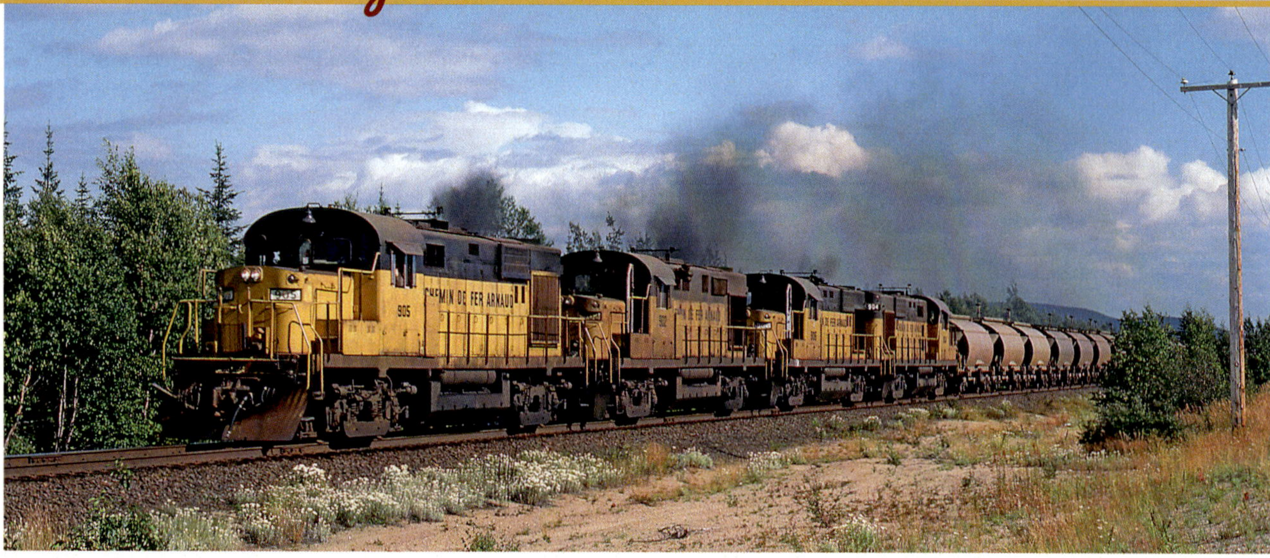

ABOVE: The Arnaud Railway, in French Chemin de Fer Arnaud, had somehow slipped from the radar as we planned the 1987 trip to northern Quebec. The chief target was the Cartier Railway with a secondary interest in the QNSL. But fortune shined on us as we investigated the Arnaud on our way from Port Cartier to Sept-Ile. As we approached the Arnaud at Pointe-Noir, we saw an eastbound train of empties about to leave. The sun was lined up perfectly as four Arnaud RS18s headed out of the yard on August 8, 1987. *(JC)*

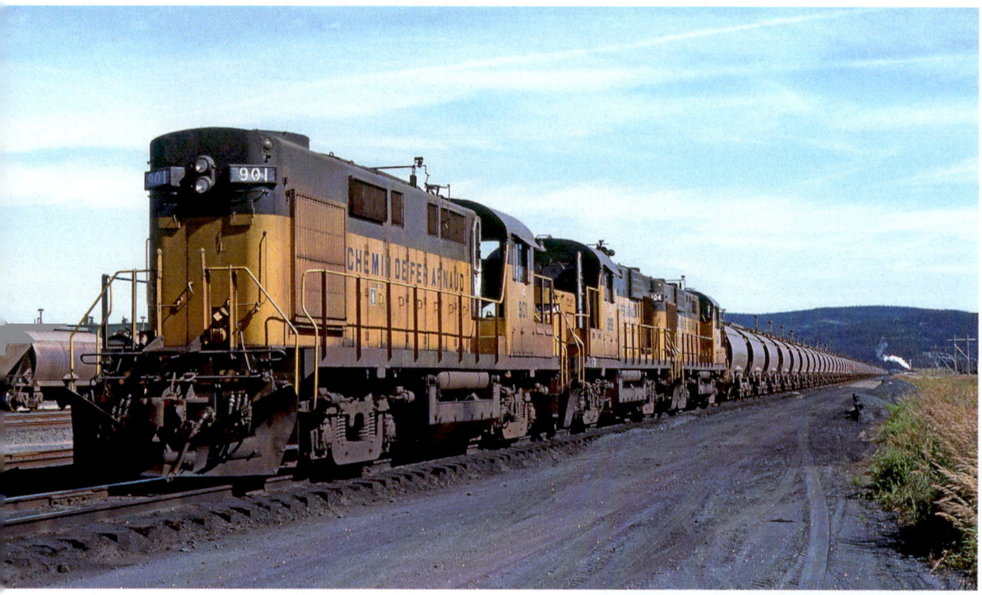

LEFT: The next day, August 9, we decided to return to see if we could get information at the Point-Noire office of the Arnaud. Language difficulties initially got in the way, but eventually we found a manager who spoke English and who generously provided a driver and car to give us a tour of the facility. The driver didn't speak any English and we had very little French, but we pointed to a train of empties made up to go out soon at the end of the yard, and he dropped us off to shoot the train with a set of three RS18s. *(JC)*

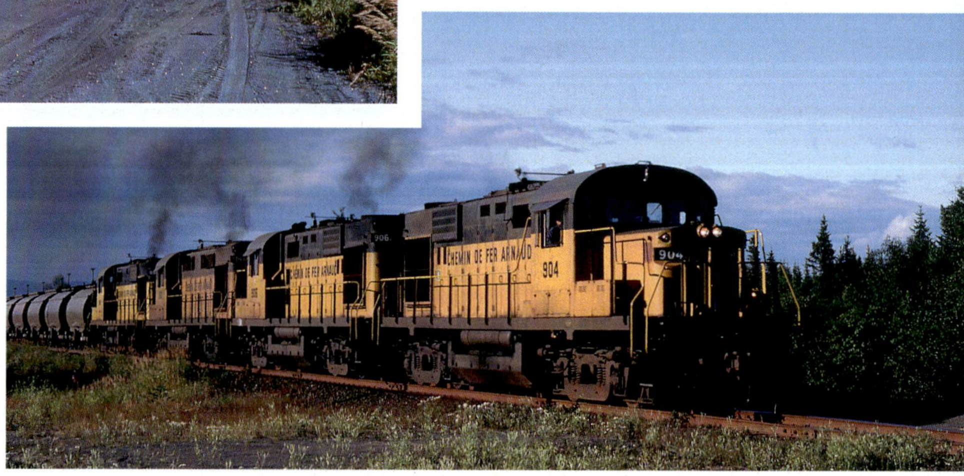

RIGHT: Later in the afternoon of August 9, 1987, we photographed the return run with loads and four RS18s about to cross the highway on the way to the plant at Pointe-Noir. *(JC)*

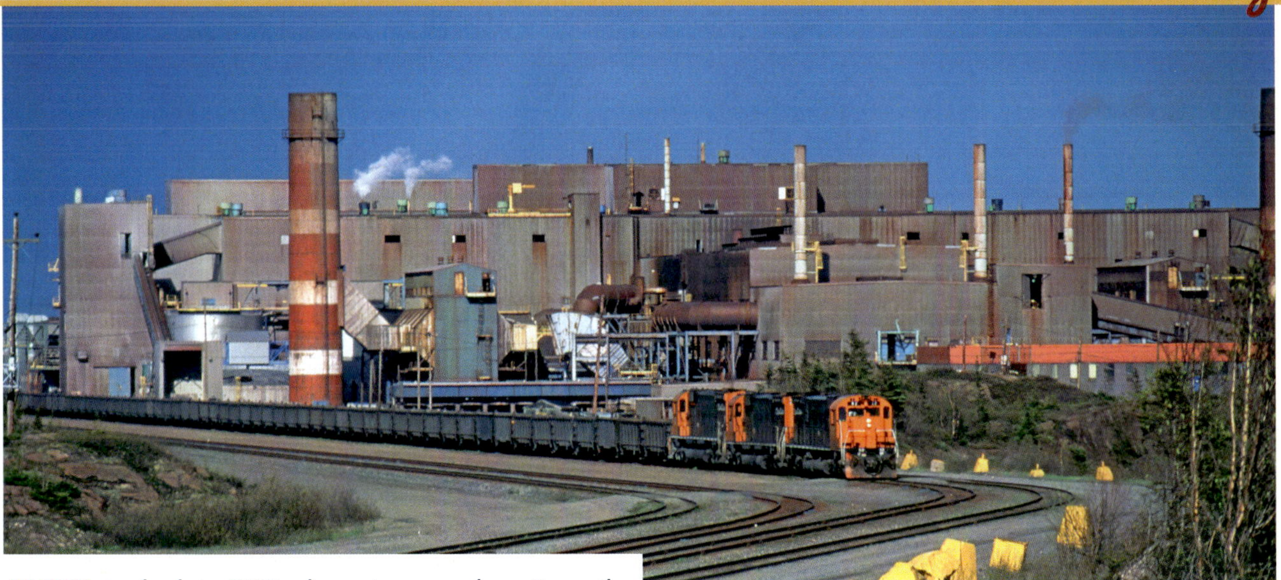

ABOVE: In the late 1950s, large iron ore deposits north of the St. Lawrence in the Quebec/Labrador Trough were opened to mining. Railways were needed to transport the ore for export from ports on the river or refineries. No existing rail lines extended so far north and east along the St. Lawrence, so the lines would be isolated from the larger North American rail network. The Quebec Cartier Mining Company, a U.S. Steel subsidiary, constructed a line from Shelter Bay, QC on the St. Lawrence to Lac Jeannine, 190 miles to the north, and opened it for traffic in December 1960. The line was extended north an additional 86 miles to a new mine at Mont-Wright, QC in 1972. The Cartier's southern terminus was the large facility at Port Cartier at a site alongside the St. Lawrence known prior as Shelter Bay. On June 3, 2000, a three-unit set of power was heading north out of the facility at Port Cartier with empties for the mine at Mont-Wright. *(BDP)*

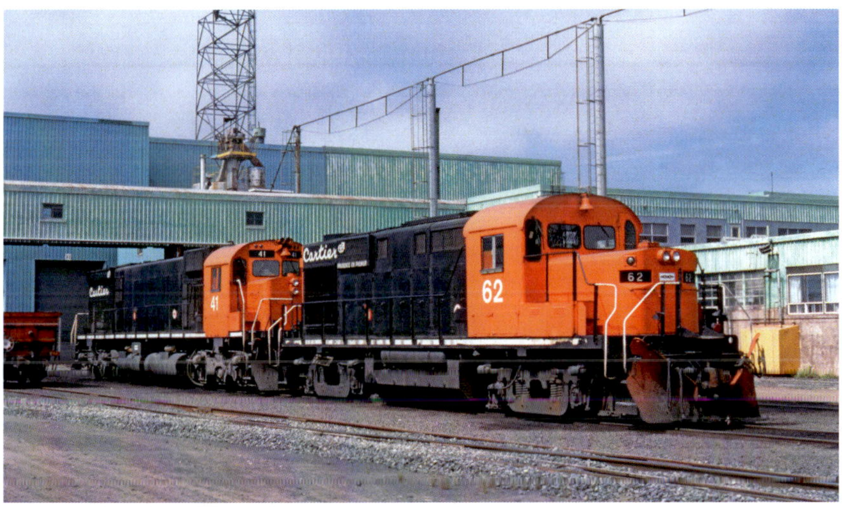

LEFT: A tour of the engine facility at Port Cartier provided us with an overview of the motive power used by the Cartier since its inception. The road dieselized with nine GMDD GP9s and eight MLW RS18s. By this time the GP9s were out of service and stored for disposition. The Cartier retained the RS18s for switching and local freight service. RS18 #62 was coupled to M636 #41 at Port Cartier in August 1987. The #41 was former CNR unit #2300. *(JC)*

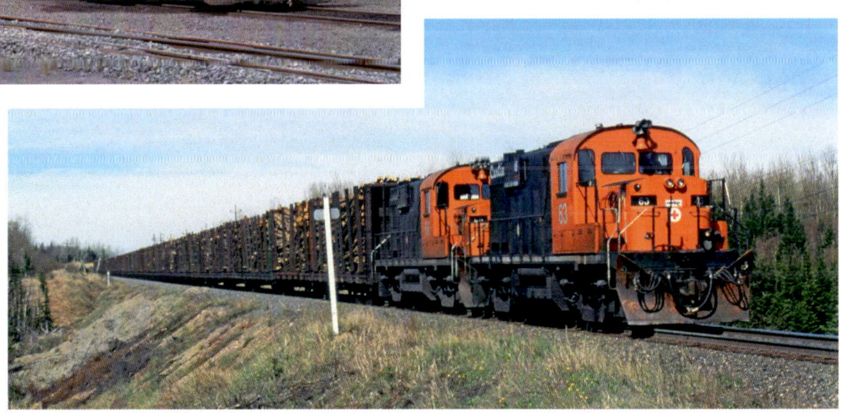

RIGHT: The Cartier was mostly a conveyor belt for iron ore, but it also brought lumber south to the Uniforet pulp and sawmill at Port Cartier. The log trains were powered by sets of RS18s, seen here nearing the mill at Port Cartier on May 30, 2000. *(BDP)*

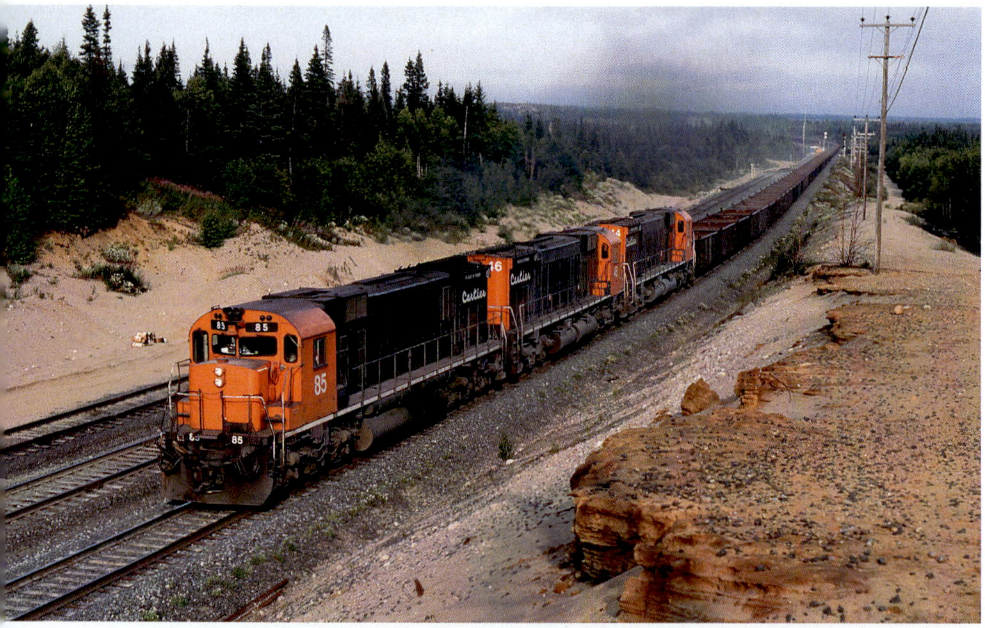

LEFT: A northbound train of empties was beginning its long run back to the mine at Able in August 1987, climbing out of the St. Lawrence Valley with the usual three-unit lash-up of six-axle Alcos. The Cartier named its 12 sidings for letters of the alphabet, from south to north, with Able the first out of Port Cartier. *(JC)*

BELOW: Brian Plant and two railfan colleagues visited the Cartier in early June 2000. It was a good time to travel around northern Quebec, before the black fly invasion of summer. The weather was generally good, and the railroad was still all Alco-powered, making for a productive trip. Southbound loads curved through MP 23 in the first week of June of 2000. The second unit wears the new maroon and gray colors adopted by the Cartier. *(BDP)*

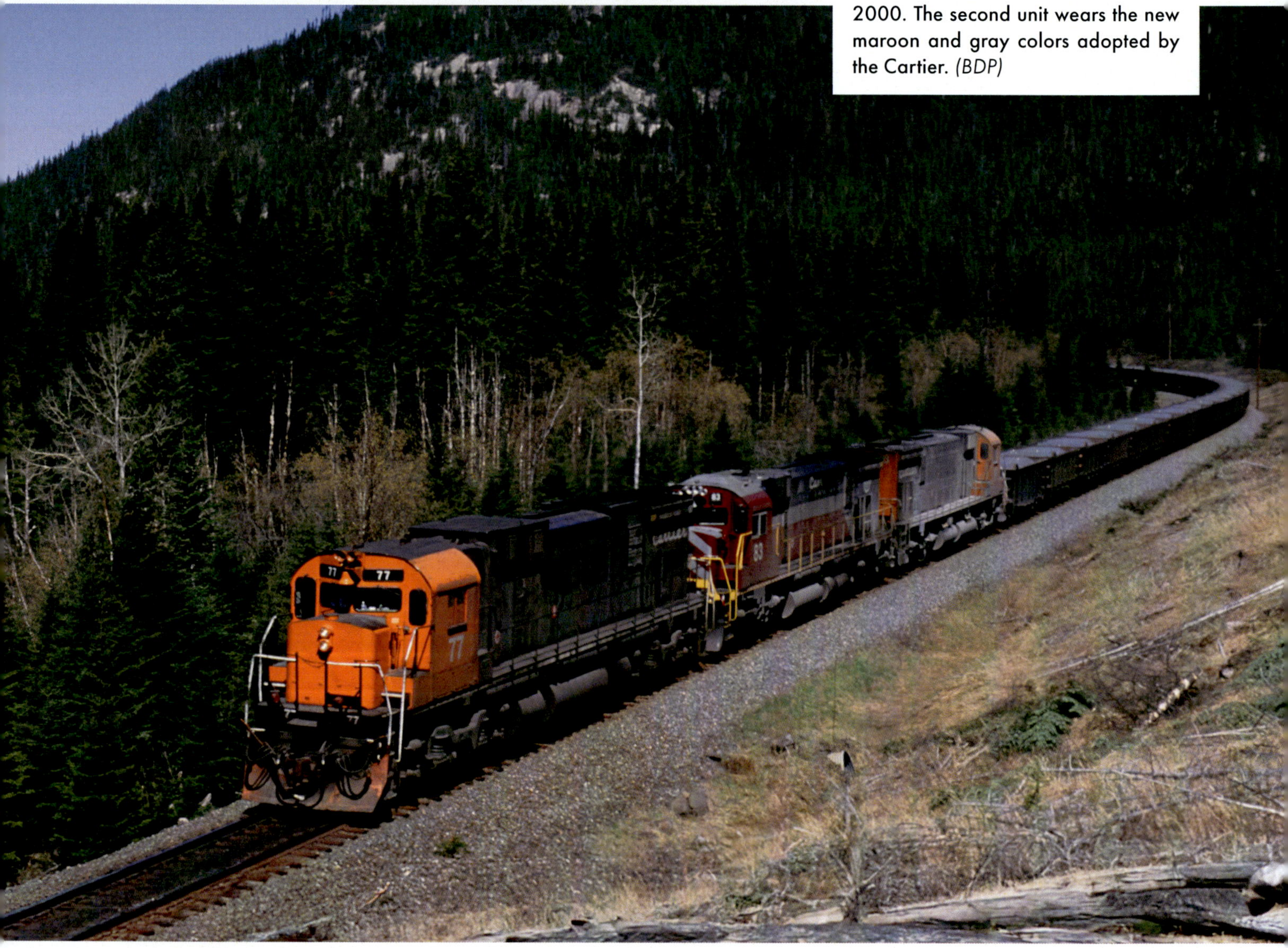

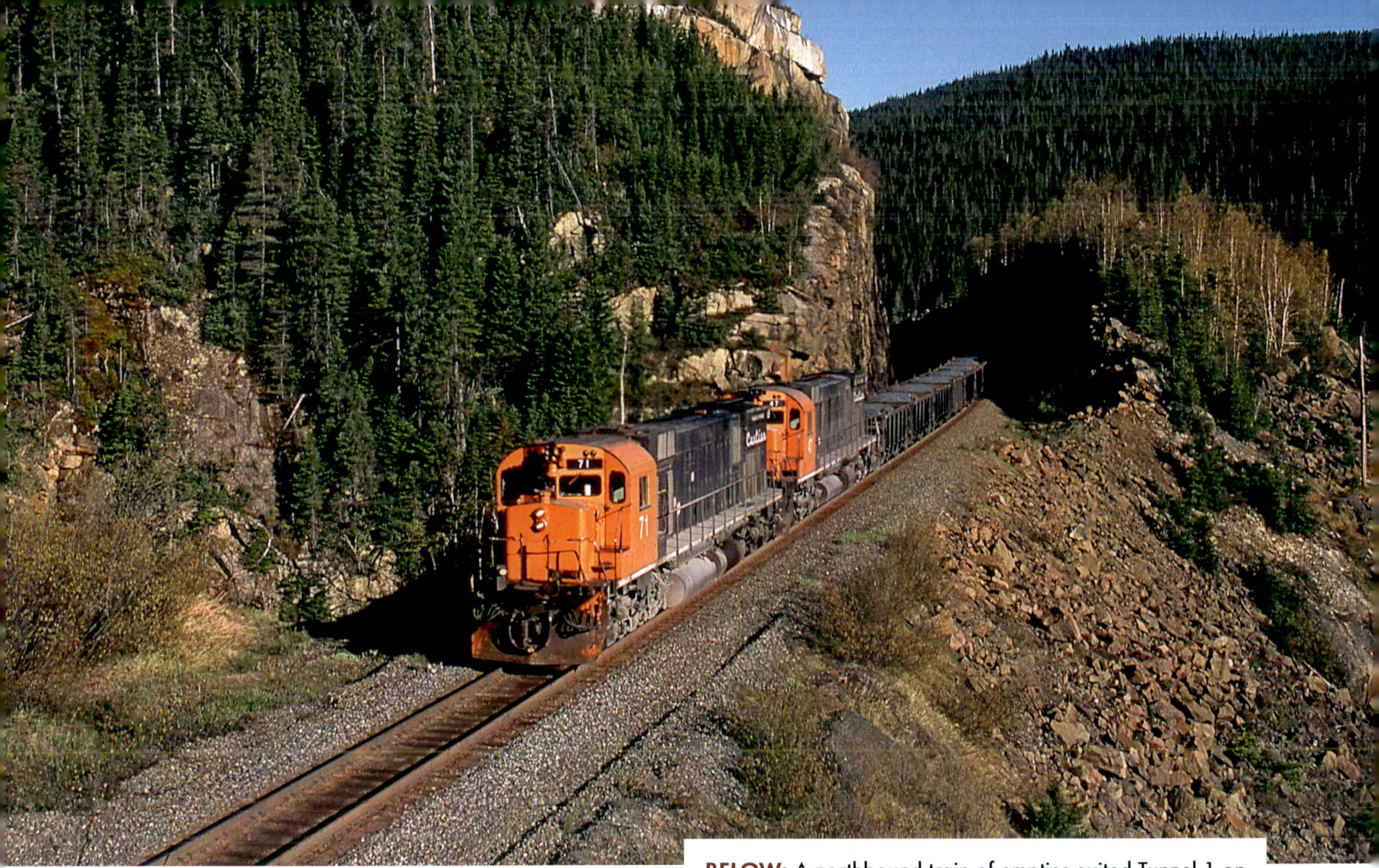

ABOVE: A pair of M636s brought a loaded ore train southward at Tunnel 1 on June 5, 2000. *(BDP)*

BELOW: A northbound train of empties exited Tunnel 1 on June 5, 2000. The Cartier numbered its tunnels from south to north as it did its mileposts. *(BDP)*

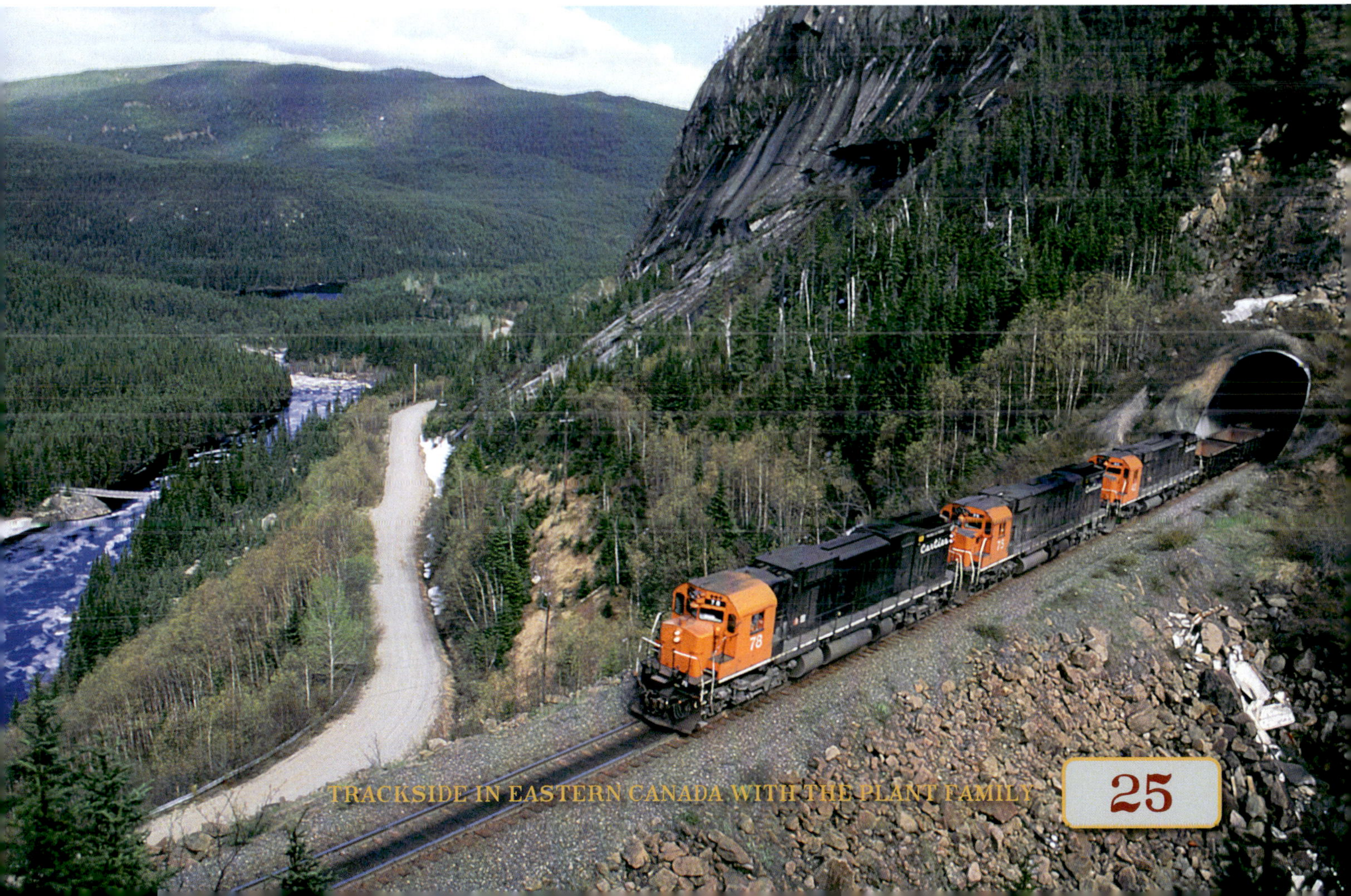

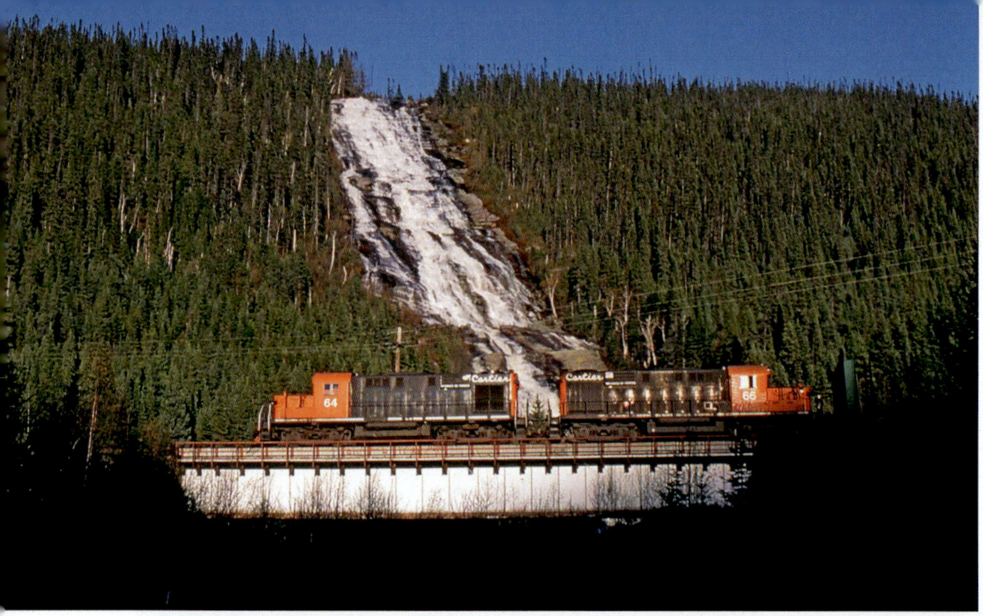

LEFT: One of the most scenic locations on the Cartier is the waterfall and bridge at MP 43, where a northbound empty log train passed behind a pair of RS18s on June 5, 2000. *(BDP)*

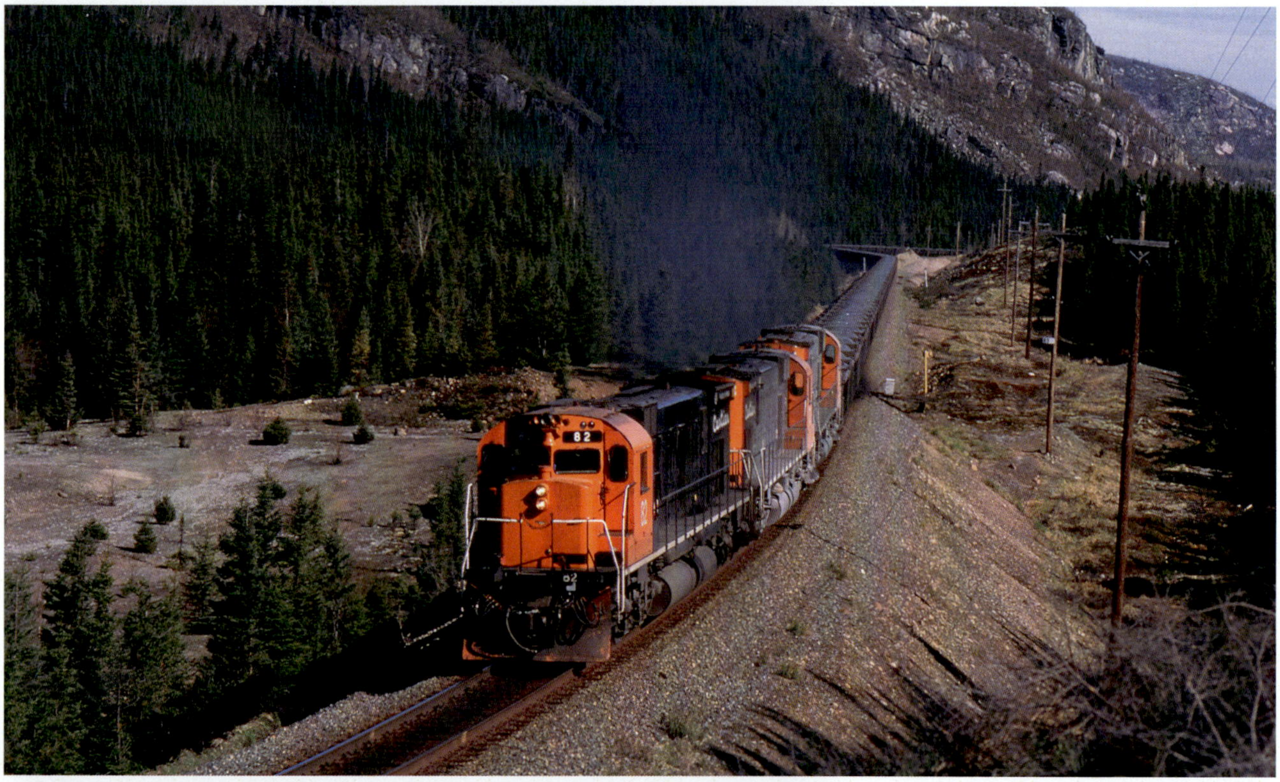

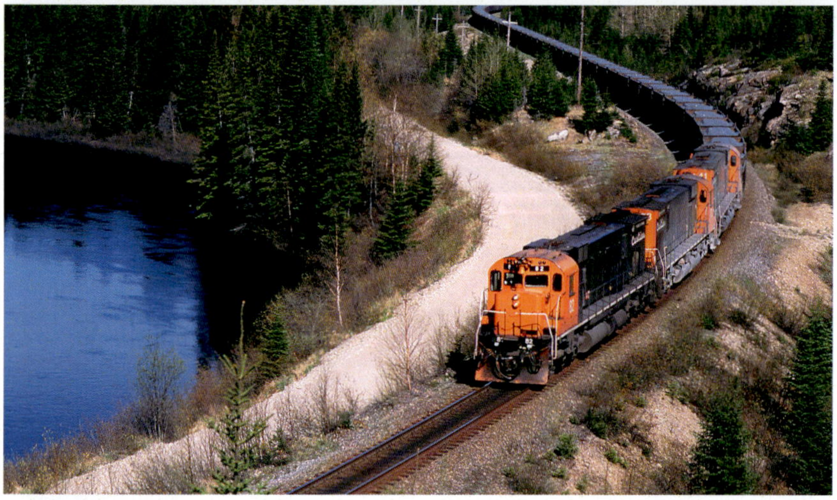

ABOVE AND LEFT: Cartier train #82 South was at MP 49, near Dog Siding, on June 3, 2000. Near Charles, it curved around a gentle S curve. The unpaved gravel access road to the left of the tracks was the only way to access the southern part of the railway. *(BDP)*

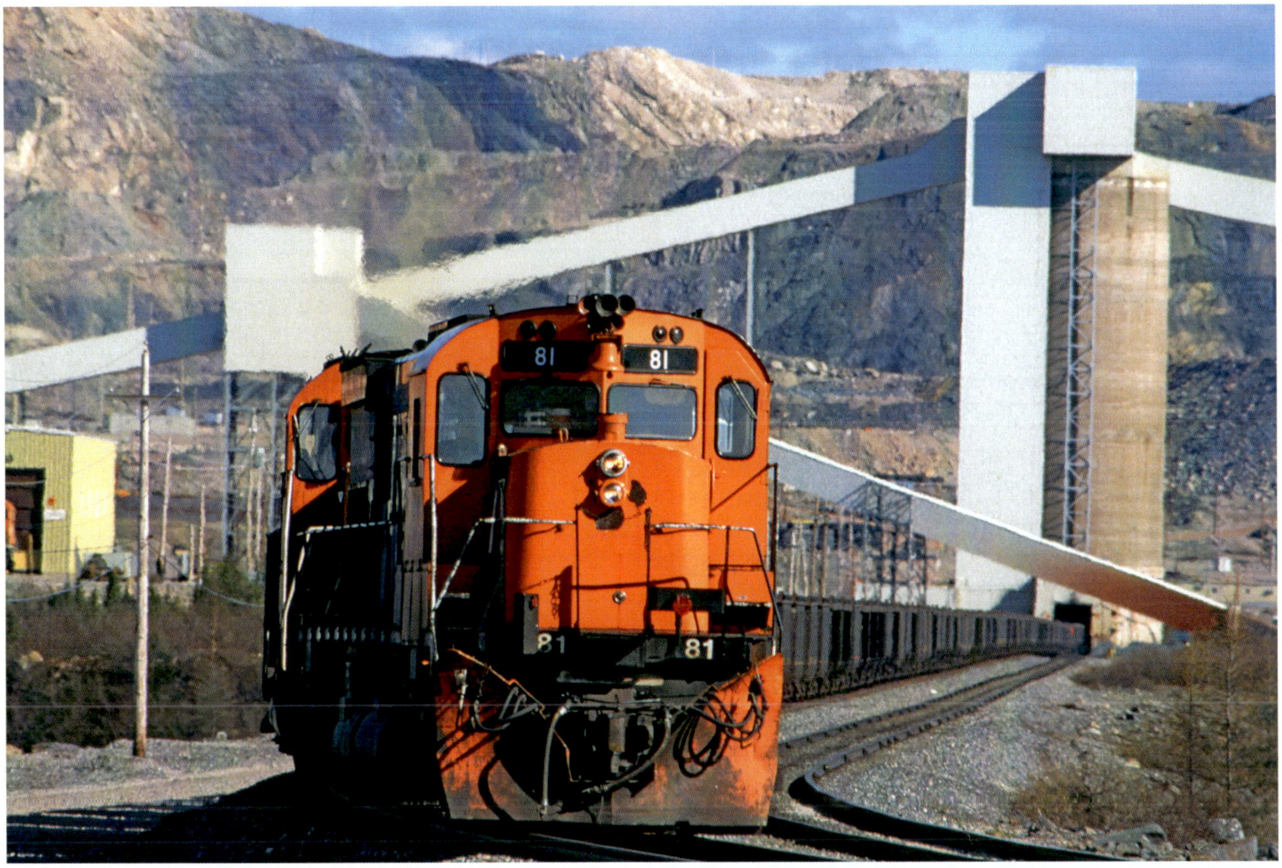

ABOVE AND BELOW: The mine at Mont-Wright was an impressive modern facility. On June 7, 2000, M636 #81 was loading at the mine prior to heading south to Port Cartier. After loading was completed, the southbound train was beginning its trip to Port Cartier at MP 247.2. *(BDP)*

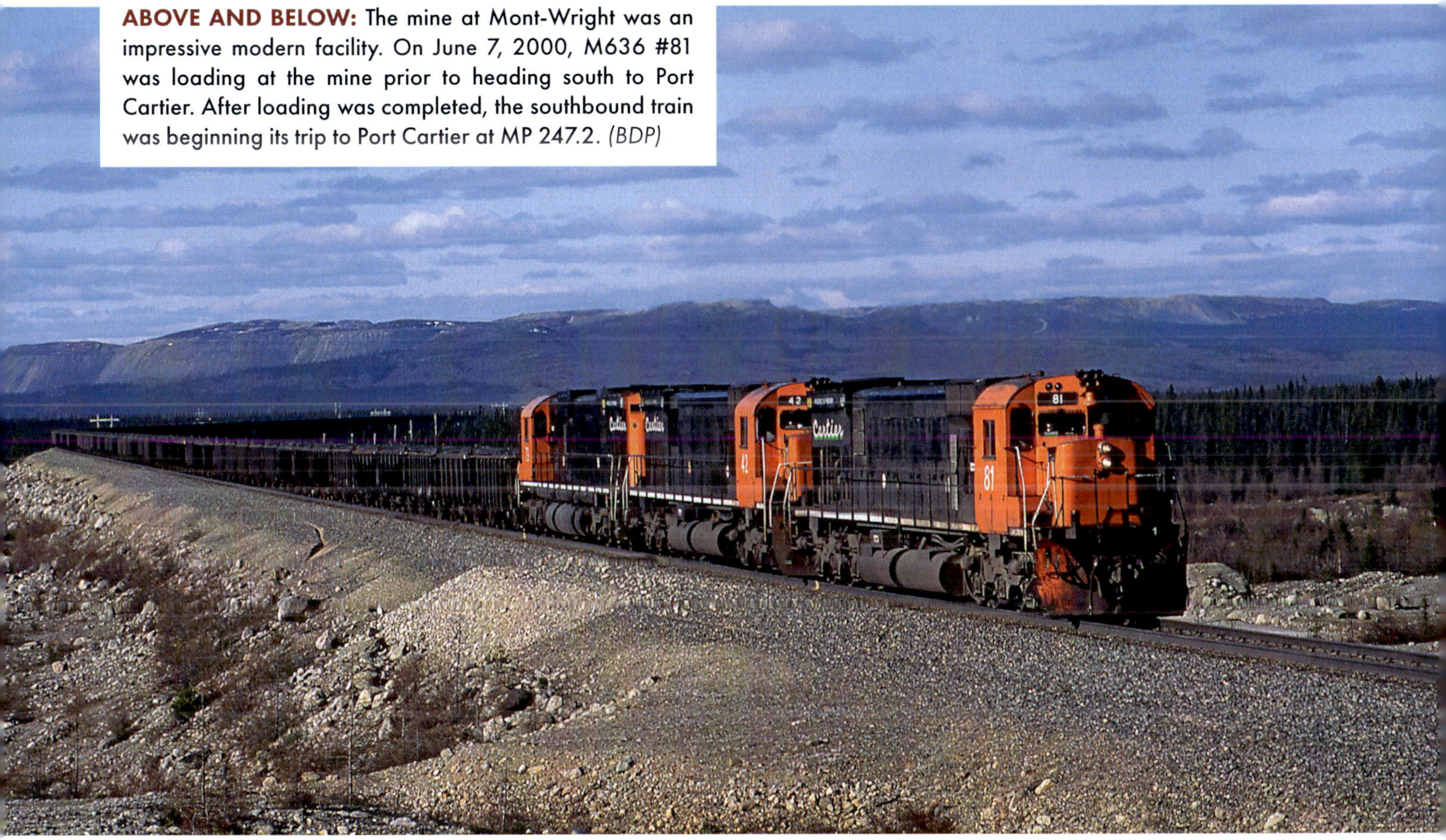

Baie-Comeau

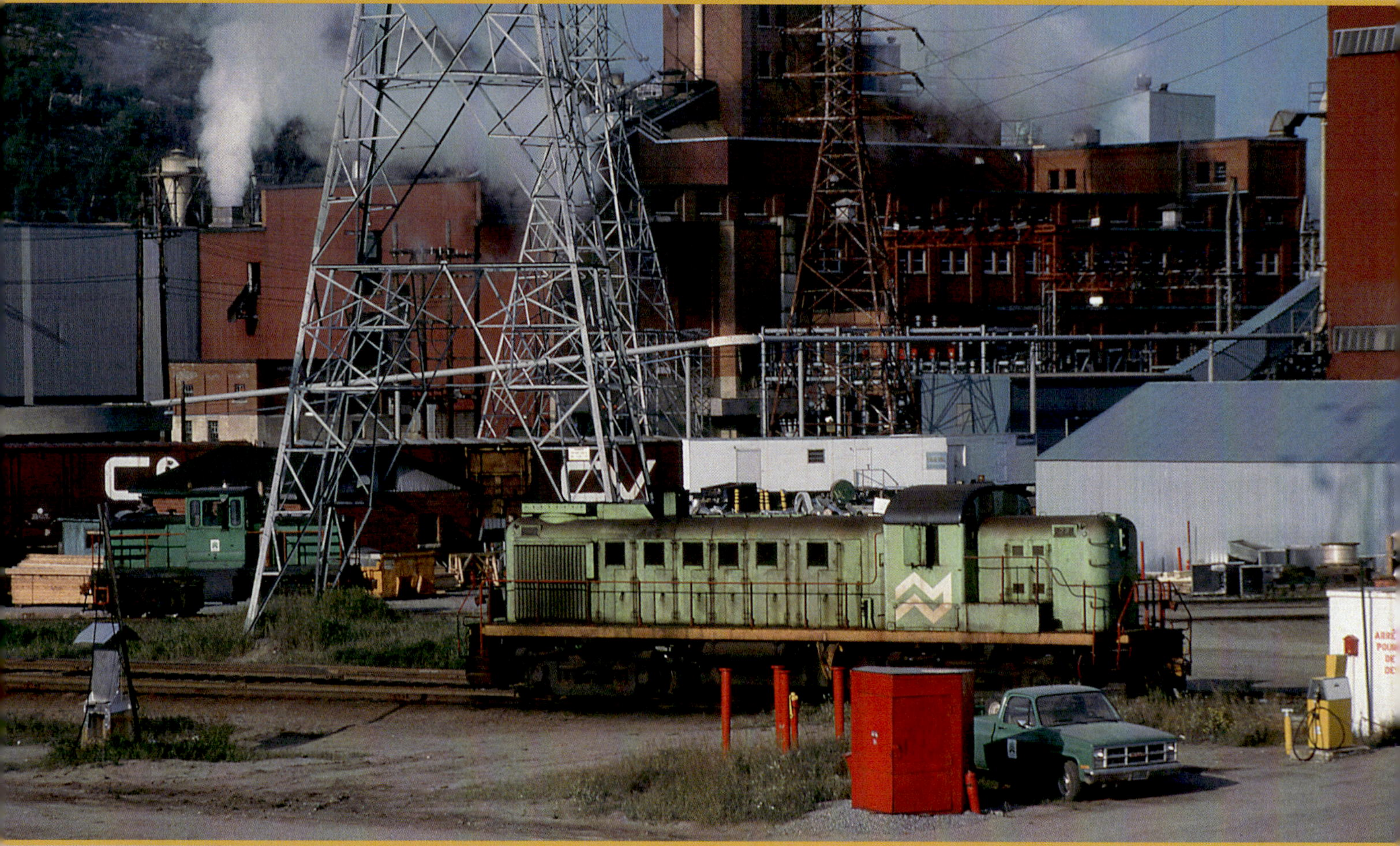

Roberval & Saguenay Railway

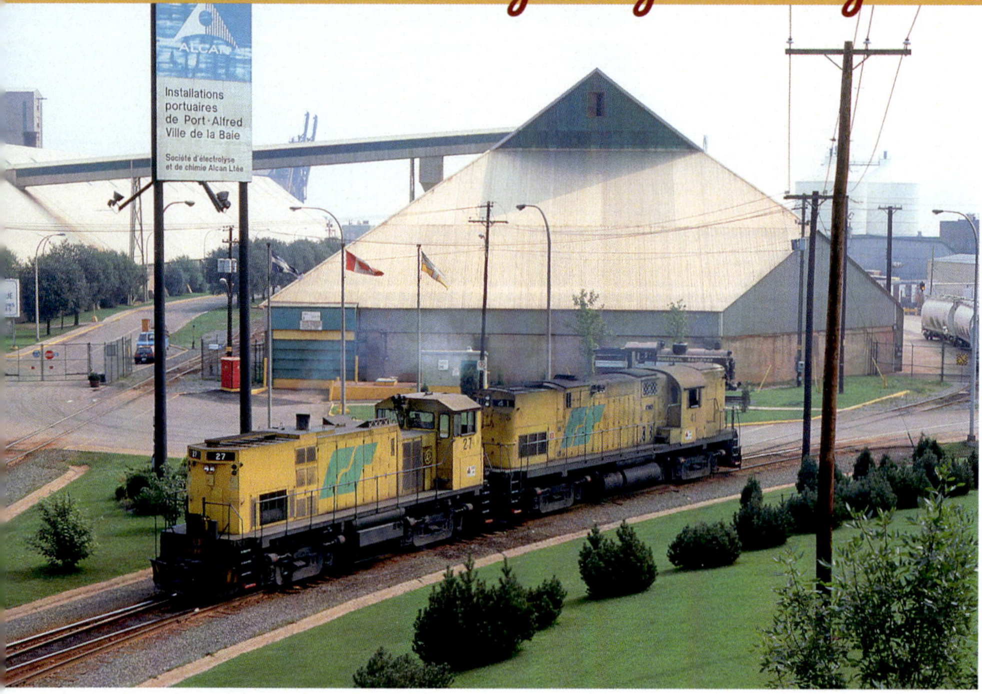

ABOVE: Quebec North Shore Paper operated a plant at Baie-Comeau, on the north shore of the St. Lawrence about 250 miles northeast of Quebec City. It used an RS3 and a center cab switcher, seen near the plant in August 1987. *(JC)*

LEFT: The Roberval & Saguenay (RS) in the modern era existed largely to service the aluminum industry in the Saguenay region of Quebec. It was owned by Alcan Aluminum and its successor, Rio Tinto Alcan. At the Alcan plant at Port Alfred, QC, M420TR #27 and C420 #41 posed before heading to nearby La Baie with a large cut of CNR boxcars in August 1987. The #27 was one of only two such units on the RS, along with sister unit #26. *(JC)*

RIGHT AND BELOW: High hood C420 #41 was a former Long Island unit, one of nine acquired by the road. It was switching at La Baie in August 1987 alongside the uniquely named Ha! Ha! Bay, where the Saguenay River meets the St. Lawrence. *(BDP)*

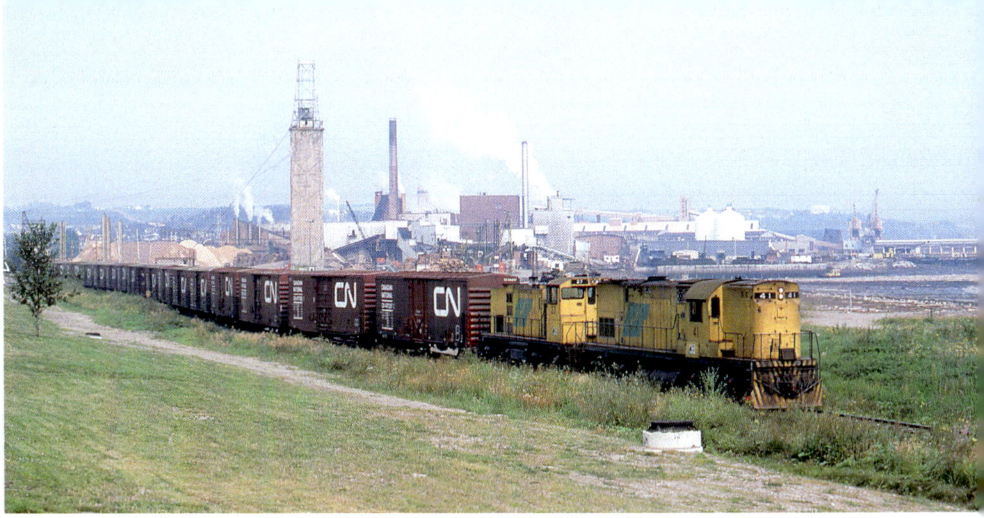

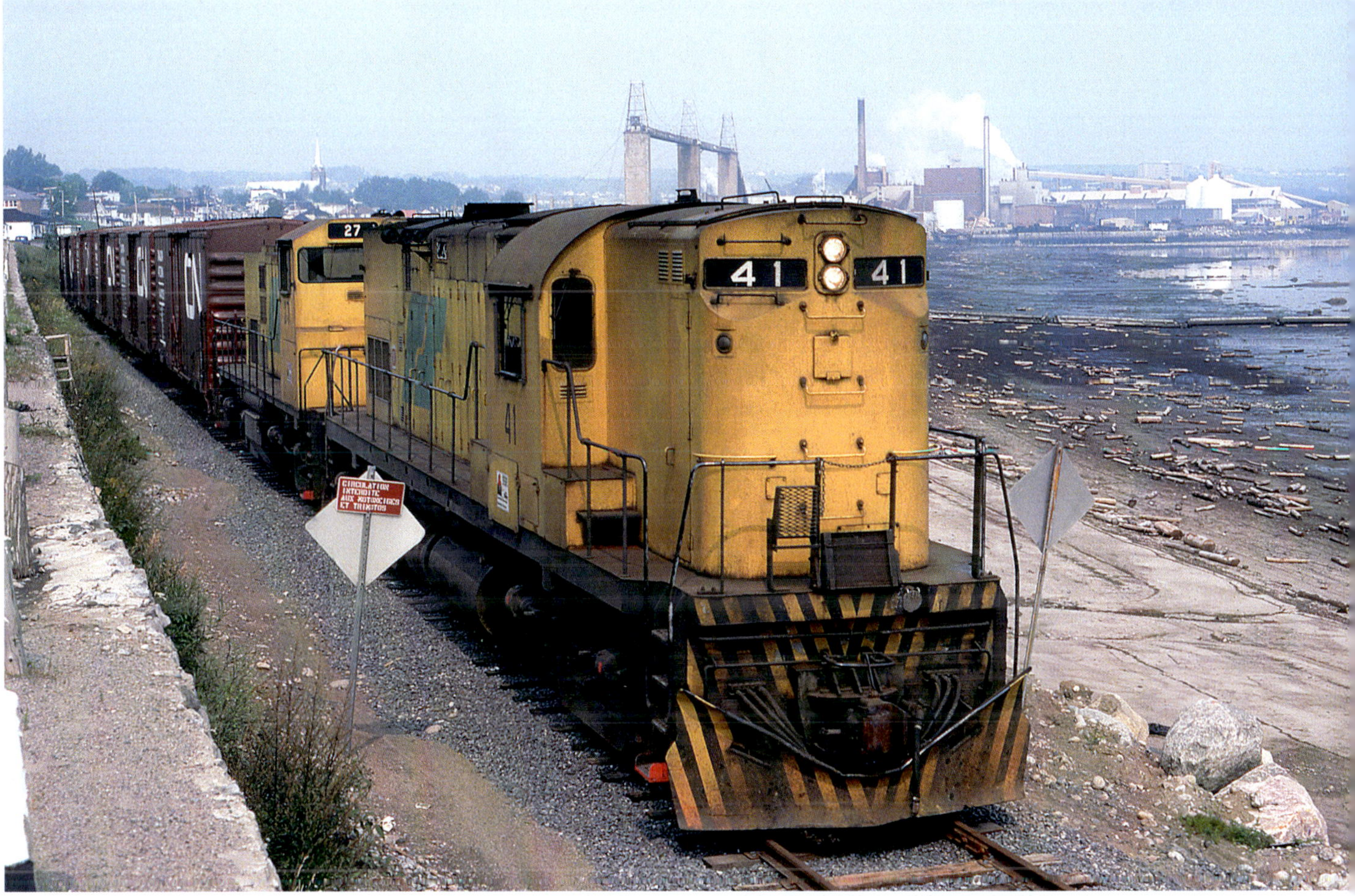

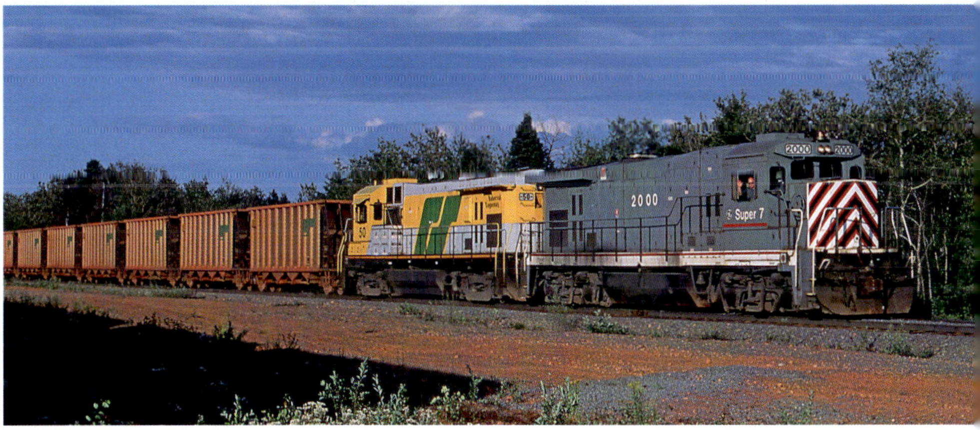

RIGHT: The RS briefly rostered General Electric "Super Seven" units, rebuilt at Montreal Locomotive Works from U23Bs. A pair was heading west about six miles west of Port Alfred in July 1993. *(JGP)*

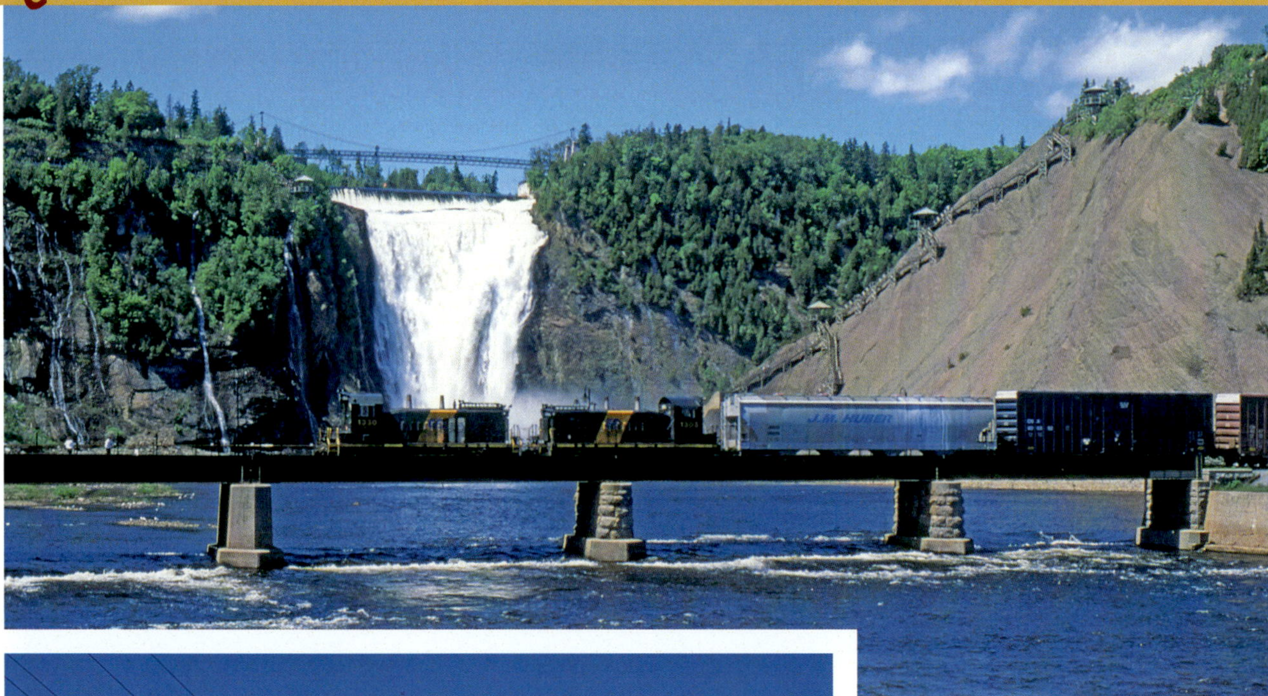

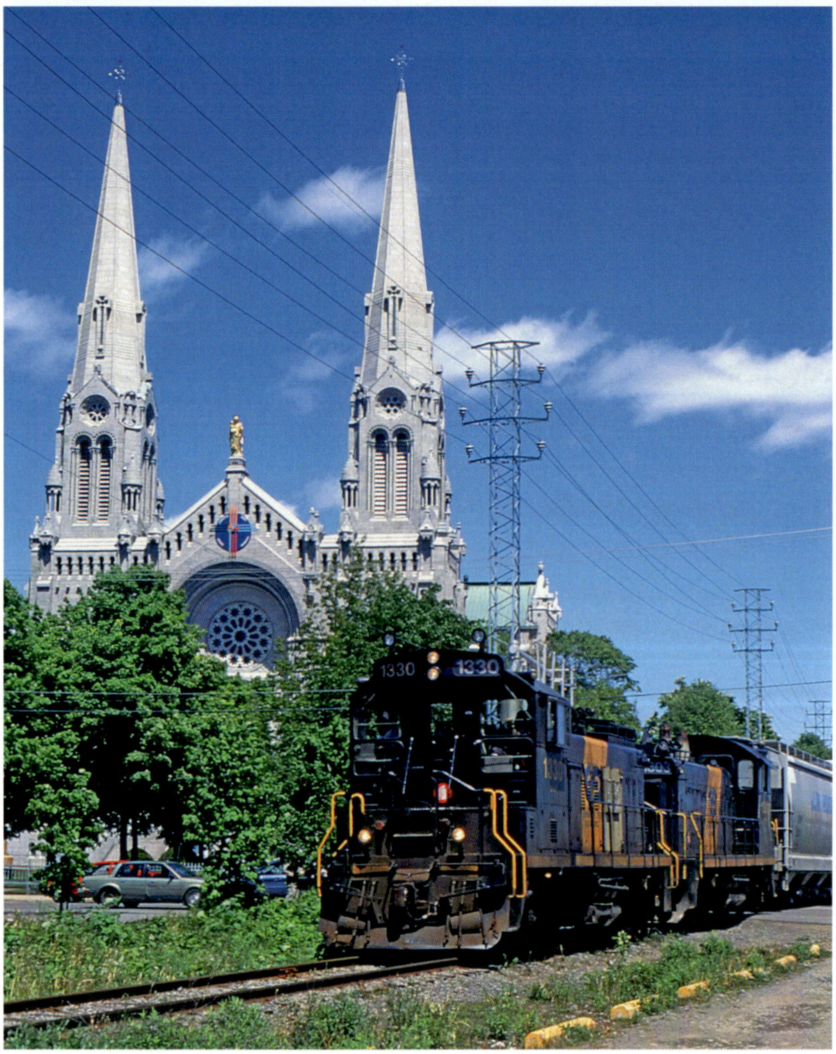

ABOVE: Less than 10 miles east of Quebec City, Montmorency Falls is one of the scenic highlights of Quebec. Higher than Niagara Falls, it provided a magnificent setting for a westbound Charlevoix Railway freight led by a pair of GMDD switchers on June 9, 2000. The railway had an interesting history. Built in the late 1880s, from 1904 to 1951 it was run as the Quebec Railway Light and Power and electrified to provide passenger and freight service. Canadian National took over the line in 1951 and sold it to the Quebec Railway Corporation in 1994, which renamed it the Charlevoix Railway (CFC). *(BDP)*

LEFT: The imposing Basilica of Ste. Anne de Beaupre rose above a westbound Charlevoix Railway freight on June 9, 2000. The shrine is a popular spot for pilgrims hoping for a miraculous cure for their ailments, with hundreds of canes and crutches left behind by the faithful. *(BDP)*

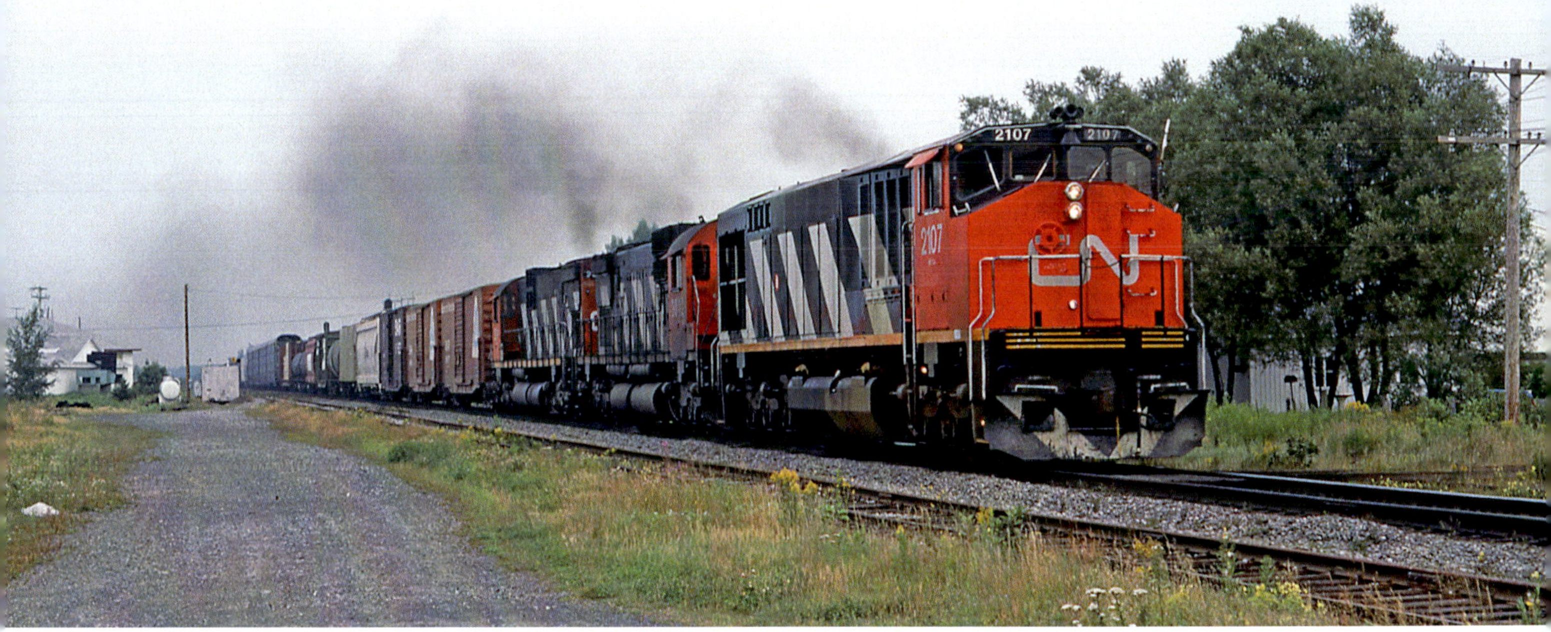

ABOVE: West of Quebec City, an eastbound CNR freight blasted by led by HR616 #2107 in August 1987. The lead unit was built by Bombardier in 1982, one of 20 rostered by the CNR. They introduced the "Draper Taper" body style, designed for good visibility by the crew in the cab looking back over the train. The HR in the model designation stood for "high reliability," unfortunately not a trait they displayed. *(JC)*

Montreal to Maine

BELOW: Closer to home for the Plant family was the CPR's line to Maine and New Brunswick. This line was made famous by the late Jim Shaughnessy, who covered it extensively in the late steam era. The line hosted through freights and the *Atlantic Limited*, trains #41 and #42, between Montreal and St. John, NB. On its usual assignment, E8 #1802 waited at Windsor Station on a rather dreary day in December 1974 before its evening departure for St. John. The CPR purchased three U.S.-built E8s for Montreal/Boston passenger service; trains long gone by the time #1802 posed for the photographer on this winter day. *(JFP)*

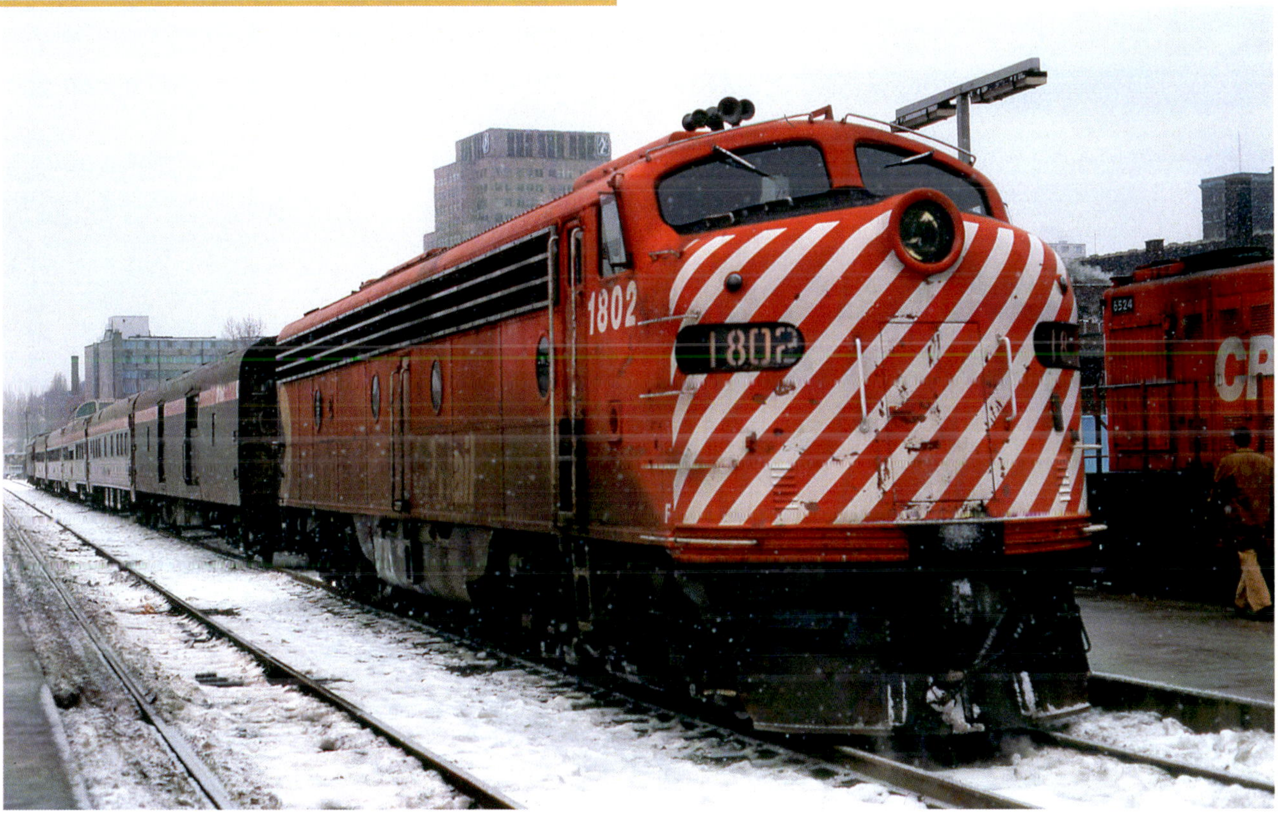

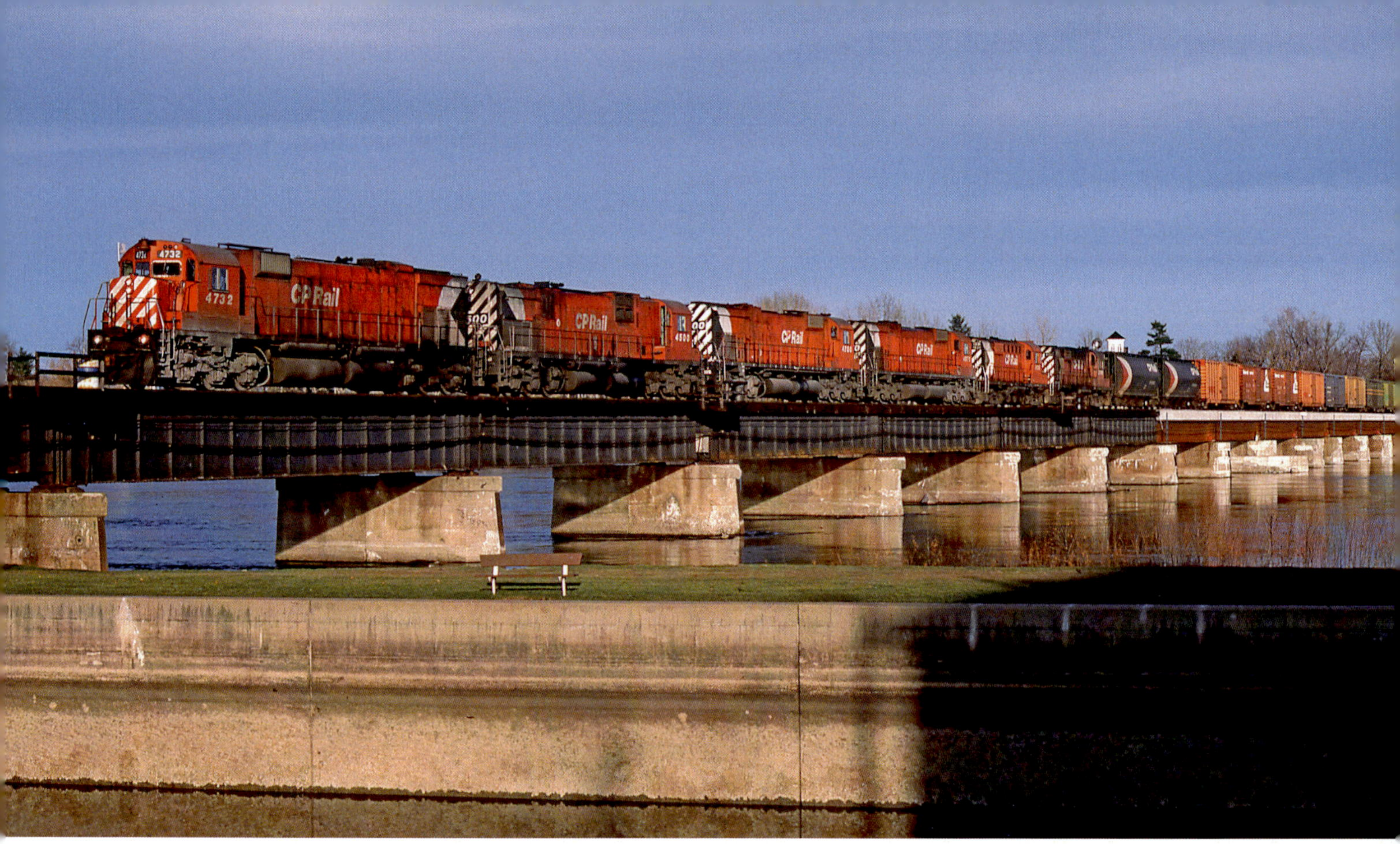

ABOVE: St. Jean sur Richelieu is a city of around 98,000 residents located roughly 25 miles east of Montreal on the Richelieu River. The CPR crossed the river on a long open-sided bridge well-set-up for good photographs of trains in either direction. In November 1987 Jeffrey caught this westbound crossing the Richelieu River in nice late-afternoon light with a six-unit set of power. *(JGP)*

BELOW: A broadside view of the bridge at St. Jean sur Richelieu was just able to fit in the six six-axle MLW units heading east in November 1987. *(JGP)*

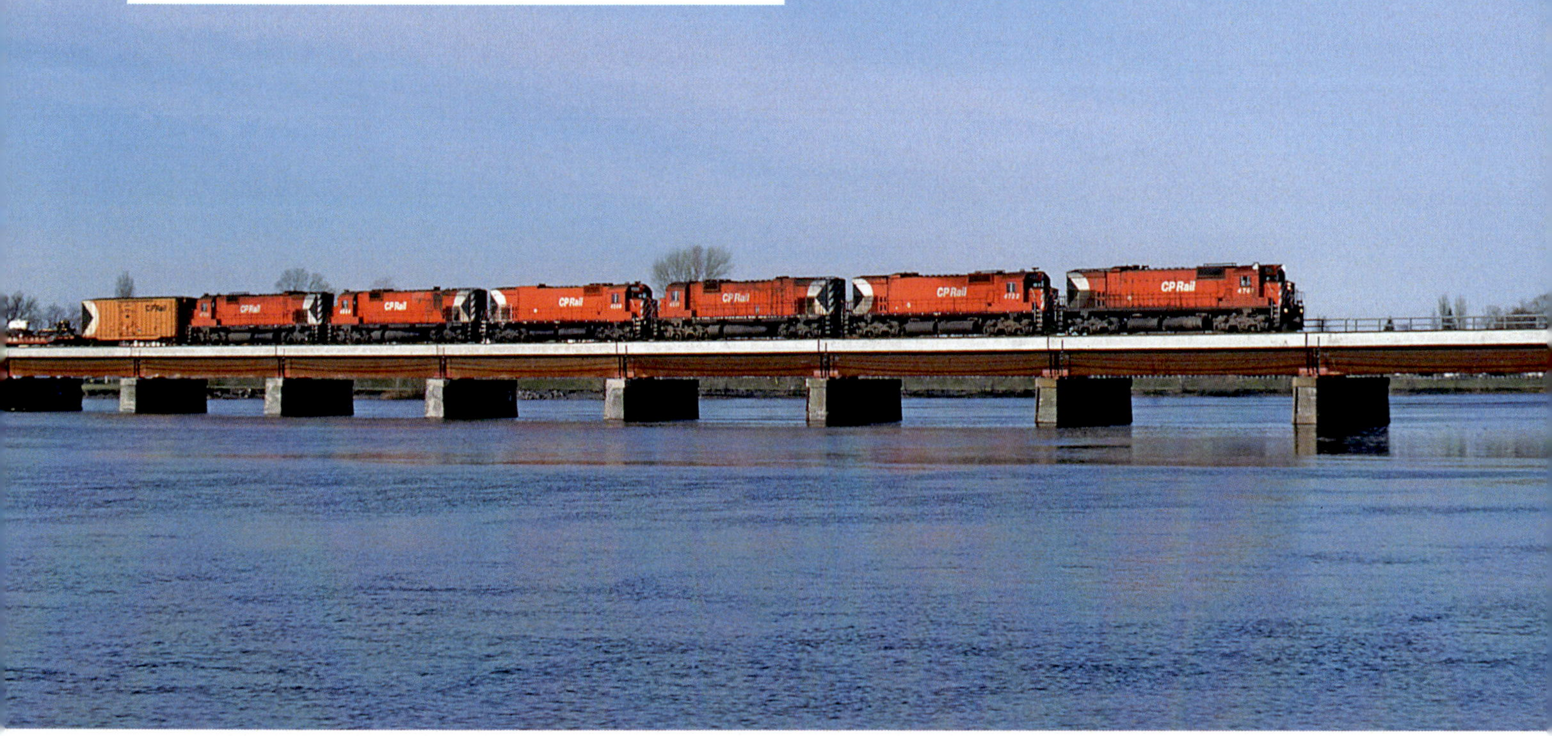

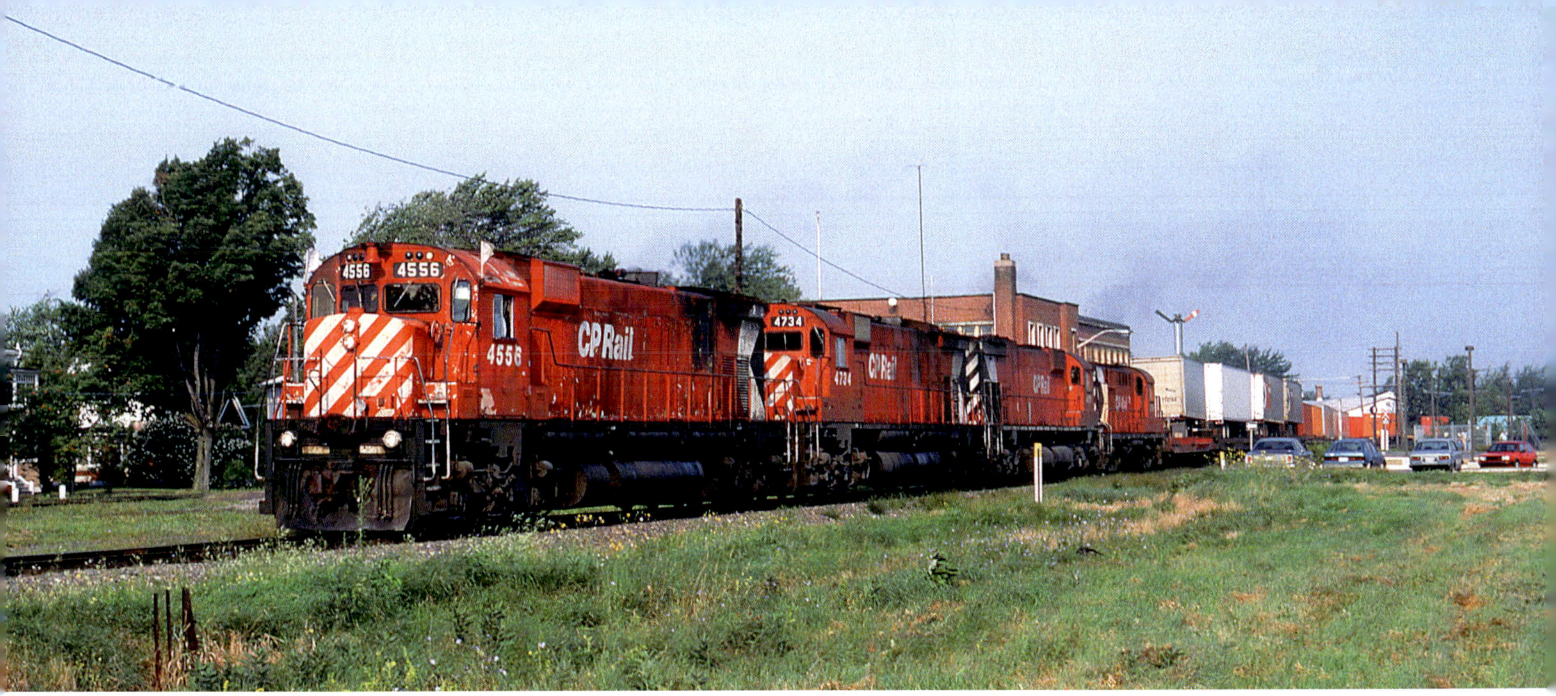

ABOVE: Farnham was an important location on the CPR, where its Montreal-St. John, NB mainline met its line to Vermont. It is on the western flank of the so-called "Eastern Townships," a region first settled by English-speaking settlers but now mostly inhabited by French-speakers. At the station at Farnham, the friendly station operators provided useful information on train movements. On August 16, 1987, train #522 headed east past the large brick station at Farnham. *(JC)*

BELOW: Eastbound train #522 paused at the Sherbrooke station for a crew change on August 16, 1987. We chased this train from Farnham to the Maine border at Megantic,QC this day. *(JC)*

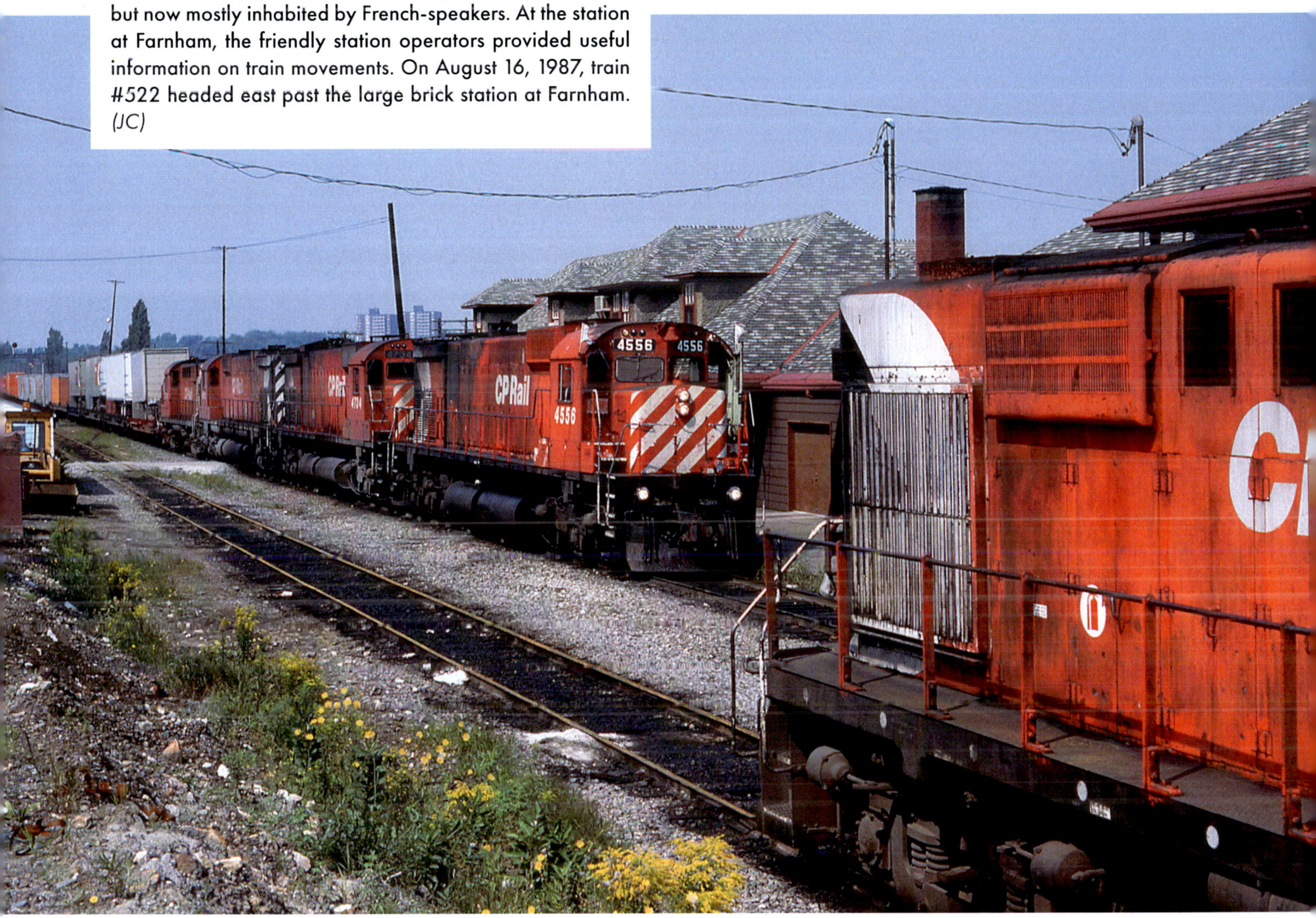

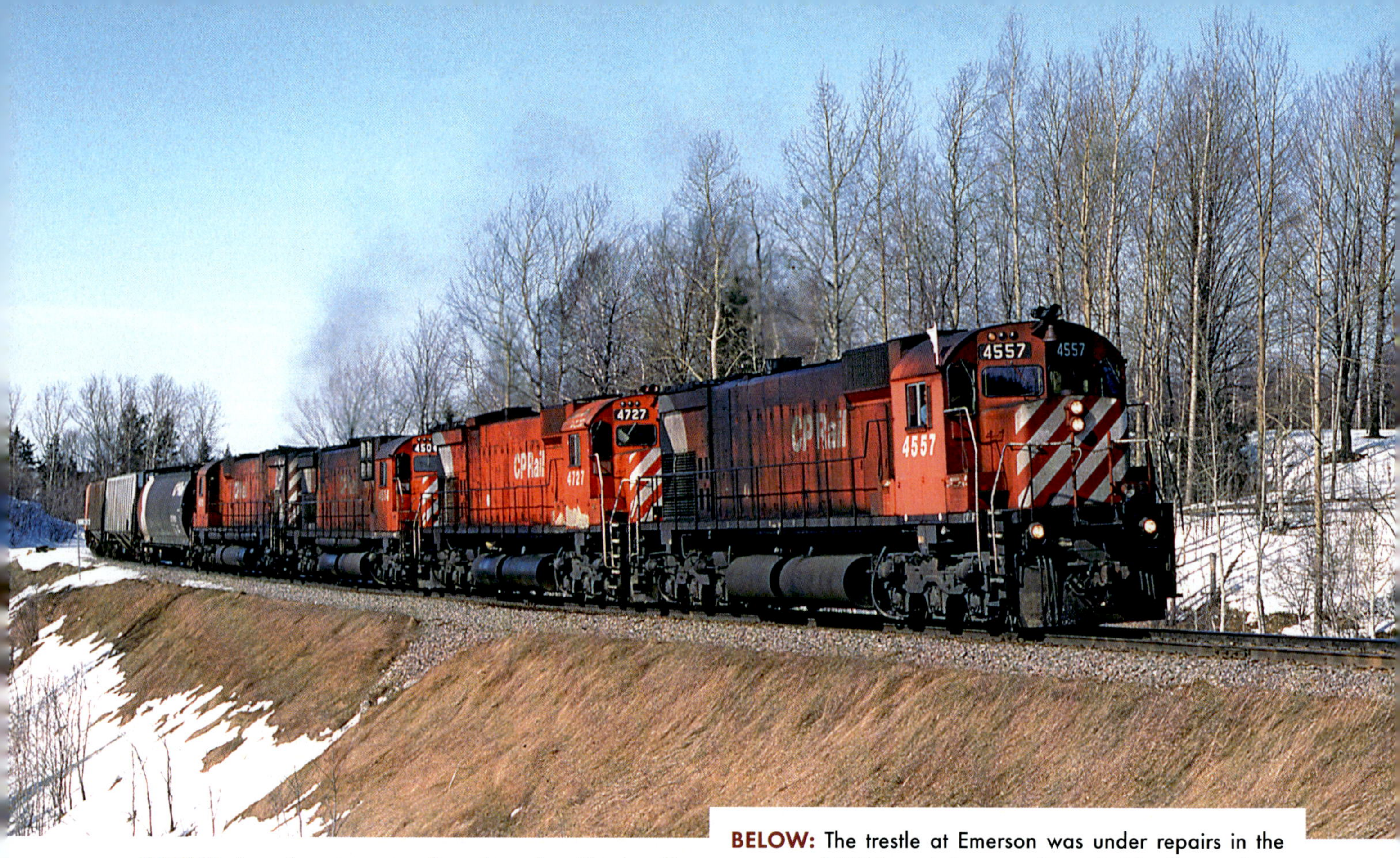

ABOVE: A grain extra passed eastbound at Huntingville with four six-axle MLW units in November 1993. *(JGP)*

BELOW: The trestle at Emerson was under repairs in the summer of 1987, restricting speed to only 10 miles per hour and providing a good opportunity to get ahead of the otherwise fast-moving train #522 on August 16, 1987. *(JC)*

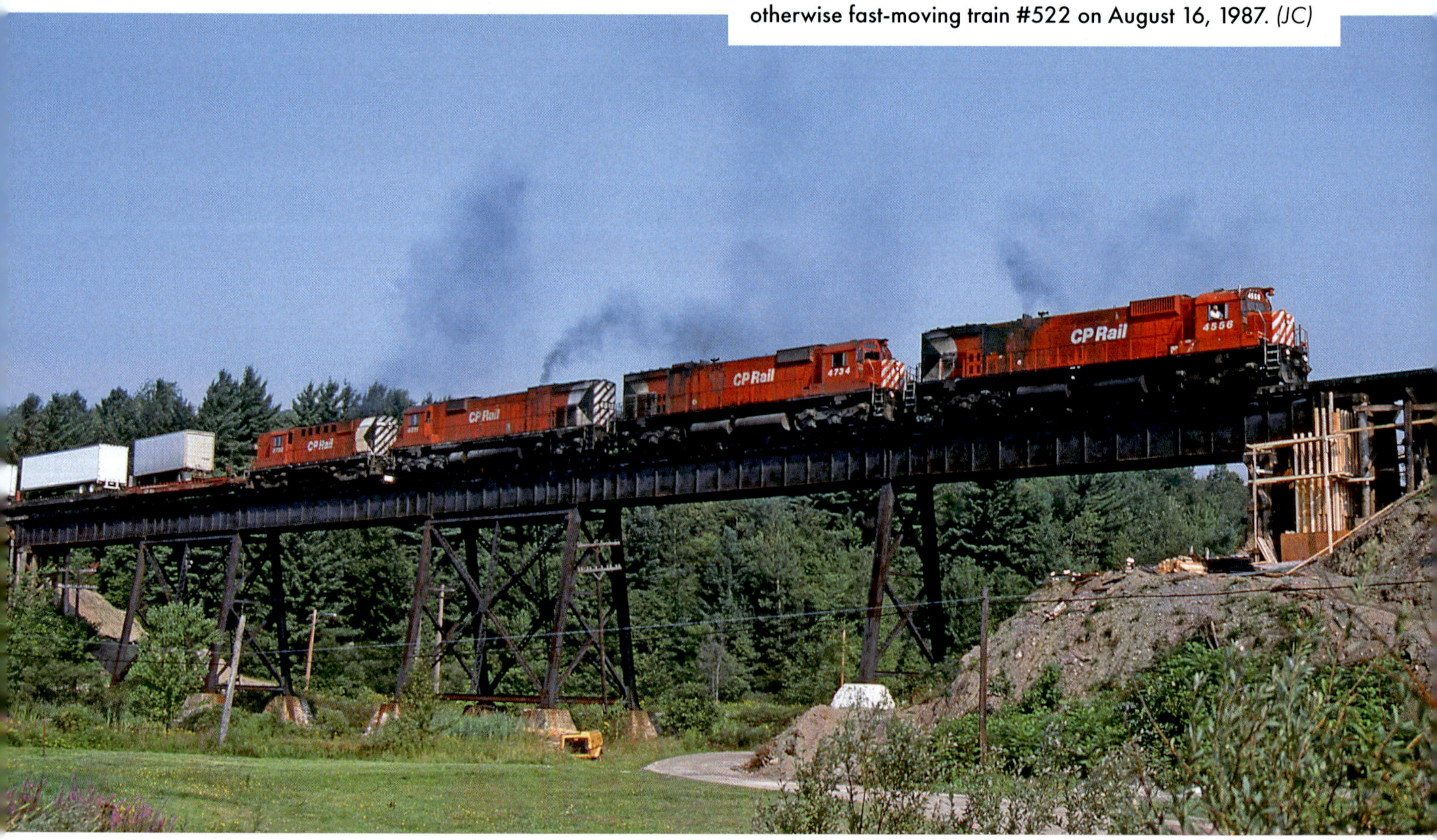

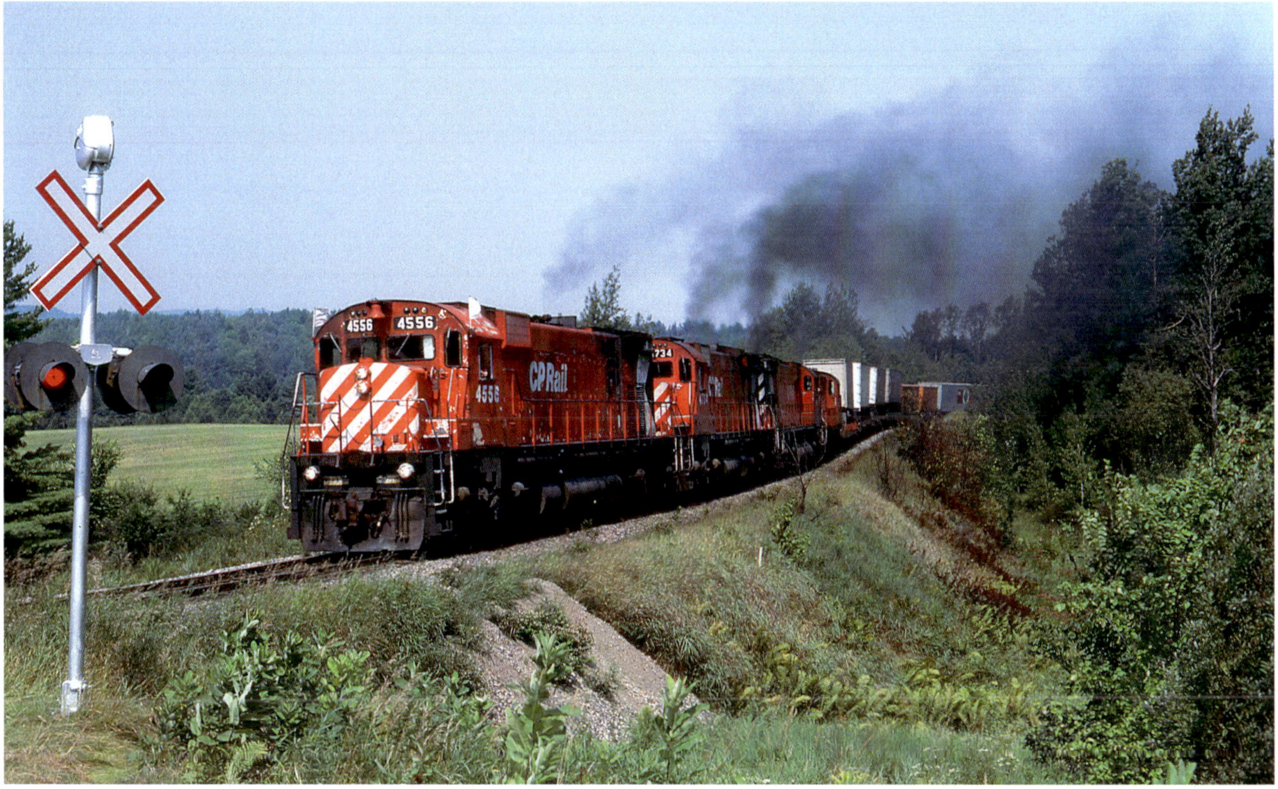

ABOVE: Train #522's four Alco units were working hard and smoking profusely as the eastbound train hit the grade outside Johnville, Quebec on August 16, 1987. *(JC)*

BELOW: Nearing the international border train #522 eased to a stop at the Megantic station on August 16, 1987. A new crew will board to take the train across the remote Maine woods to the next crew change point, Brownville Junction, ME. Things seem happy and serene at the little border town as the train enters; it would be a scene of terror and destruction in the early morning hours of July 6, 2013 as an unattended train of oil cars derailed and exploded, destroying much of downtown Megantic and killing 47 of its residents. By that time, CPR had sold the line and the operator was the Montreal, Maine & Atlantic Railway. *(JC)*

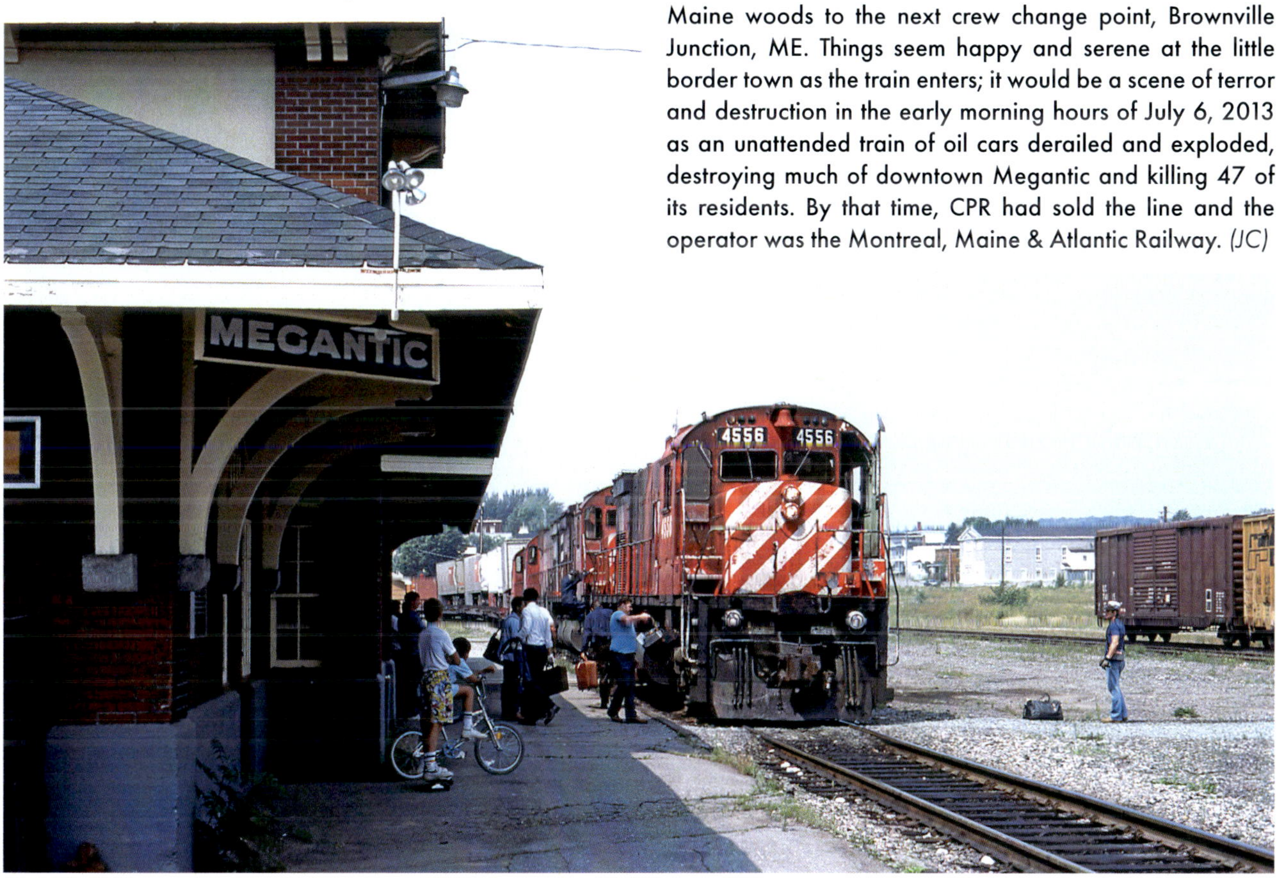

Ottawa River Bridge: Canadian Pacific

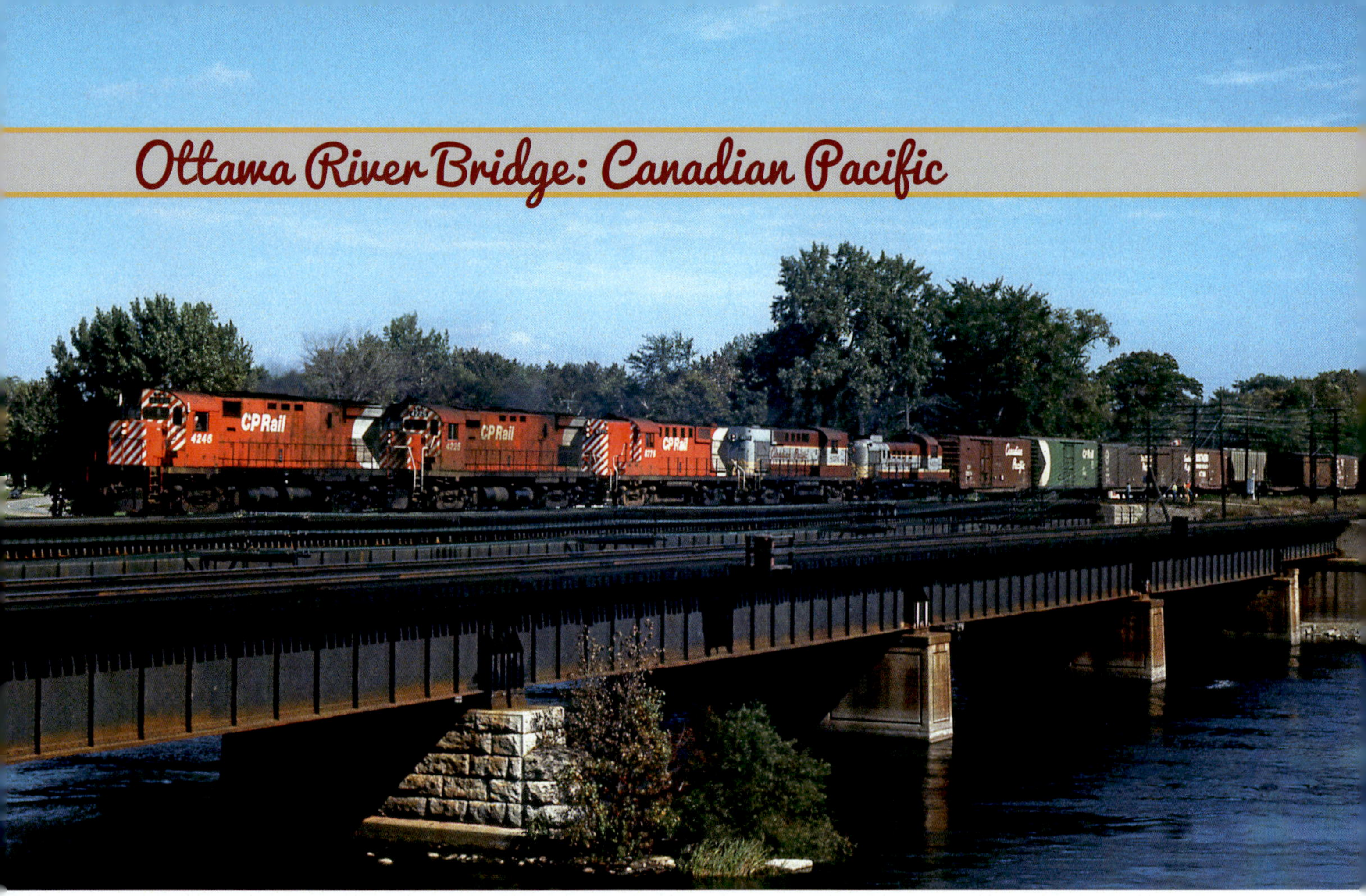

ABOVE: One of the busiest and most photogenic locations for rail photography in Eastern Canada was the crossing of the Ottawa River west of Montreal. The main lines of the CNR and CPR crossed on parallel, open-sided bridges ideal for photography. A highway bridge with sidewalk also paralleled the railway bridges, providing easy and safe access. In the summer of 1970, the CPR was still in a transition from Tuscan and Gray to Action Red diesel color schemes. This westbound freight from September of that year is evidence of that change as a mixed set of MLW units crossed the Ottawa River en route to Smiths Falls with a pair of C424s leading two RS18s and an RS3. *(JC)*

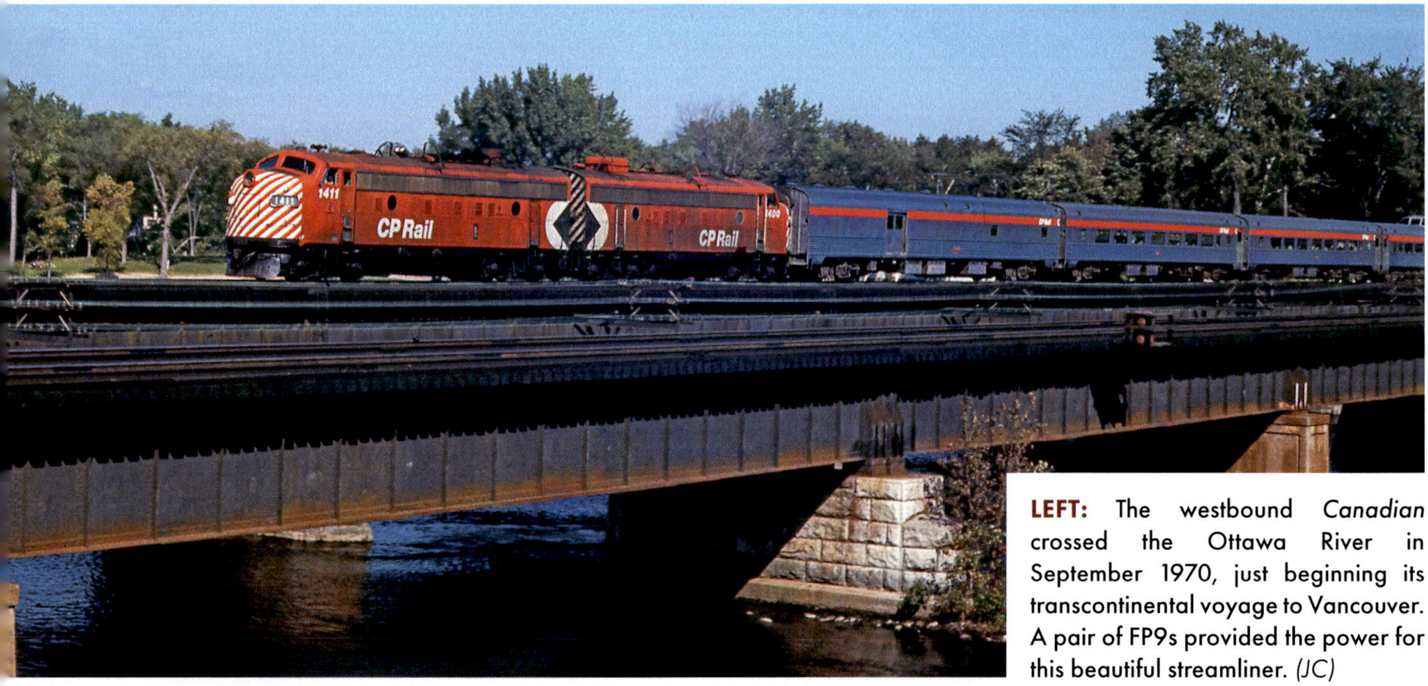

LEFT: The westbound *Canadian* crossed the Ottawa River in September 1970, just beginning its transcontinental voyage to Vancouver. A pair of FP9s provided the power for this beautiful streamliner. *(JC)*

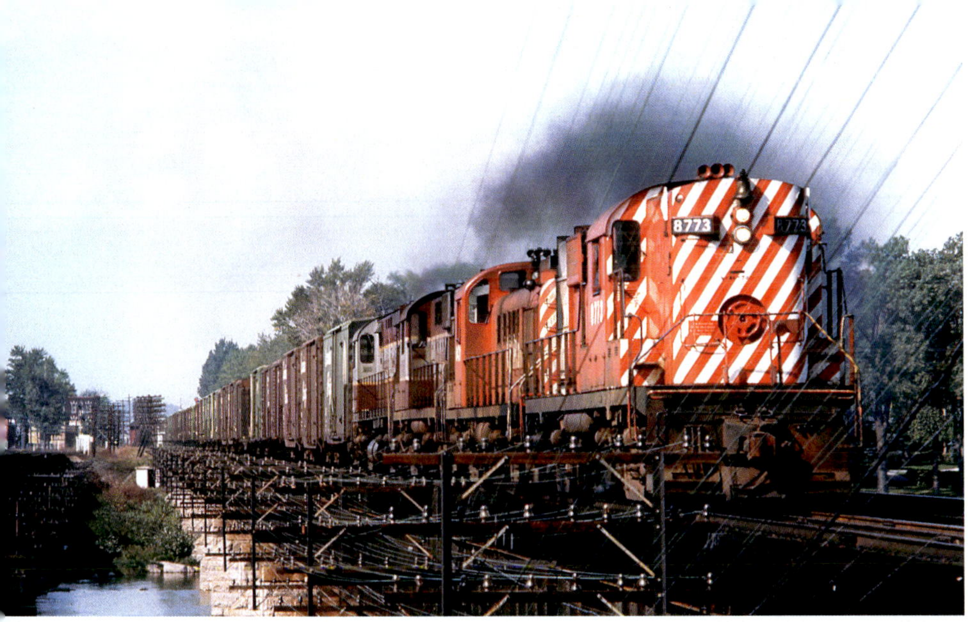

LEFT: In September 1971, RS18 #8773 led an all-Alco set of power eastward ahead of RS3 #8431, RS10 #8595 and C424 #4217. *(JC)*

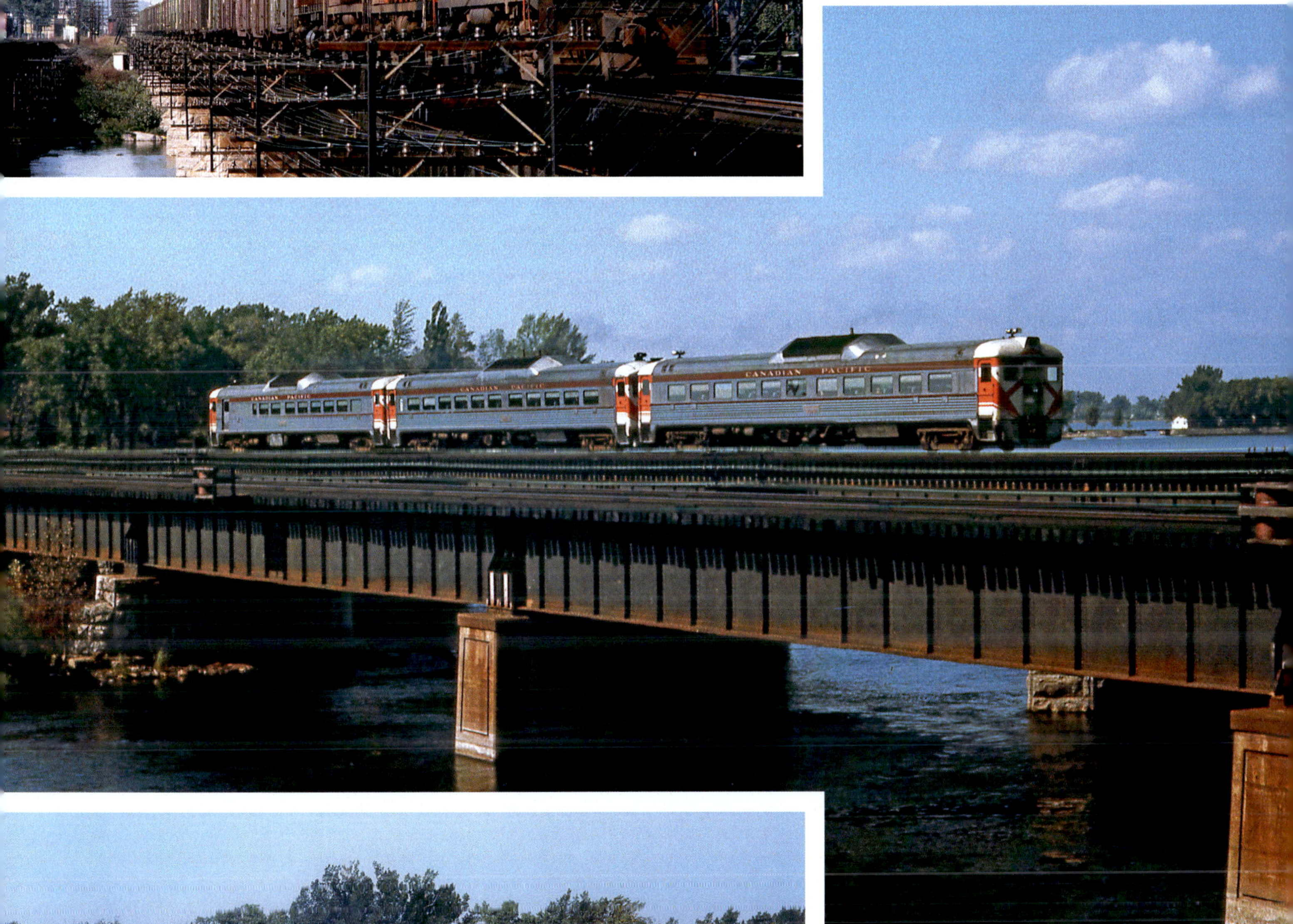

ABOVE: Budd *Dayliners* covered much of the Montreal-Ottawa passenger service for CPR in the 1970s. A trio crossed the Ottawa River bridge westbound in September 1970, showing off the old and new CPR schemes. *(JC)*

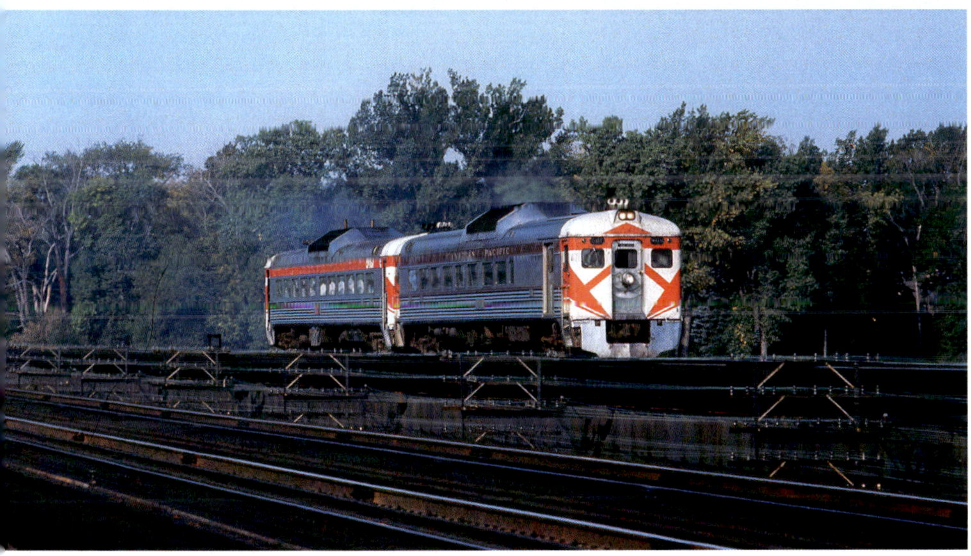

LEFT: A pair of *Dayliners* headed toward its Montreal destination in September 1970. *(JC)*

Ottawa River Bridge: Canadian National

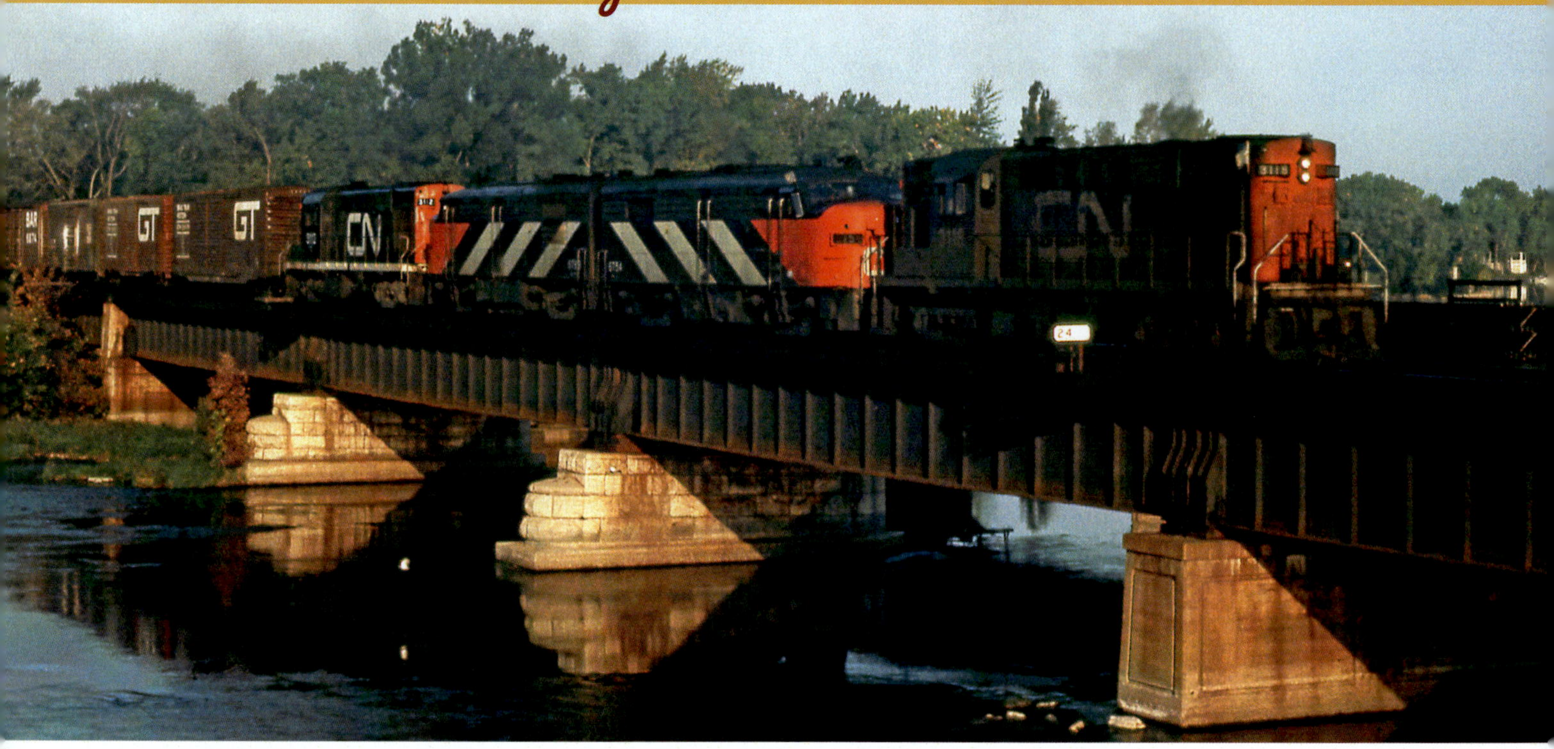

ABOVE: On an early September morning in 1971 the sun had just begun to light the bridges over the Ottawa River as an unusual set of power, two RS18s bracketing a pair of FPA-4s, led an eastbound freight toward Montreal. This was the only time that the Plants found CNR Alco cab units on a freight movement. *(JC)*

BELOW: A trio of RS18s led a mixed freight over the bridge that September morning in 1970. The RS18 was one of the success stories for Montreal Locomotive Works, a reliable and versatile locomotive that enjoyed a long career on the CNR, which purchased 225 of the 1,800 horsepower road switchers. *(JC)*

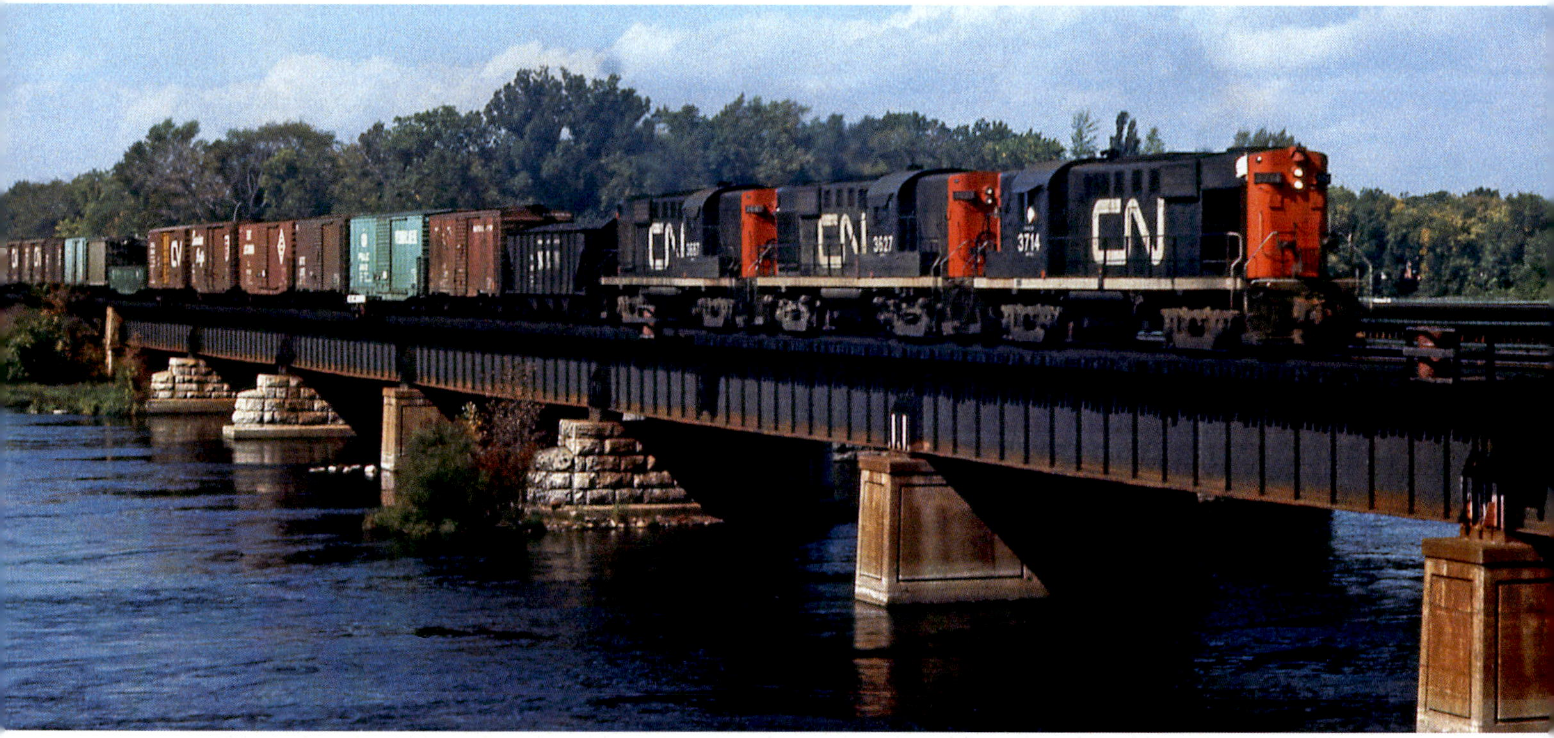

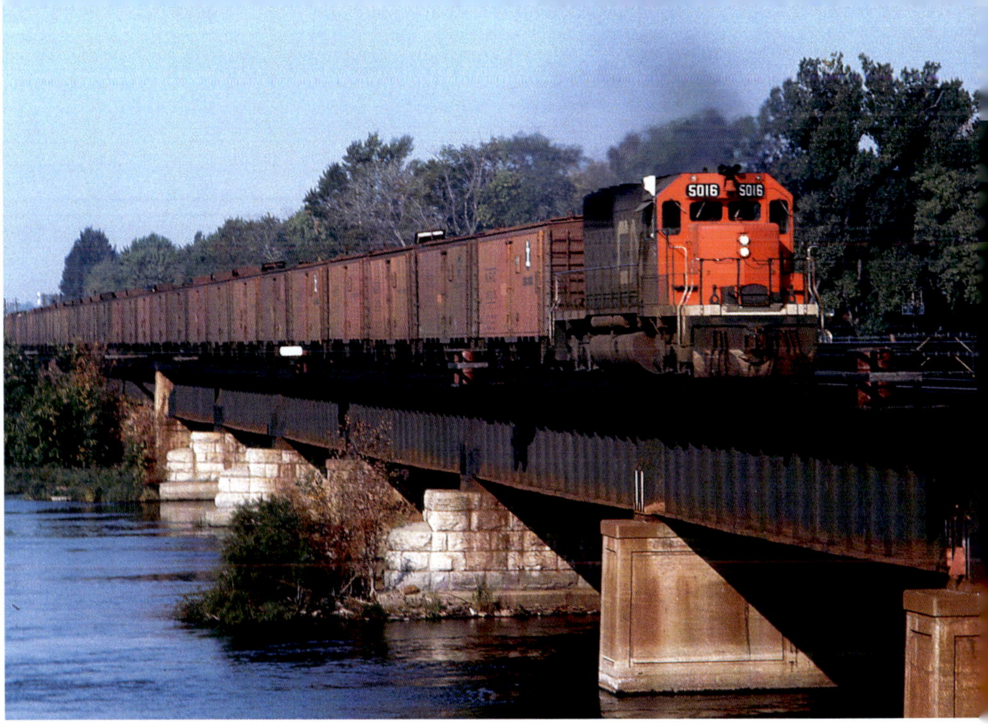

RIGHT: SD40 #5016 led a solid train of refrigerator cars over the blue waters of the Ottawa River in September 1970. *(JC)*

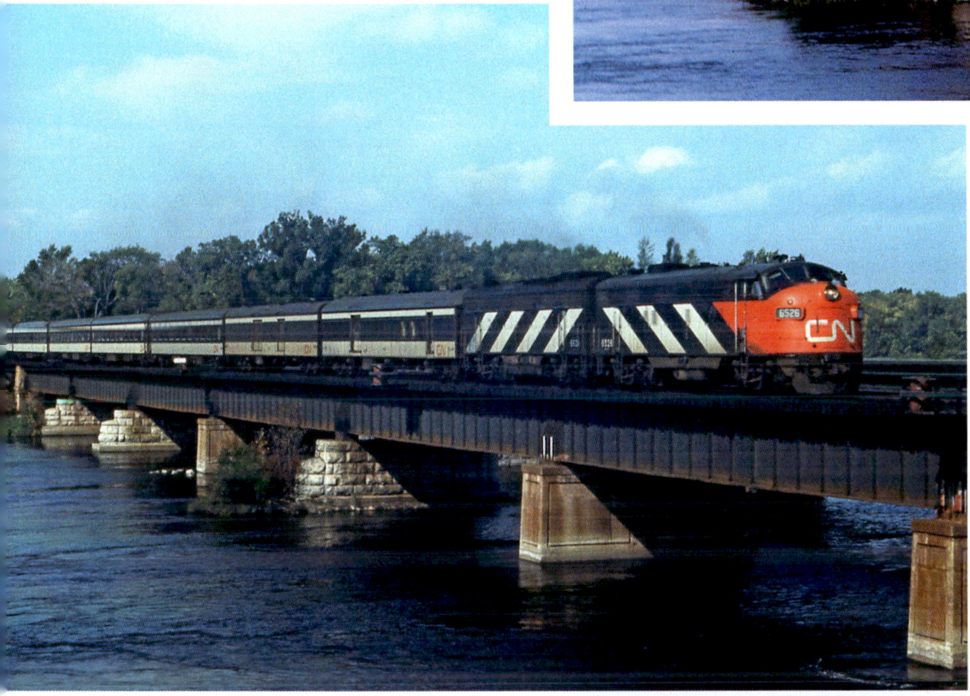

LEFT: An A/B set of FP9s headed toward Montreal on this September morning in 1970. *(JC)*

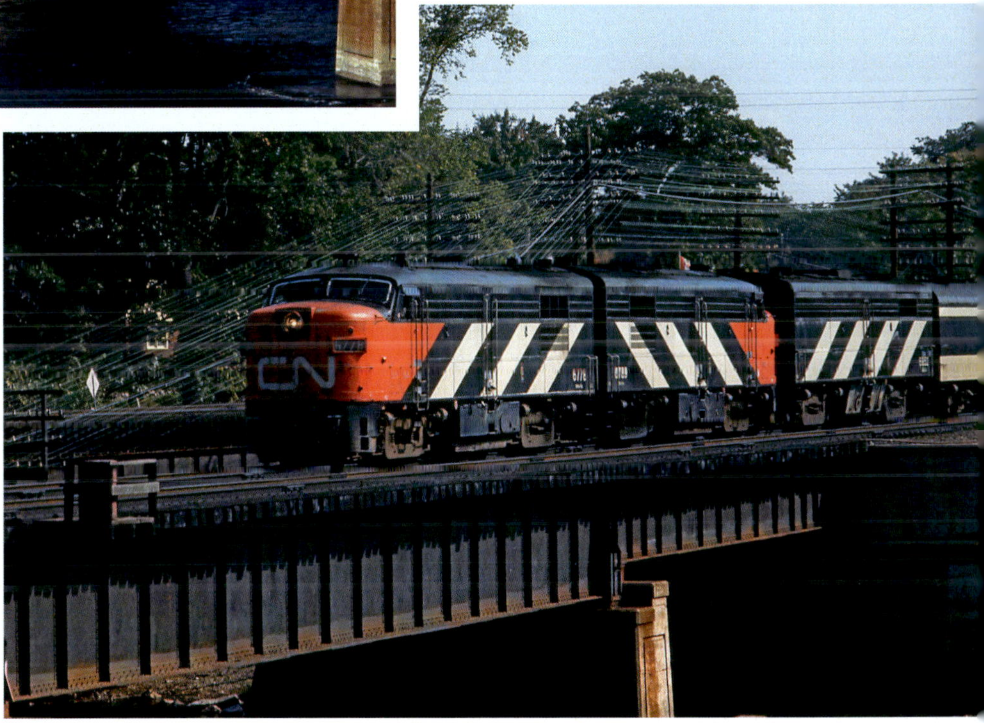

RIGHT: An oddly arranged set of three MLW cab units crossed the bridge over the Ottawa River westbound in September 1970. *(JC)*

Vaudreuil-Dorion

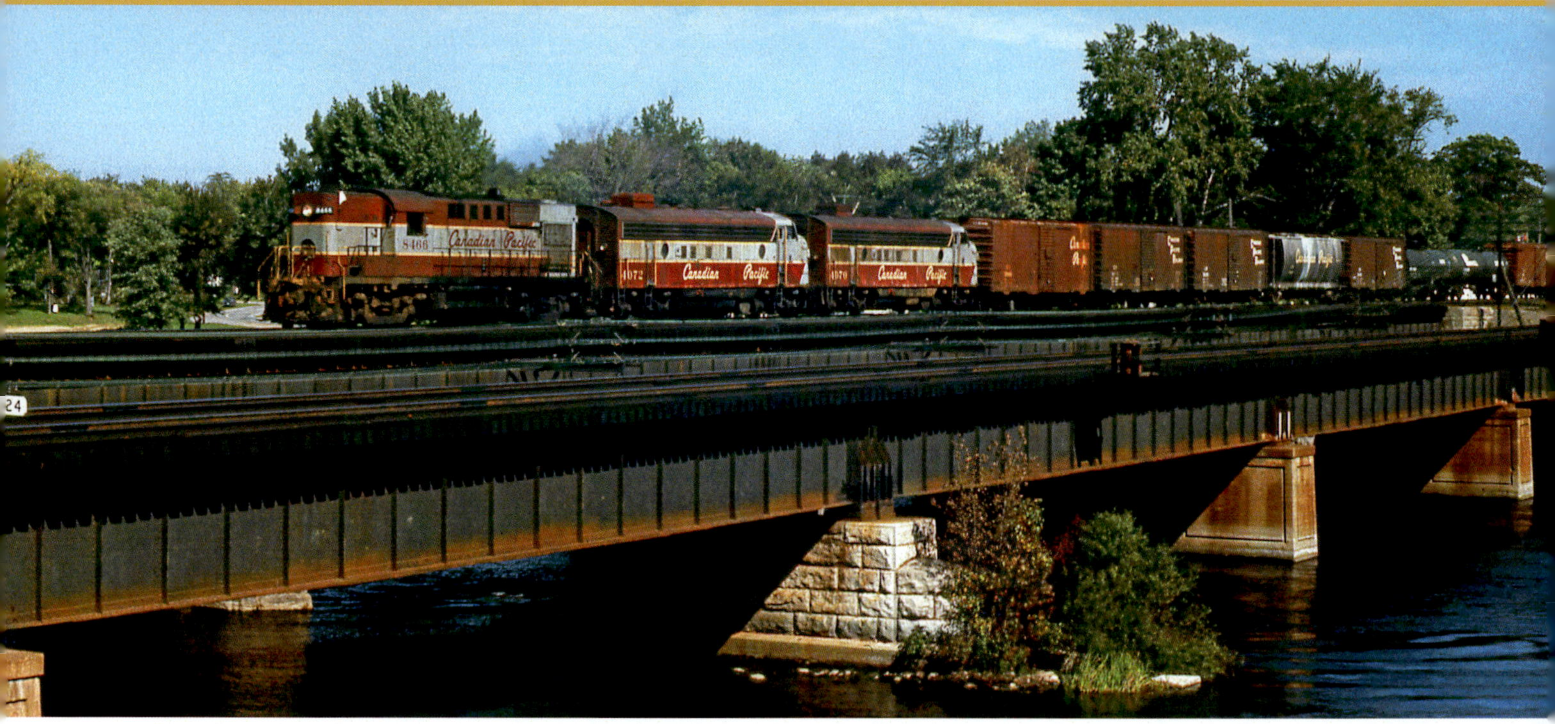

ABOVE: The CPR assigned a fleet of FP7s for the Montreal commuter service. On Sundays a westbound local pulled the FP7s from their servicing at Montreal to Vaudreuil to line up for Monday's commuter runs. It was crossing the Ottawa River this pleasant day in September 1970. *(JC)*

BELOW: After dropping off the FP7s, the "Cornwall Swing" pulled past the station at Vaudreuil to do some switching at the small yard there. RS10 #8466 is operating with the short hood leading as the crew prepare to do its work. *(JC)*

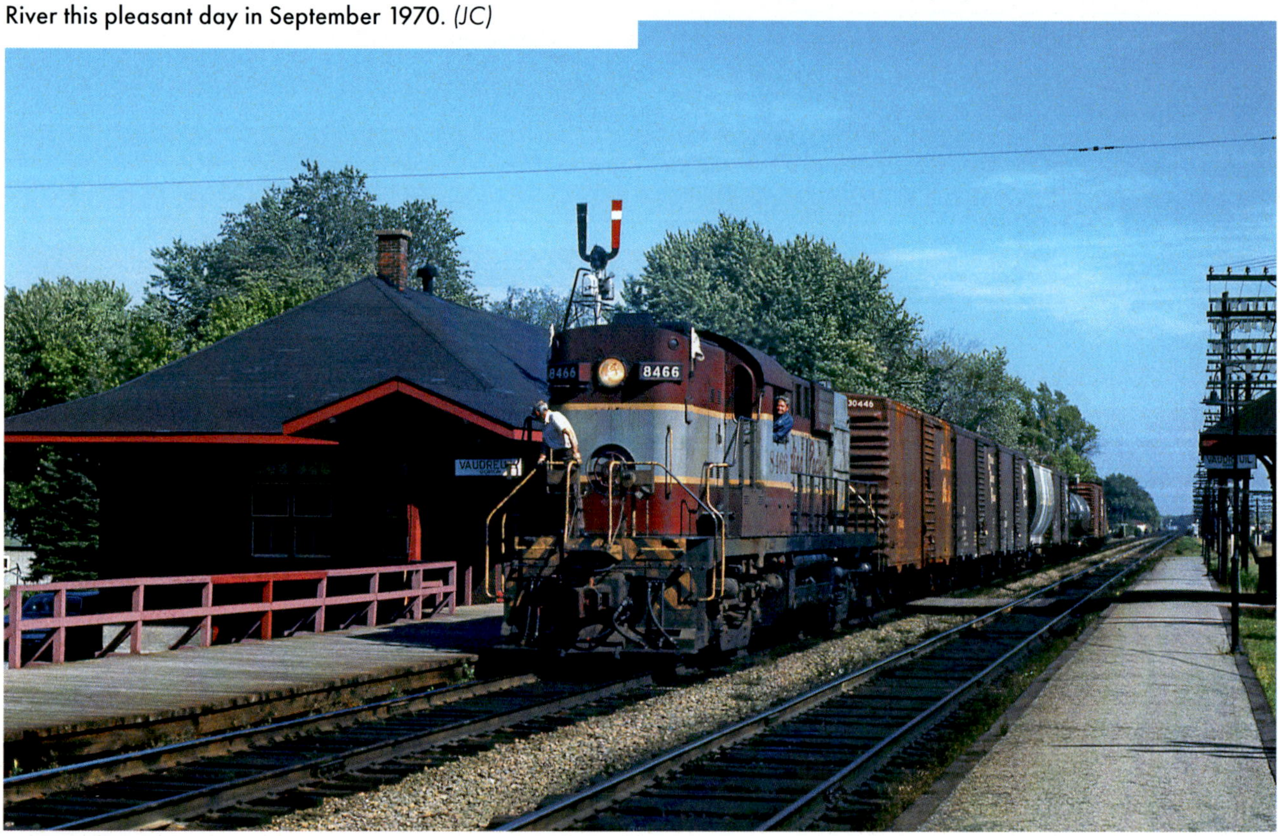

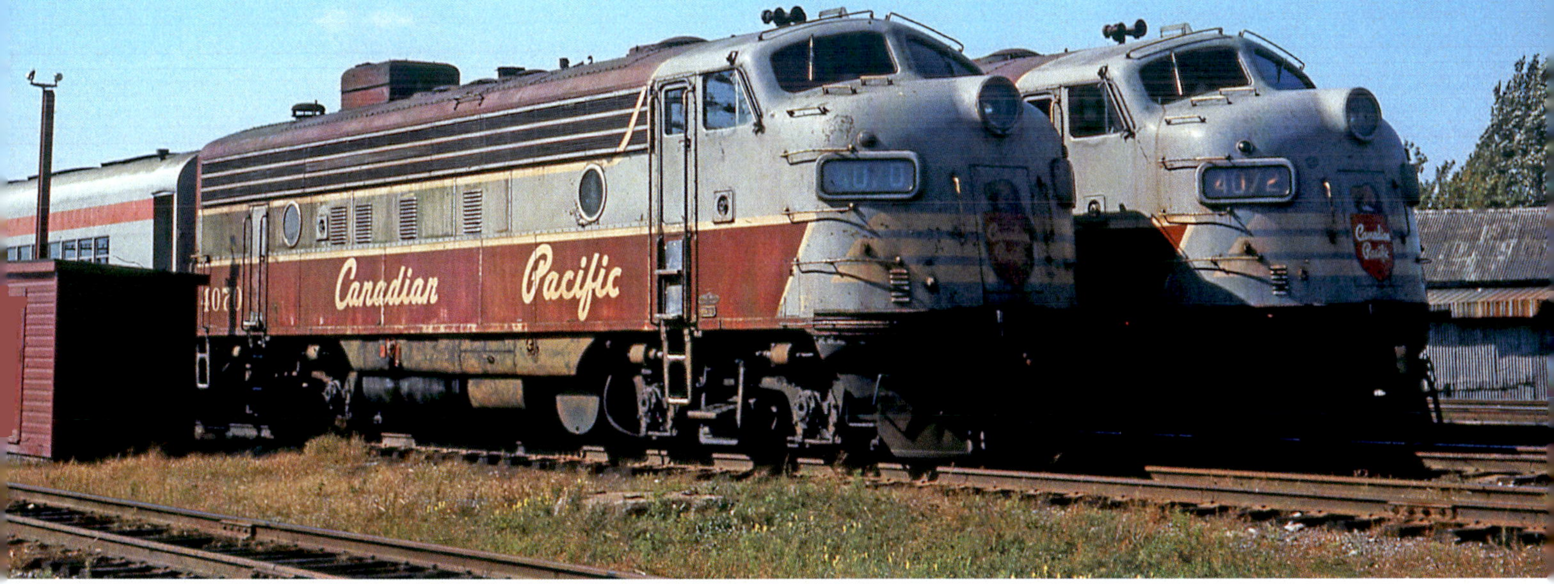

ABOVE: Two FP7s rested at Vaudreuil on a Sunday afternoon in September 1970, awaiting a return to service on Monday morning to bring commuters into Montreal. Both #4070 and #4072 were built in 1952. *(JC)*

BELOW: In the soft evening light of August 17, 1981, a westbound commuter train entered the Vaudreuil station behind FP7 #4075 repainted into the 1970s Action Red scheme. *(JFP)*

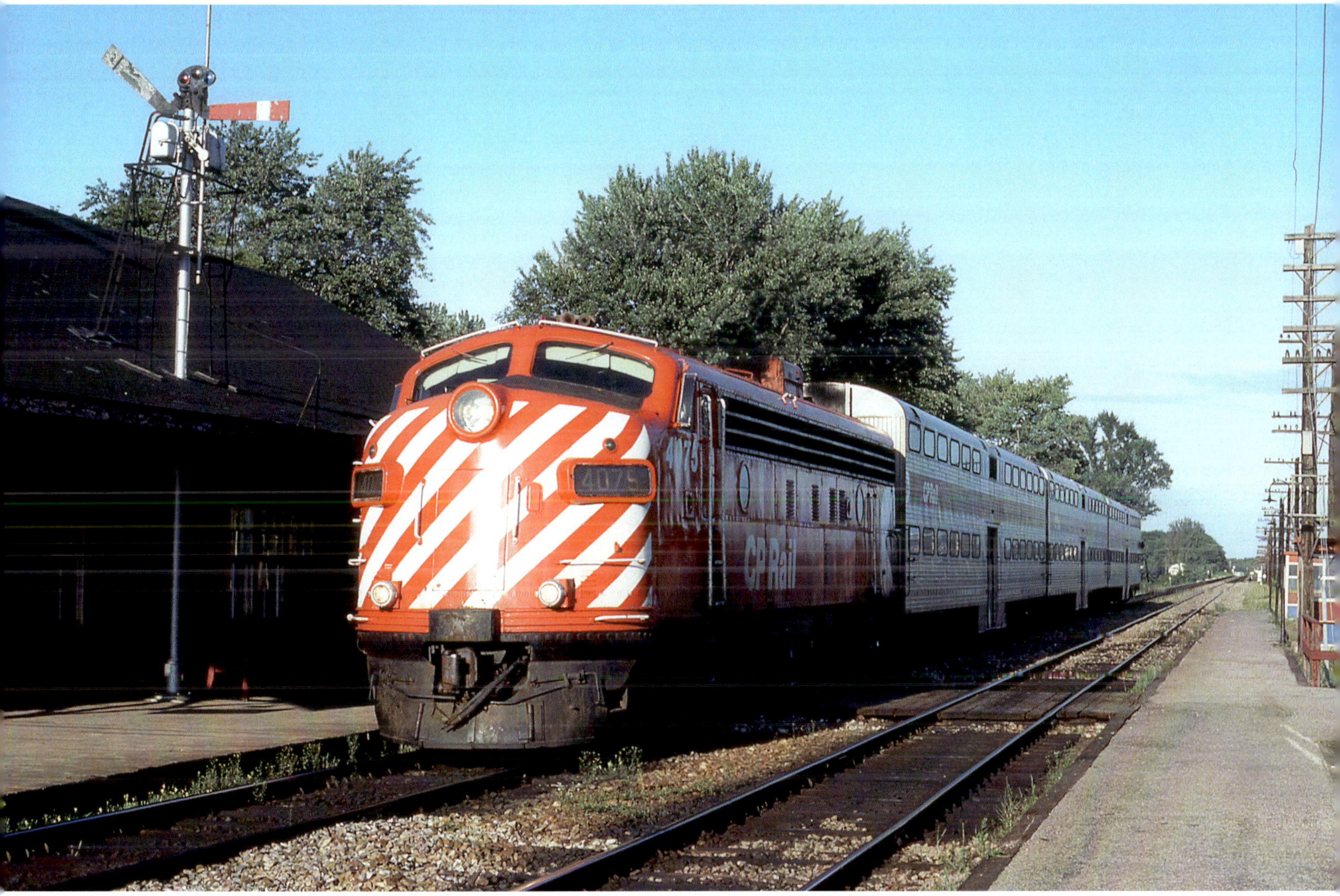

Via Rail

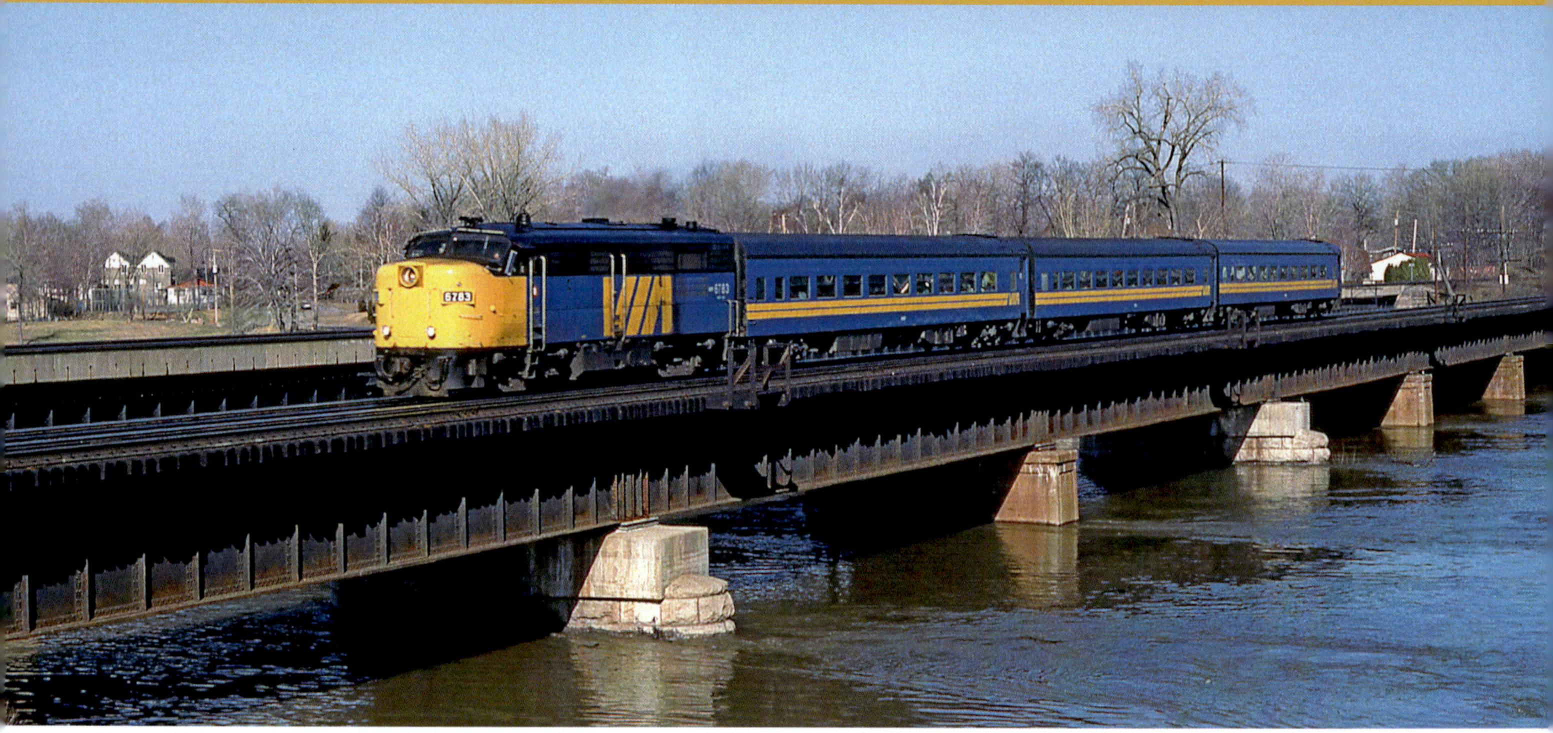

ABOVE: VIA Rail FPA-4 #6783 led a short westbound passenger train over the swollen Ottawa River in April 1988. FPA-4 #6783 sports ditch lights on its nose, without VIA markings. *(JFP)*

BELOW: A weary-looking Turbo Train headed west over the blue waters of the Ottawa River in the summer of 1981. This was its next-to-last year of operation; the final run of a Turbo was on October 31, 1982. *(JFP)*

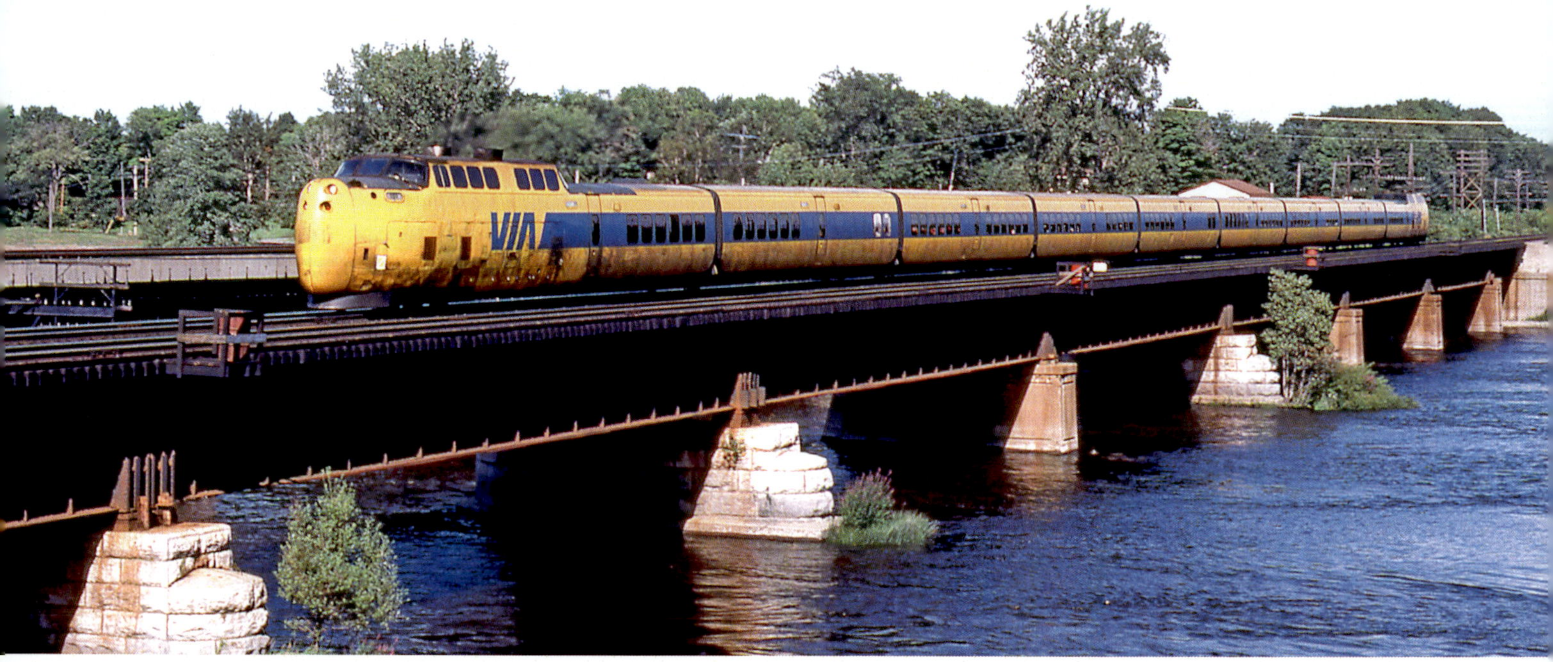

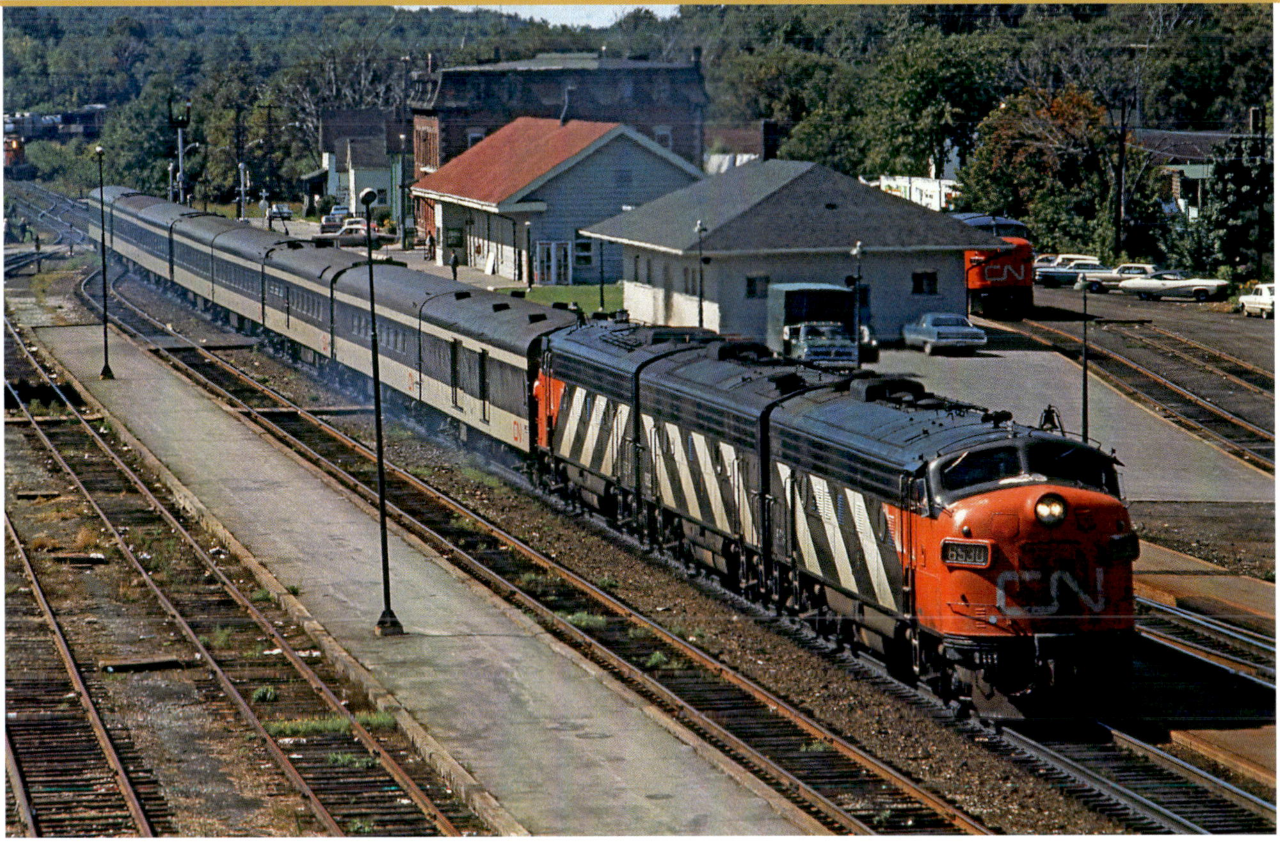

ABOVE: Moving west from Quebec into Ontario, we examine the rail activity at the city of Brockville. Brockville was, along with Gananoque and Smiths Falls, one of the three locations in eastern Ontario most often visited by the Plant brothers in the 1970s. Brockville was a great place to photograph the frequent freight and passenger trains on CNR's Montreal-Toronto corridor and the connecting trains to and from Ottawa that utilized the CPR's branch from Smiths Falls. CPR stationed a switcher, usually an Alco S3, near the station and if lucky, the CPR local from Smiths Falls would add some CPR action to what otherwise was a CNR town. Switching cars between the corridor and Ottawa trains provided several photo opportunities, as did crew changes at the CNR depot. In our first visit to Brockville in September 1970, a long eastbound train rolled through town behind an A/B/A set of FP-9s while a GP-9-powered freight waited west of the crossing and a single FPA-4 waited behind the station on the CPR branch for the run to Ottawa via Smiths Falls. *(JFP)*

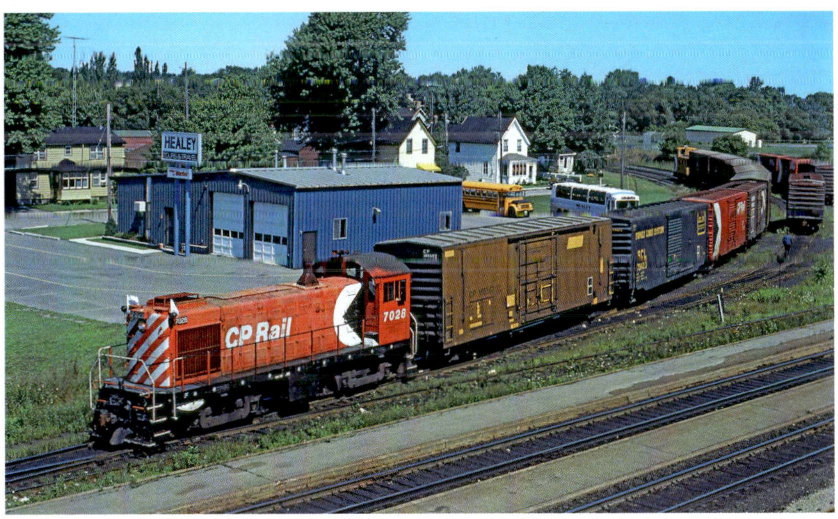

RIGHT: The CPR local from Smith Falls rolled into Brockville on August 11, 1979. *(JFP)*

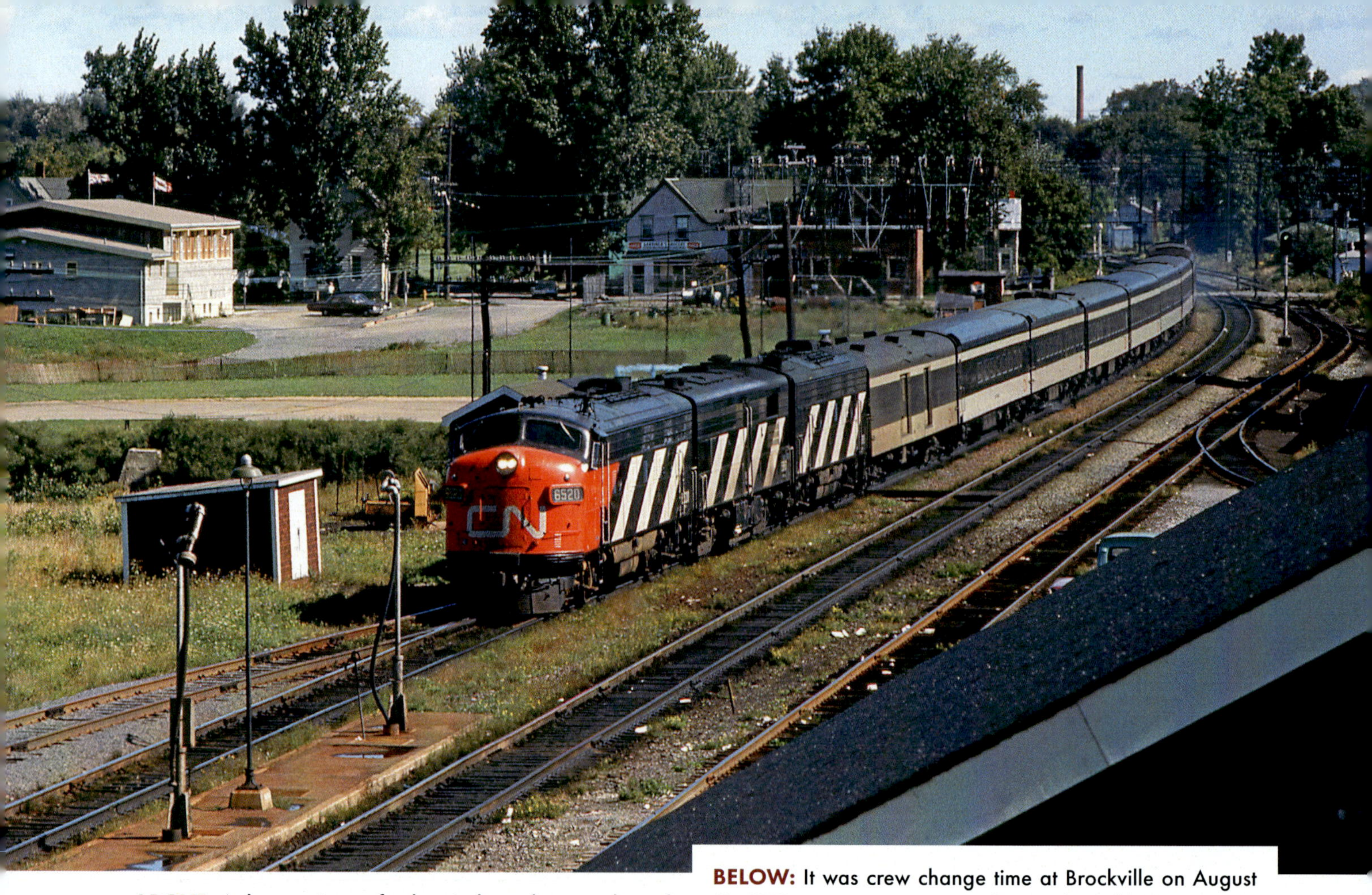

ABOVE: A three-unit set of cab units brought a westbound into Brockville on a pleasant and sunny day in September 1970. The mix of GMDD and MLW units was not unusual at this time. *(JFP)*

BELOW: It was crew change time at Brockville on August 11, 1979, as a new crew was about to board M420 #2545 to continue west to Toronto. The CNR purchased 80 of this type in the 1970s with the crew cab design for enhanced comfort, safety, and visibility for crews. *(JFP)*

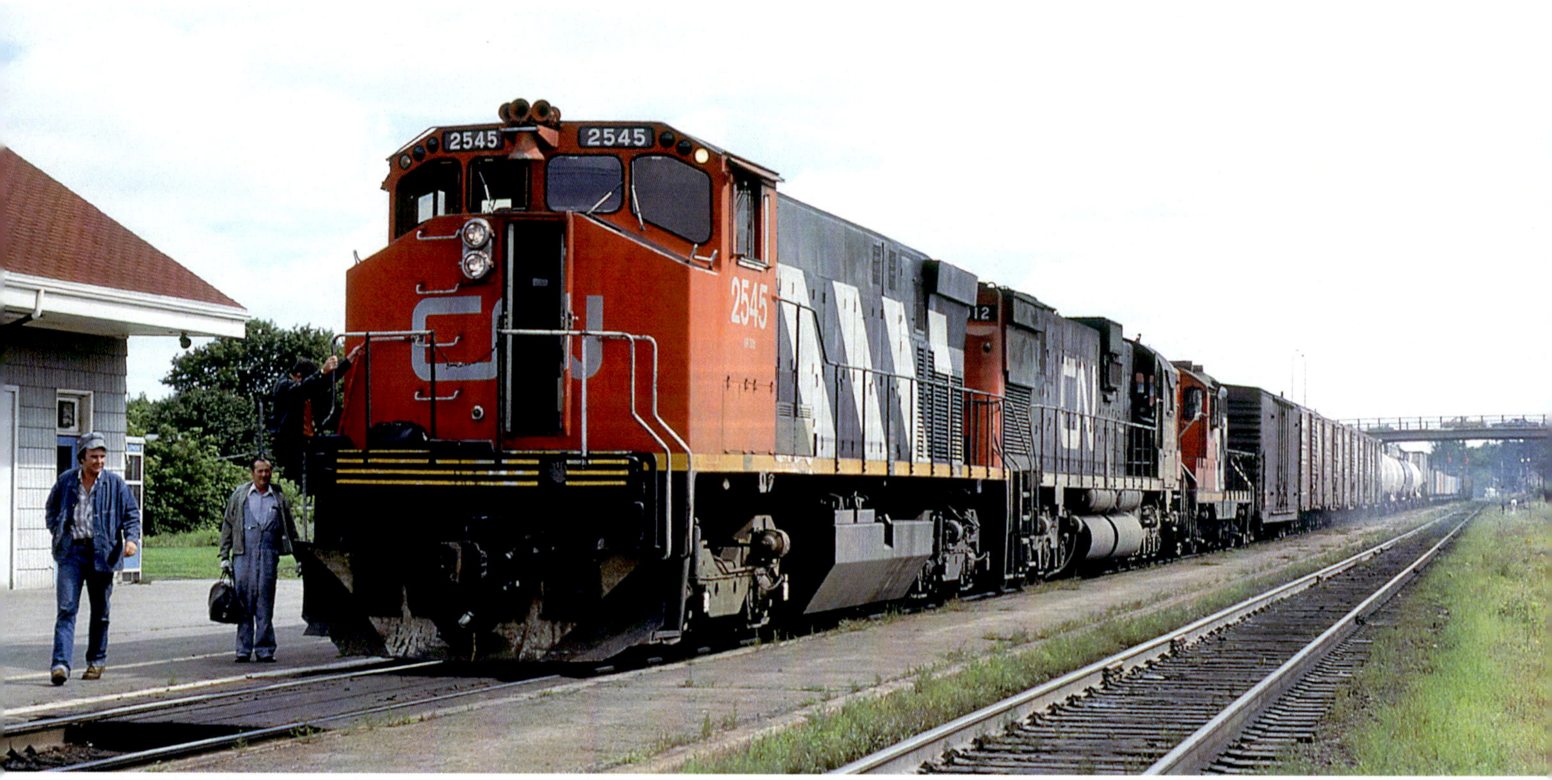

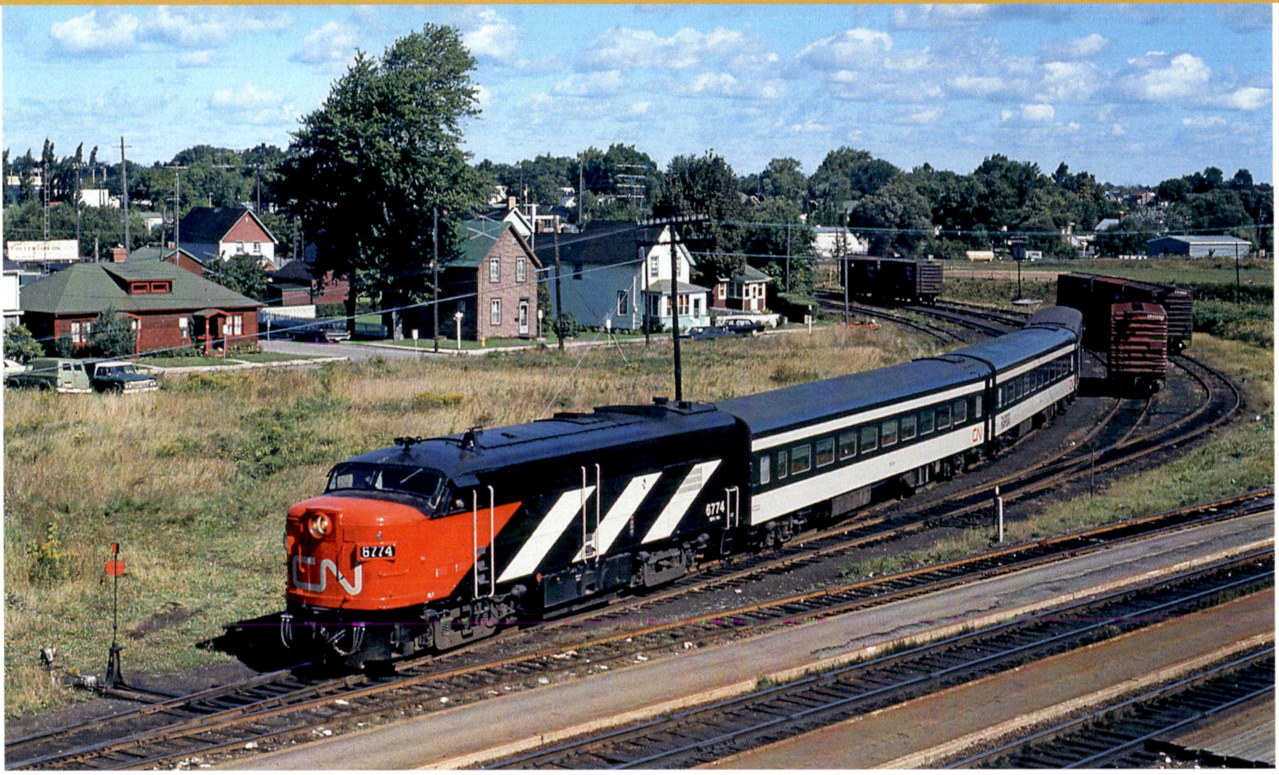

ABOVE: In September 1970, FPA-4 #6774 brought southbound train #41 from Ottawa into Brockville on the CPR branch line from Smiths Falls. *(JFP)*

BELOW: RS18 #3107 was substituting for the usual cab unit as it headed out of Brockville for Smiths Falls and Ottawa on August 11, 1979. *(JFP)*

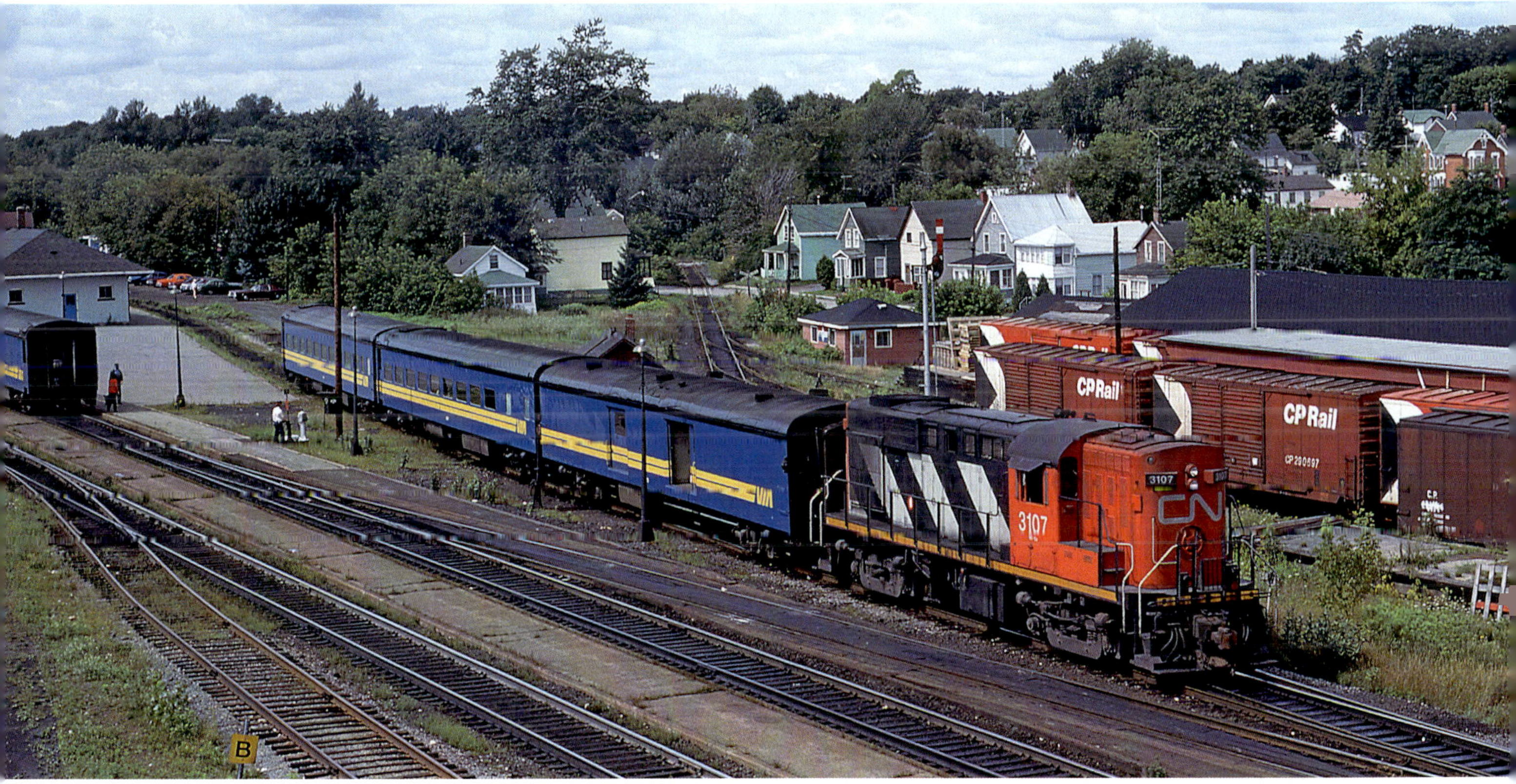

A Rainy Day in Brockville

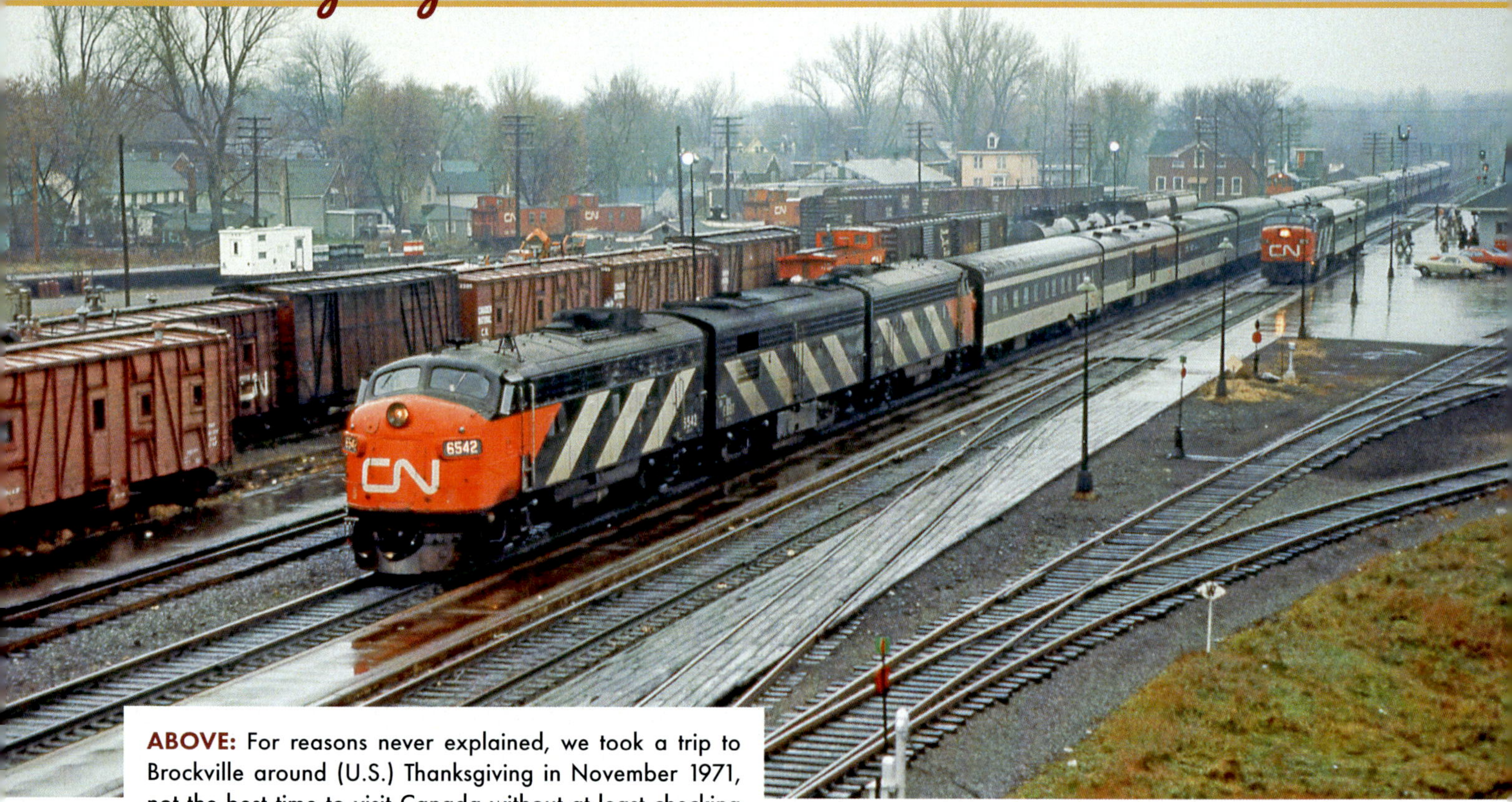

ABOVE: For reasons never explained, we took a trip to Brockville around (U.S.) Thanksgiving in November 1971, not the best time to visit Canada without at least checking the weather report. The first day we were in Brockville, it was a mix of rain and freezing rain and in the high 30s. Of course, with weather like this the rail activity was almost non-stop. Given some help from Photoshop, the day's output was exceptional for both freight and passenger action. FP9 #6542 led a three-unit set eastward. *(JC)*

BELOW: The station stop completed, the #6776 curved onto the CPR branch for the run to Smiths Falls and connection with the CNR line to Ottawa on this November 1971 afternoon. *(JC)*

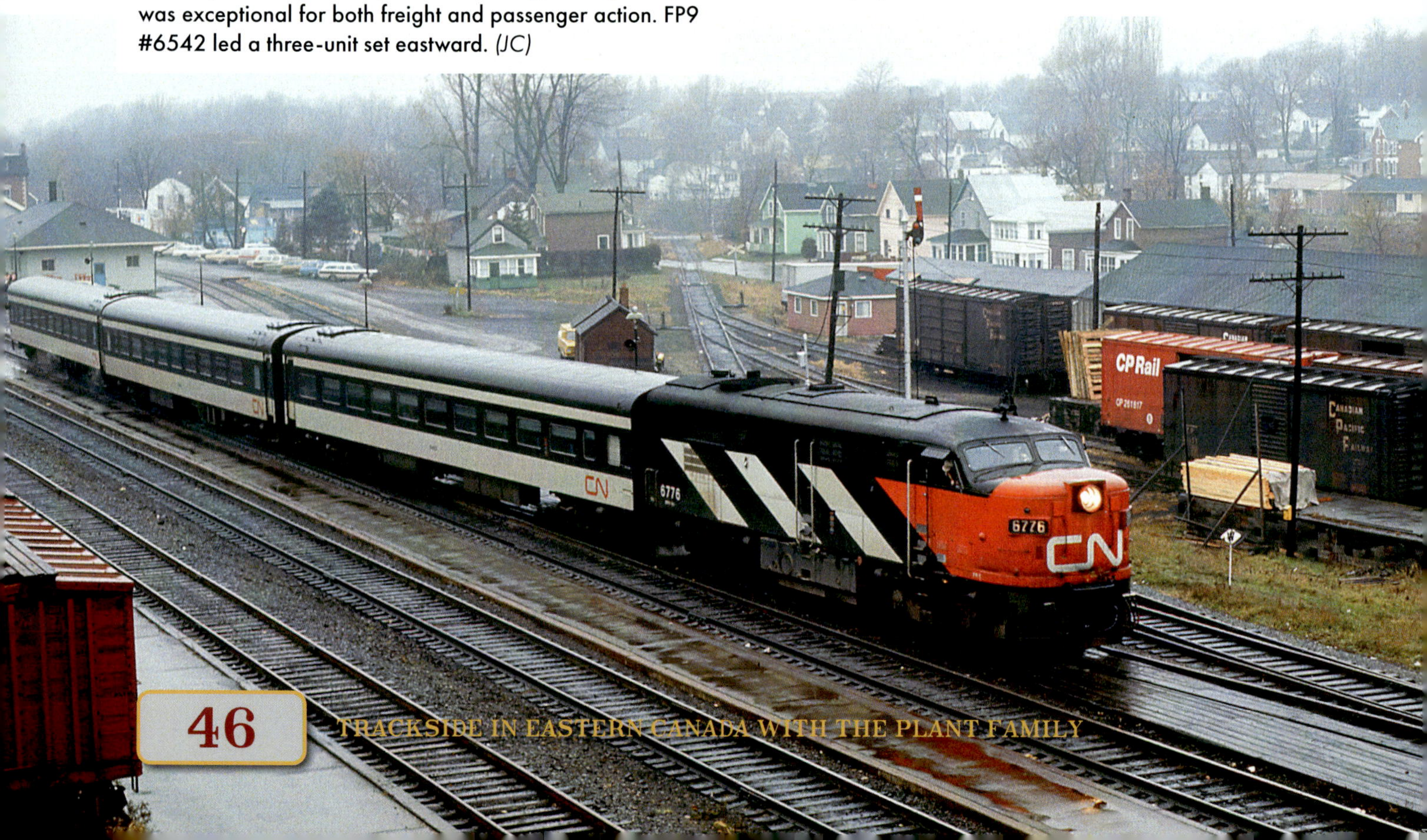

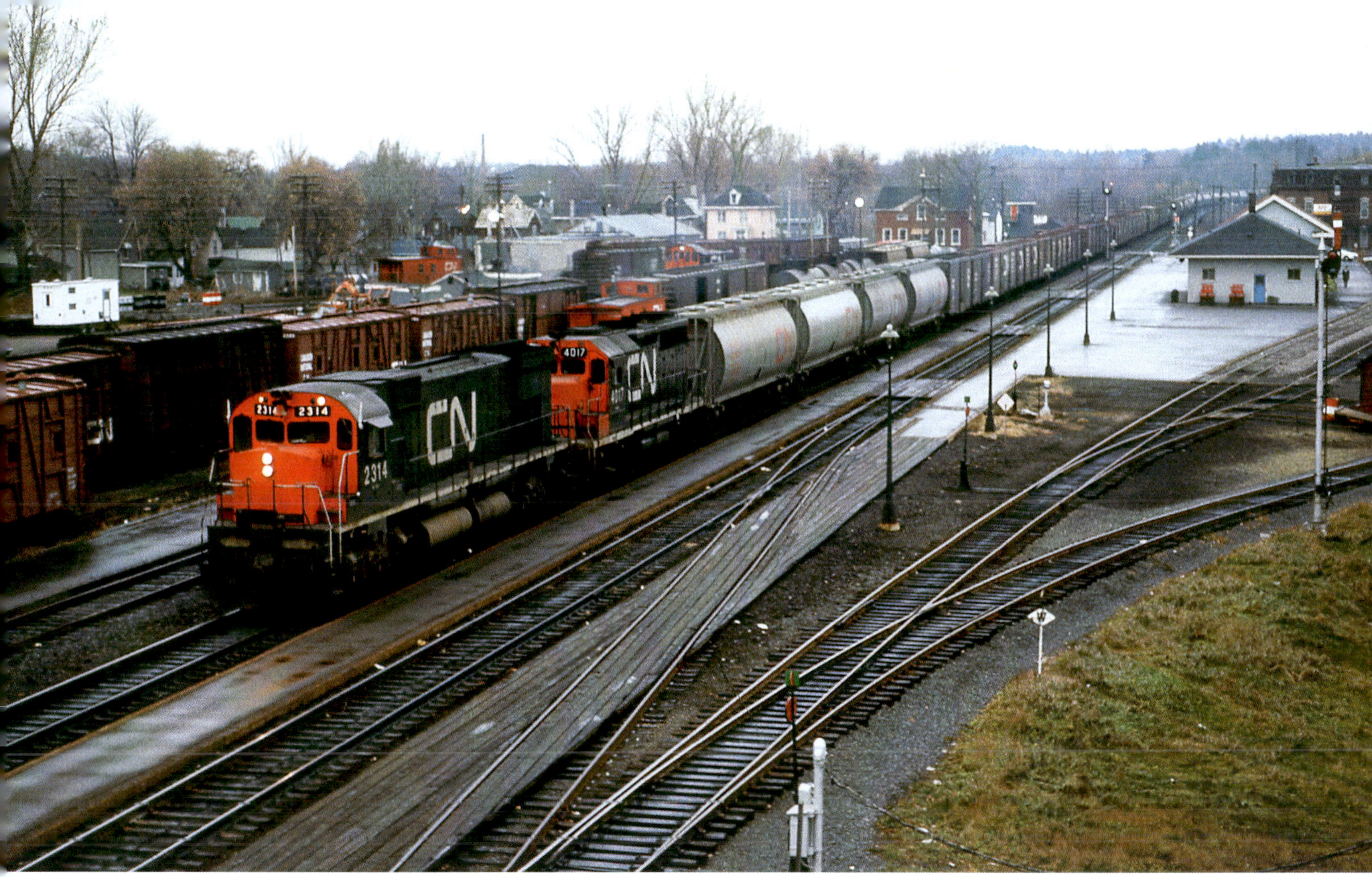

ABOVE: A cold rain was falling on this late November day in 1971 at Brockville as an eastbound freight passed with lead unit M636 #2314 displaying both marker lights and flags for an extra movement. *(JC)*

BELOW: A pair of RS18s was assigned to switching duties at Brockville on this raw November day. The train was in the siding as a green signal - still a semaphore at this relatively late date - was set for a westbound freight. *(JC)*

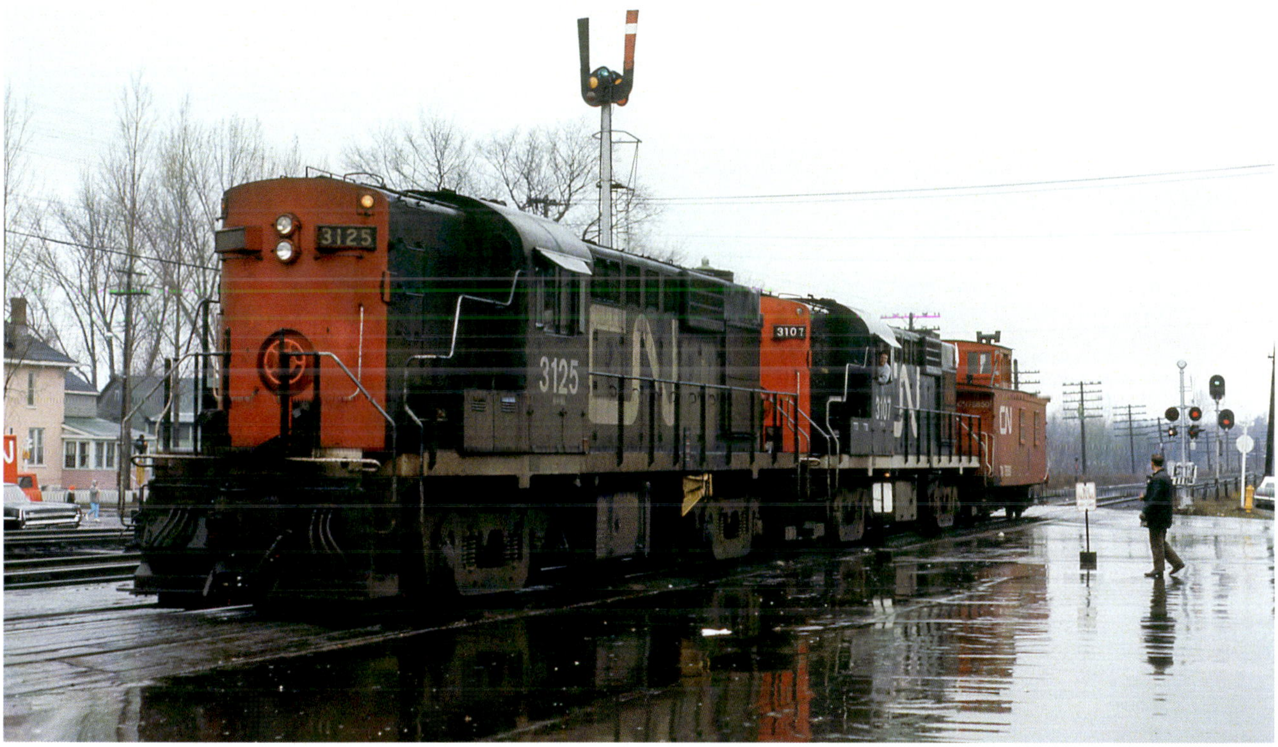

Via at Brockville

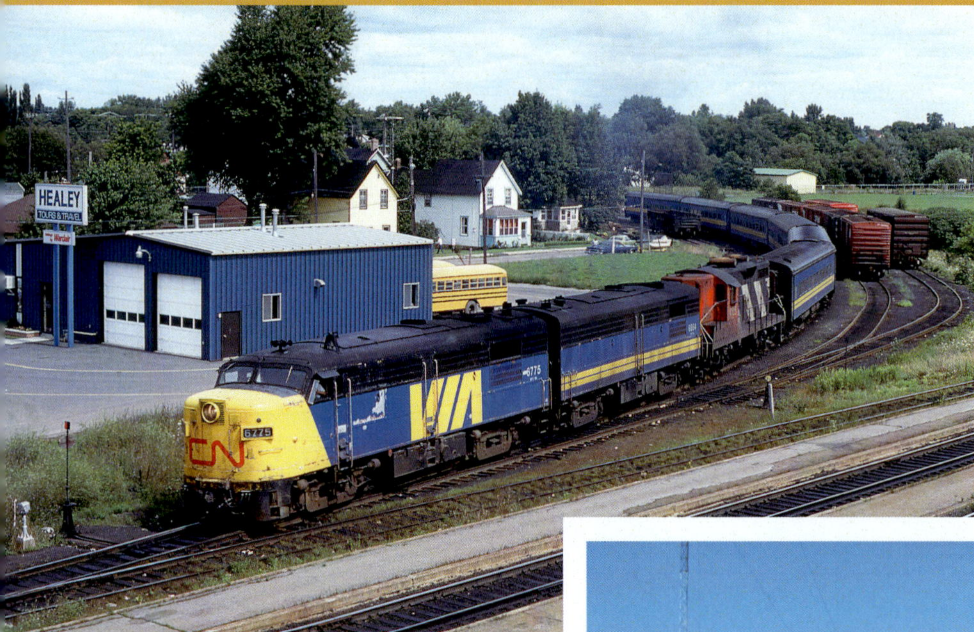

LEFT: In 1976, CNR adopted a blue and yellow paint scheme for its passenger diesels and cars and a new name and logo, VIA. At first, the colorful diesels carried the CNR logo on their nose, as shown by FP-4 #6775 curving into Brockville on August 11, 1979. *(JFP)*

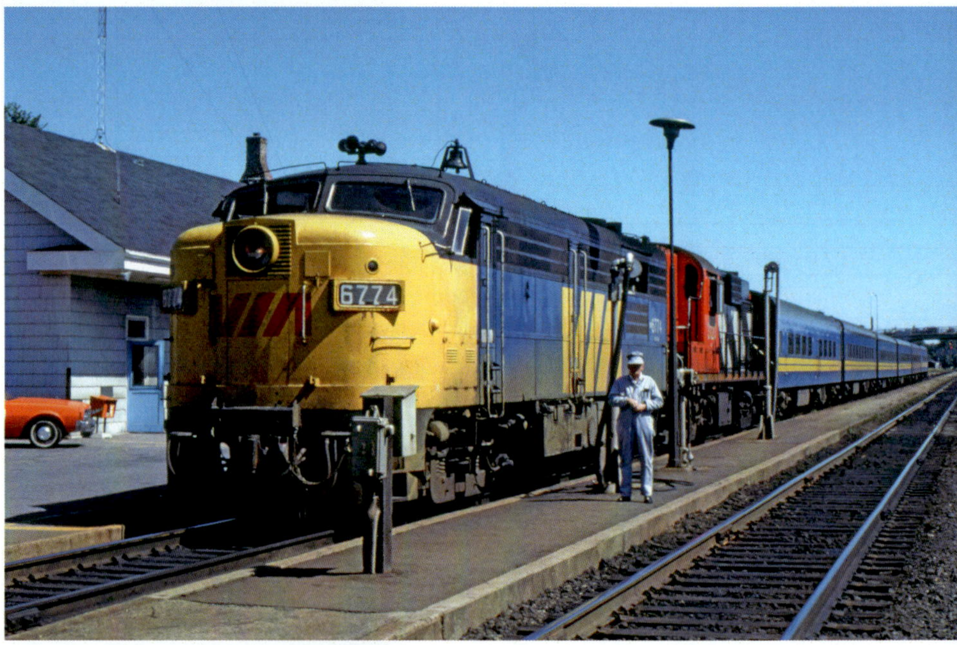

RIGHT: In 1978, VIA was made a crown corporation, and CNR no longer was responsible for its operations. The VIA logo began to replace the CNR doodle on the nose of locomotives. FPA-4 #6774 and a CNR RS18 stopped for passengers and a new crew at the Brockville station on August 11, 1979, before heading west for Kingston and Toronto. *(JFP)*

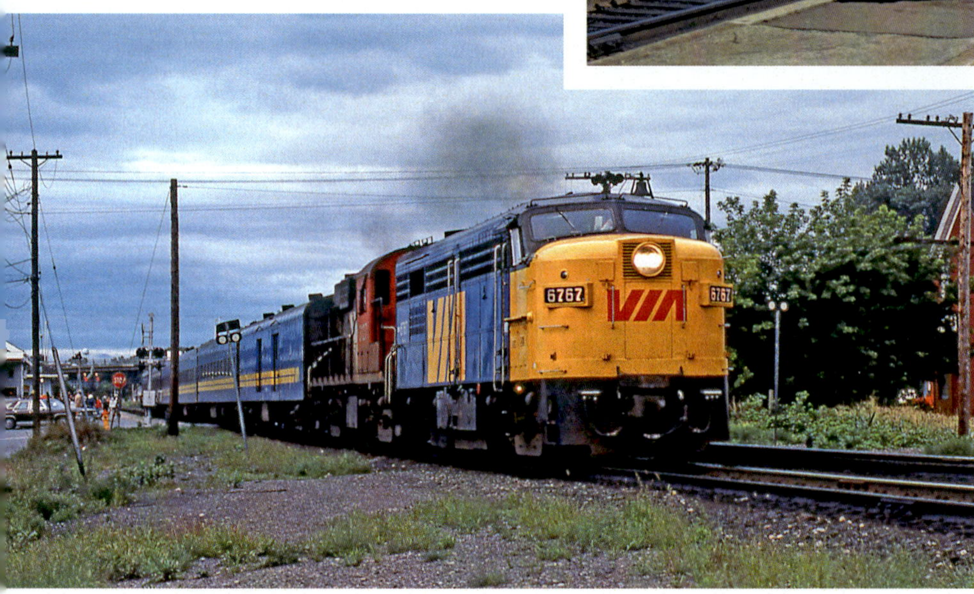

LEFT: VIA FPA-4 #6767 accelerated out of Brockville on August 11, 1979, after a sizeable number of passengers had disembarked at the station in the background. *(JFP)*

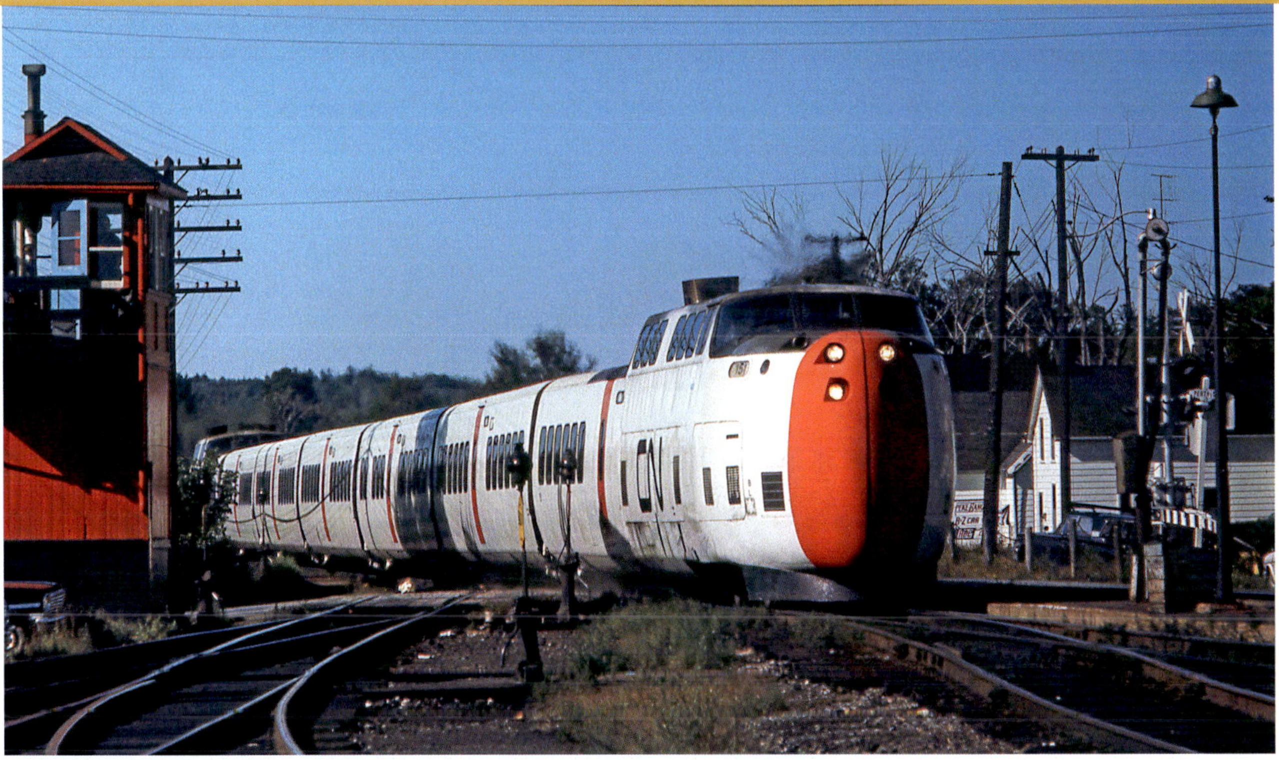

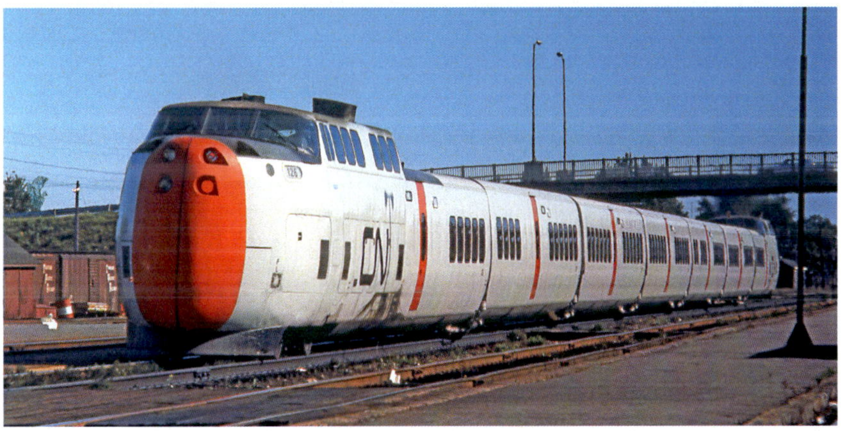

ABOVE AND LEFT: Wearing its white CNR livery, the Turbo Train blasted through Brockville without stopping on its run between Toronto and Montreal in September 1970. The Turbos were to have a checkered career on the CNR and later with VIA. Designed by United Aircraft Company, they never operated at the top speeds originally intended, and had issues with reliability that caused them to be rebuilt and reconfigured in the early 1970s. *(JFP)*

RIGHT: Now wearing VIA Rail's blue and yellow colors, the eastbound Turbo Train rounded the curve on the west side of Brockville on August 17, 1981. *(JFP)*

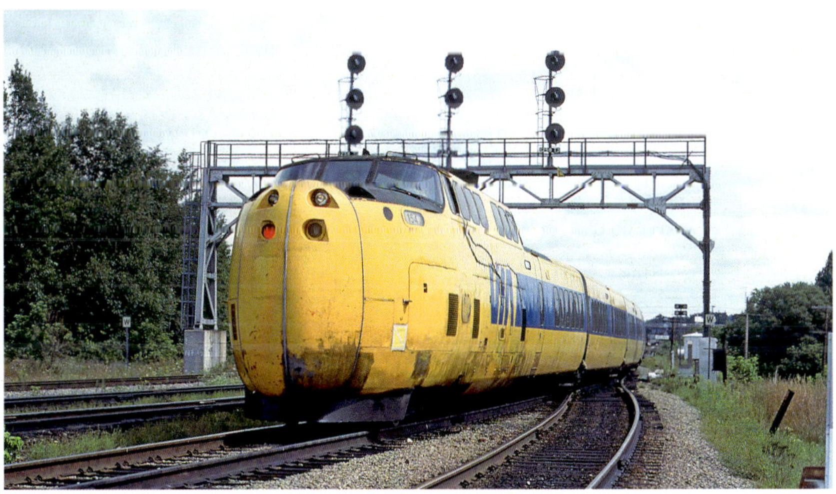

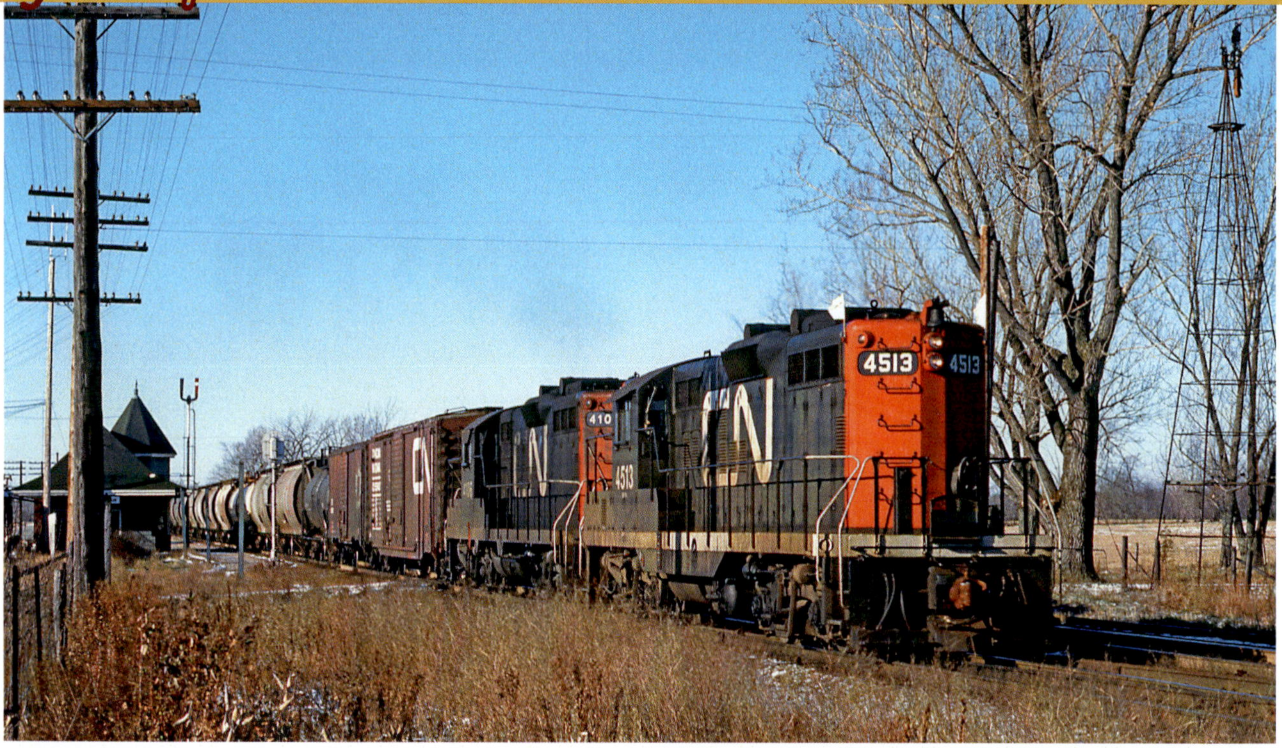

ABOVE: The CNR station at Gananoque was a favorite location for the Plant brothers to shoot in the 1970s. Situated a few miles north of the city of Gananoque at rural Gananoque Junction, the 1915-built station was a stop on the busy Toronto-Montreal corridor for all but the *Rapidos* and Turbo Trains. Its rural location provided a variety of photo opportunities at or nearby the depot. In November 1973, an eastbound freight behind a pair of GP9s passed the station and the venerable windmill at the nearby farm. *(JC)*

BELOW: On a sunny and warm October day in 1974, an eastbound freight passed the station behind SD40 #5065 leading GP40-2LW #9434. Someone has chalked a well-rendered elephant on the nose of the lead unit. *(JC)*

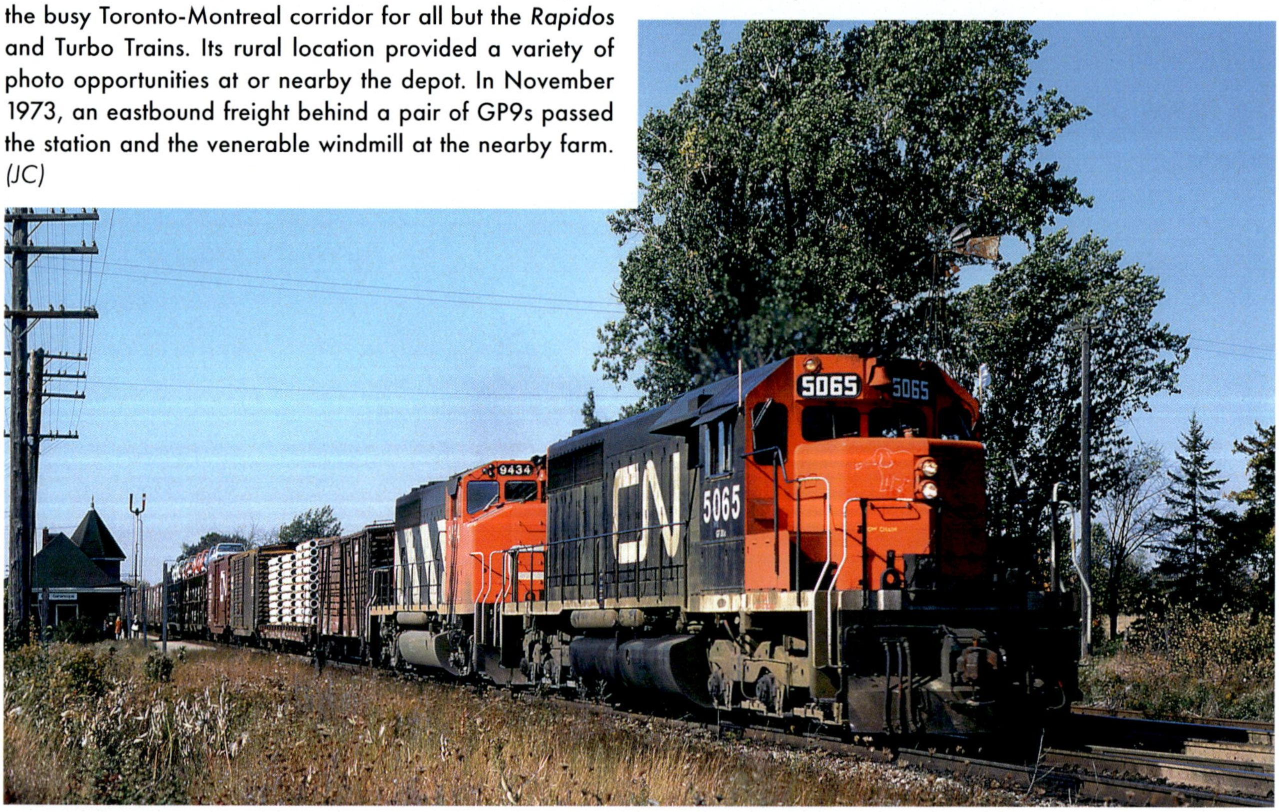

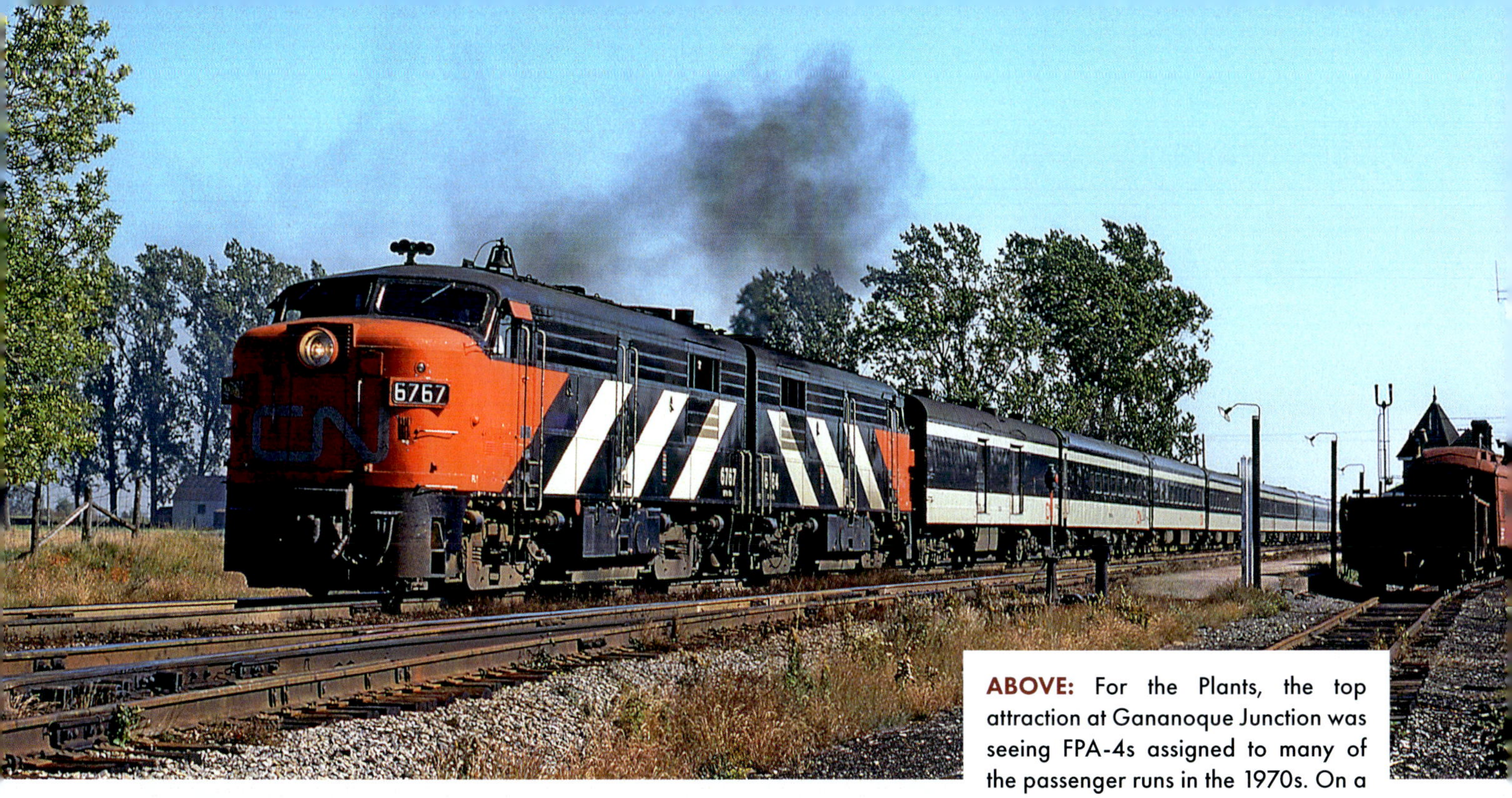

ABOVE: For the Plants, the top attraction at Gananoque Junction was seeing FPA-4s assigned to many of the passenger runs in the 1970s. On a warm but windy October day in 1974 a pair of FPA-4s accelerated toward Kingston and Toronto with westbound train #51, the *Lakeshore*, after making a brief stop at the station. *(JC)*

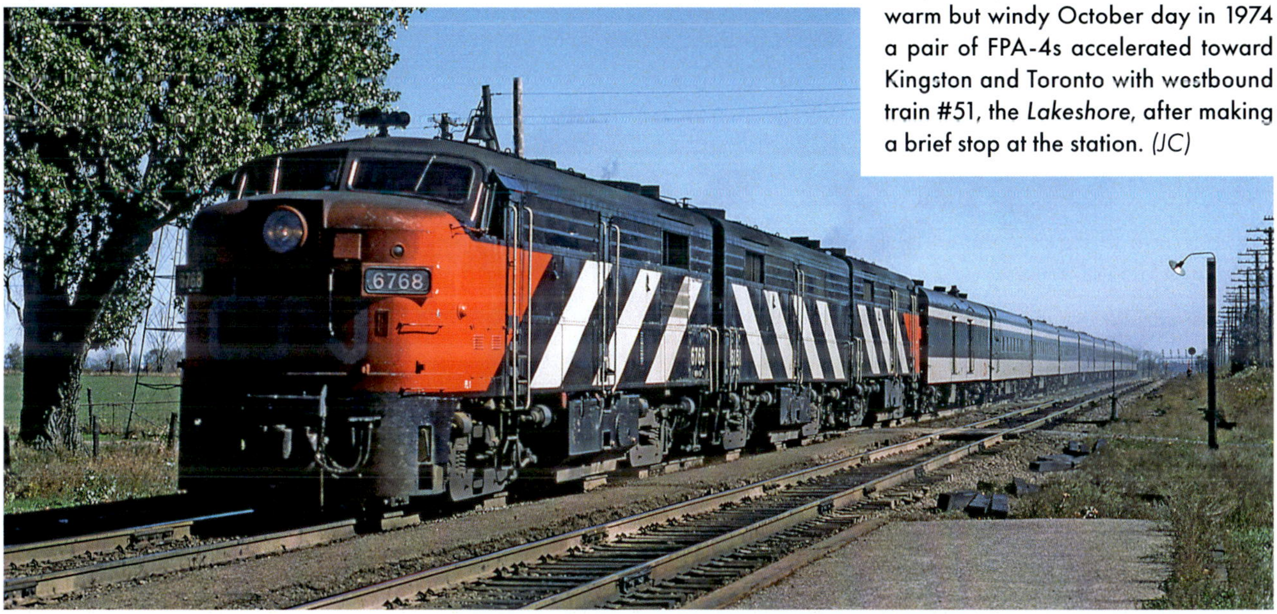

ABOVE: In October 1975 a perfect A-B-A set of Montreal-built cab units slowed for the stop at the Gananoque station with a westbound train. *(JC)*

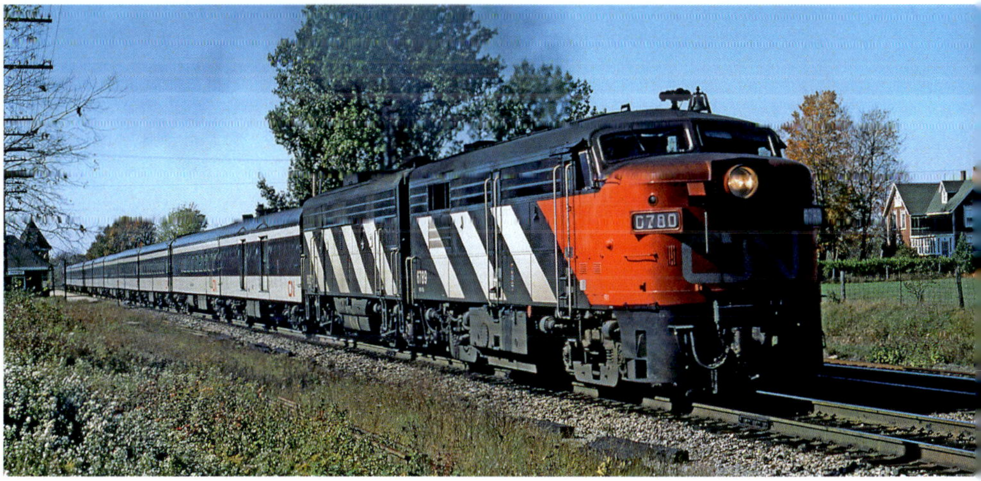

RIGHT: The CN frequently mixed and matched its GMDD and MLW cab units. In October 1975, FPA-4 #6789 led an FP9B east from the Gananoque station on train #50, the *Lakeshore*. Next stop is Brockville. *(JC)*

Canadian Pacific at Smiths Falls

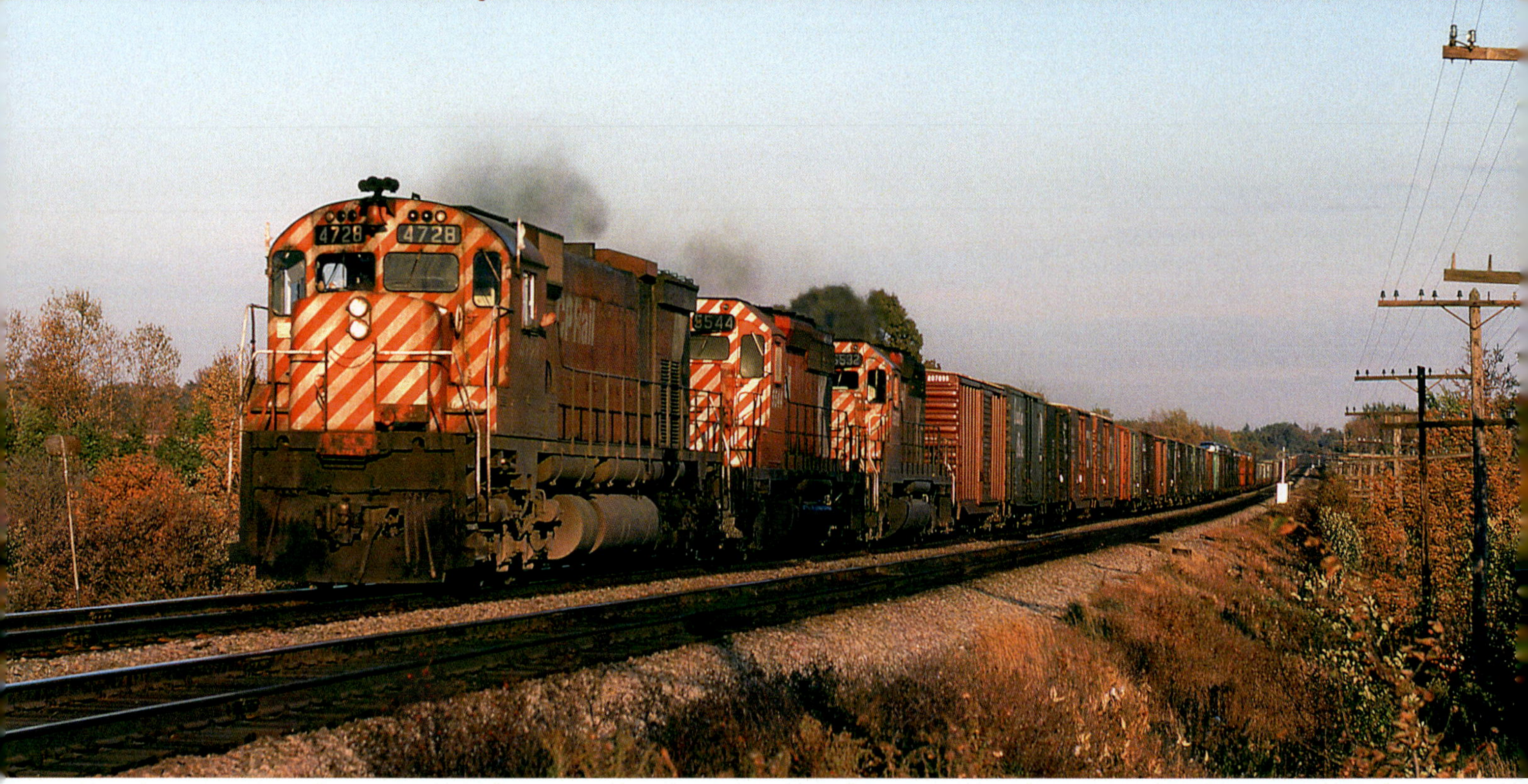

ABOVE: On our weekend trips to Ontario, from Gananoque we usually headed north to Smiths Falls, ON, a major yard and crew change point for CPR. The CPR's Winchester Sub connects the Montreal area with Smiths Falls, roughly 130 miles to the west, and was favored by railfans in the 1970s for its frequent train movements powered by Alco locomotives. In the warm light of an October afternoon a westbound freight glowed on a perfect fall day in 1974. M636 #4728 led a pair of SD40s on the final miles into the yard at Smiths Falls. *(JC)*

BELOW: This westbound freight was pulling into the east end of the yard at Smiths Falls in October 1974 behind a trio of Alco units arranged neatly by age: the newest on the lead is C424 #4212, followed by RS10 #8593 and an FB-2. *(JC)*

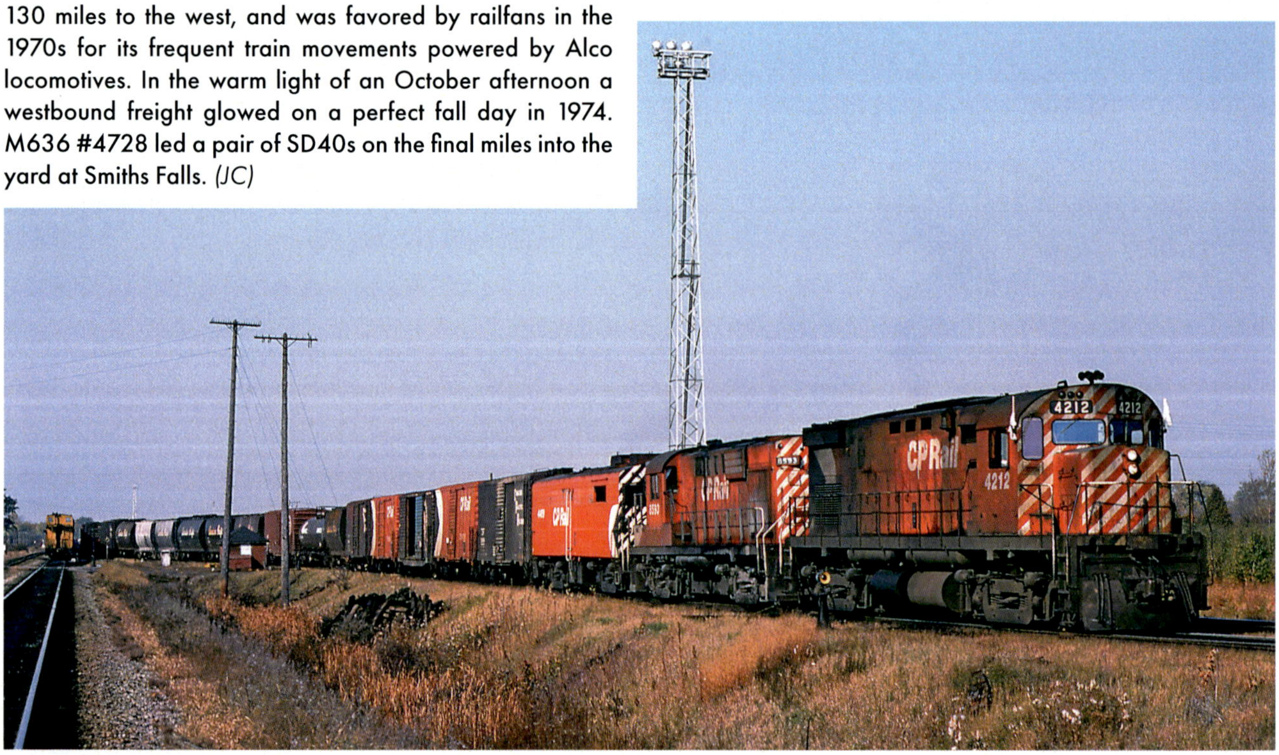

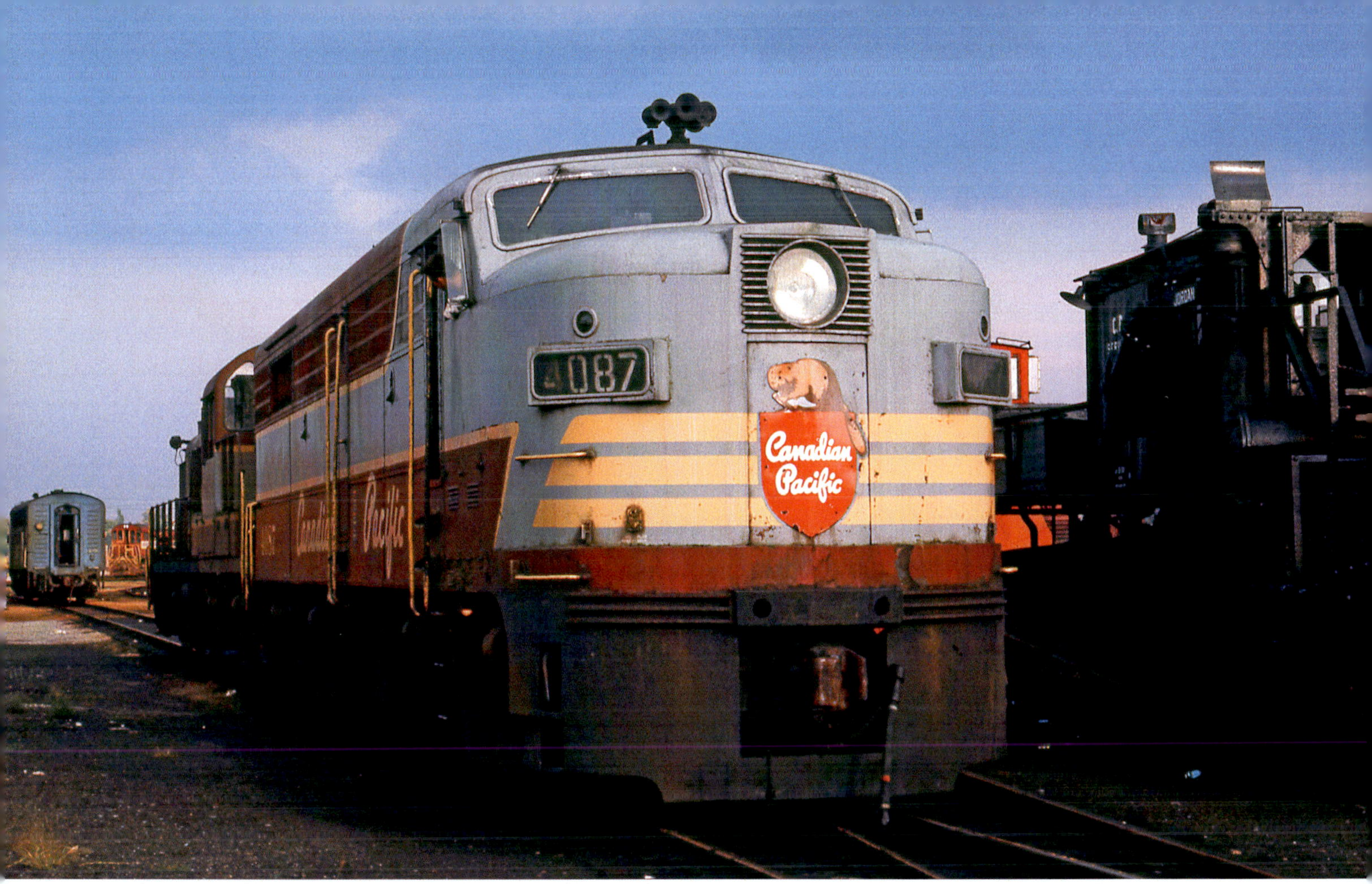

ABOVE: Compared to the busy feel of the CN on the Montreal/Toronto corridor the CPR seemed more relaxed, a bit more traditional in feel and appearance. The CPR was generally tolerant of responsible railfans, and the order board in the Smiths Falls station provided a good sense of train movements at this crew change point. Best of all, almost all power was Montreal-built Alcos (until GP35s and SD40s began to appear in numbers, as discussed below). The prized catch in the early 1970s was an FA cab unit such as FA-2 #4087, still in the Tuscan and Gray scheme with cursive lettering on this day in September 1970. *(JFP)*

BELOW: Wearing a fresh coat of Action Red paint, FA-2 #4087 waited for its next assignment at Smiths Falls along with fellow Montreal Locomotive Works alumni in November 1973. *(JGP)*

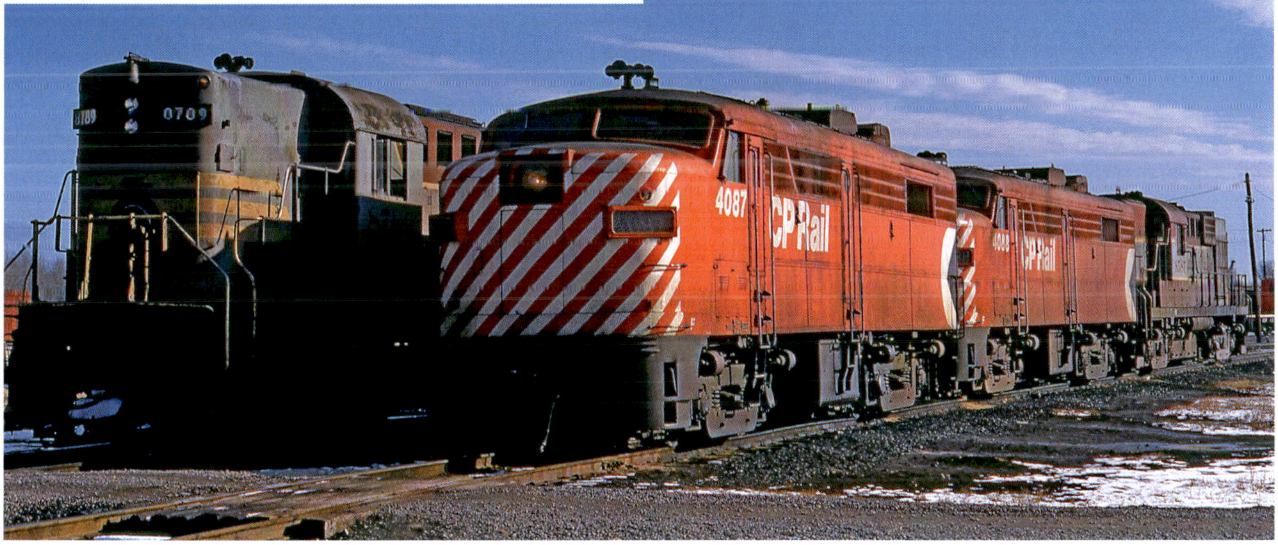

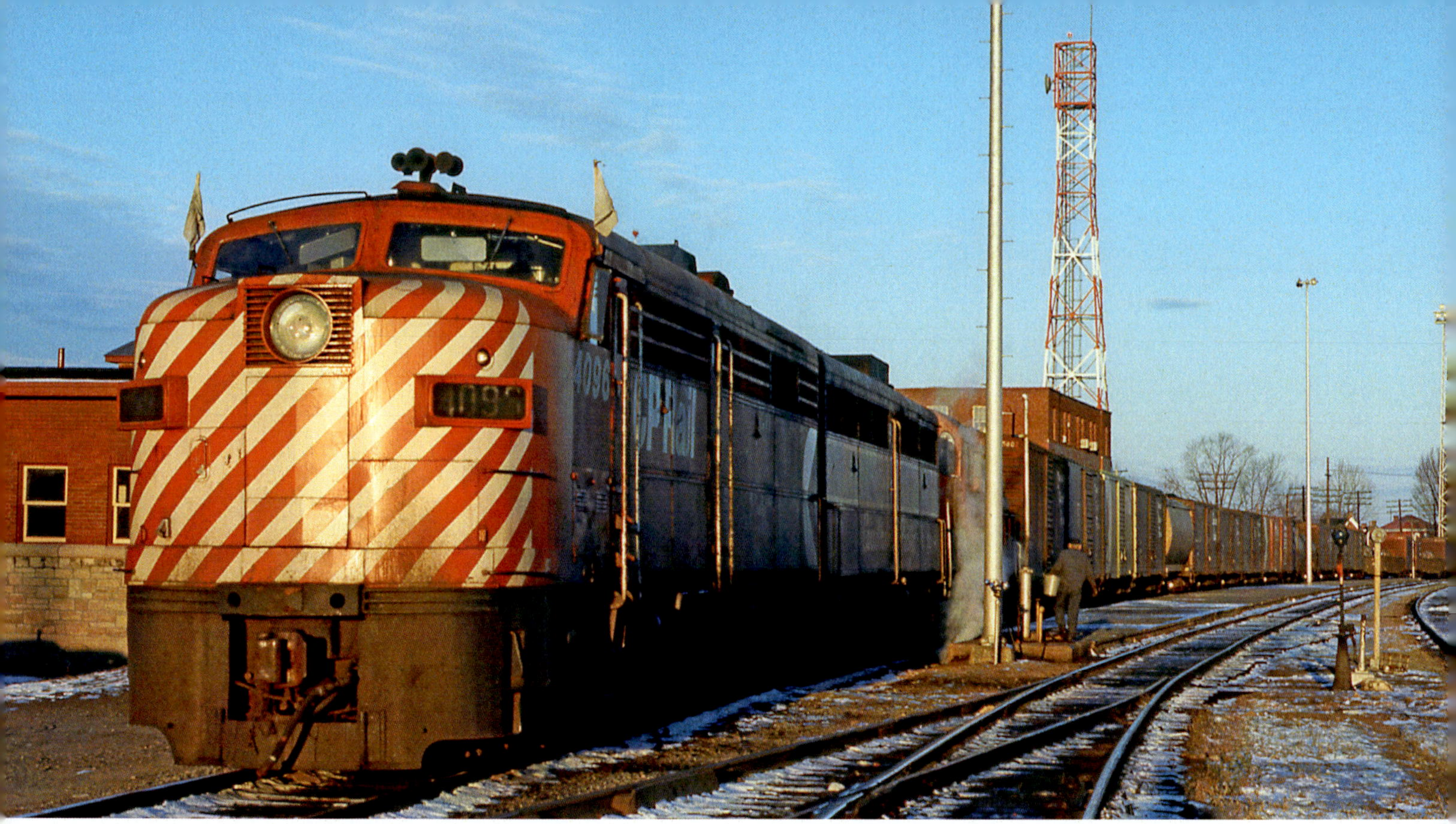

ABOVE AND BELOW: An eastbound train passed the station and stopped at the east end of the yard at Smiths Falls in November 1973, with FA-2 #4096 leading an FB-2 and RS3. *(JC)*

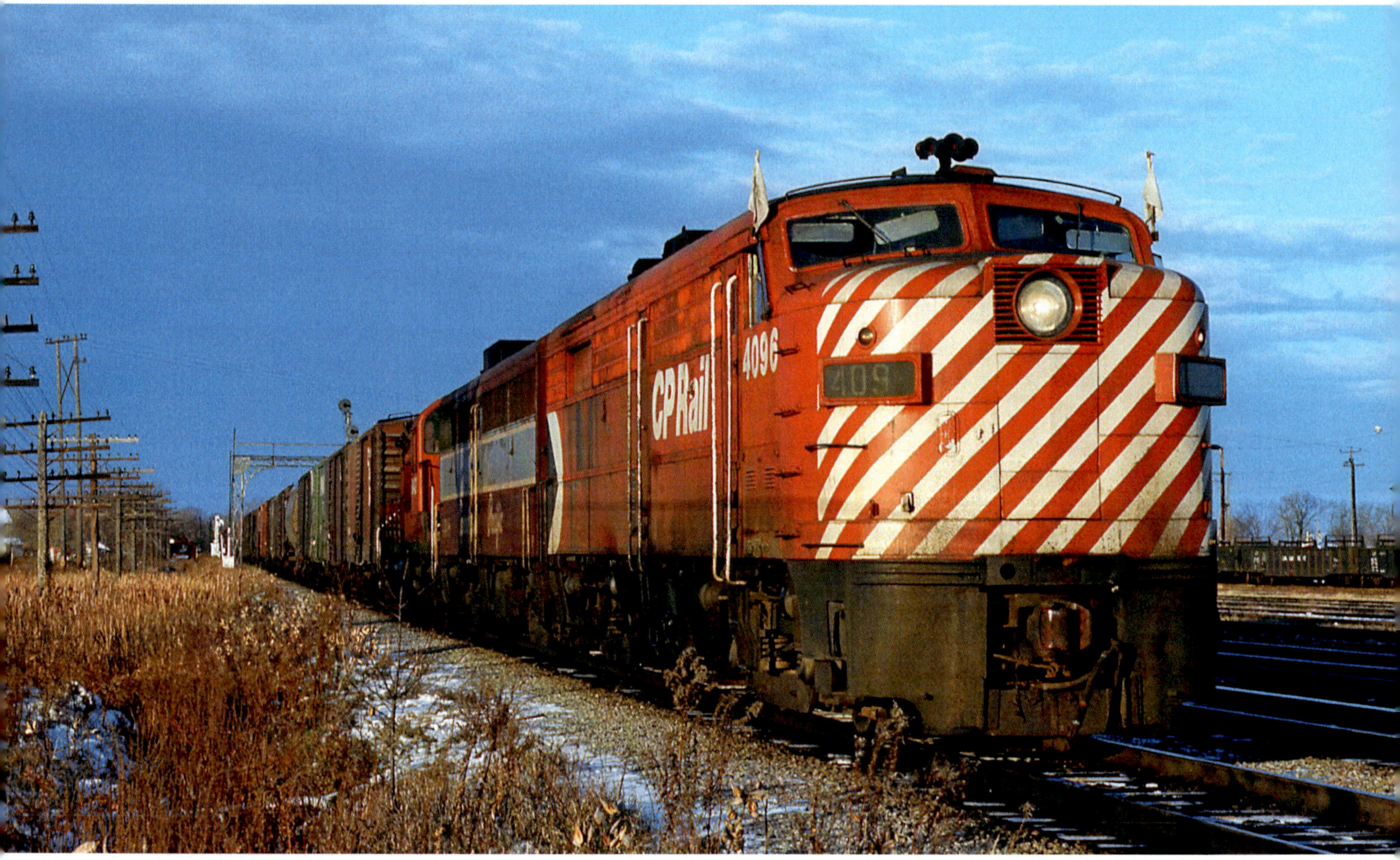

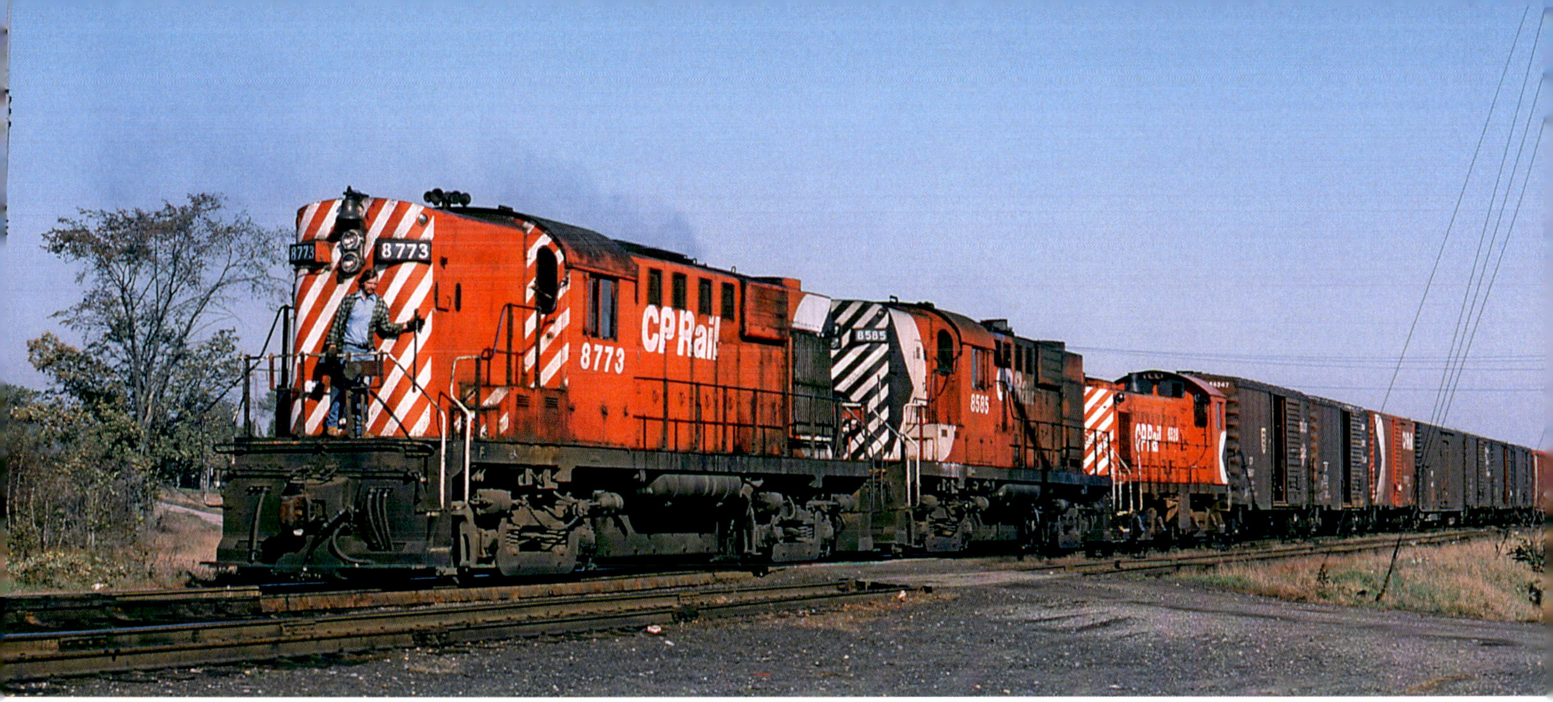

ABOVE: RS18 #8773 led RS10 #8585 and an S3 into the yard from the east in October 1975. The two lead units show the differences in Multi-Mark paint schemes, with the RS18 set up to run short-hood forward and the RS10 long-hood forward. *(JC)*

BELOW: The CPR rostered 101 S3 switchers, numbered #6500 to #6600. One of the 660-horsepower units, #6591, showed off a very clean Tuscan scheme at Smiths Falls in November 1973. *(JGP)*

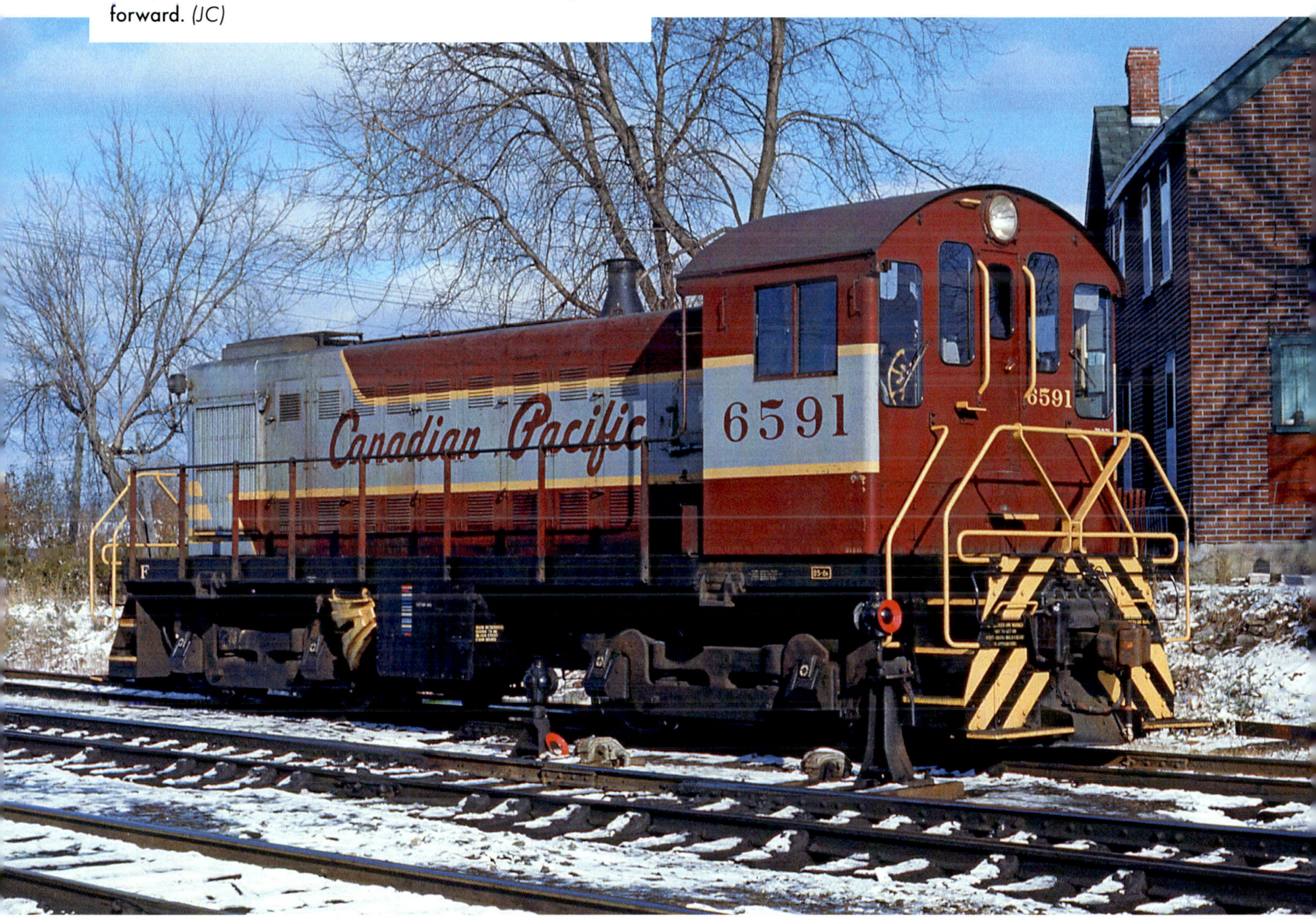

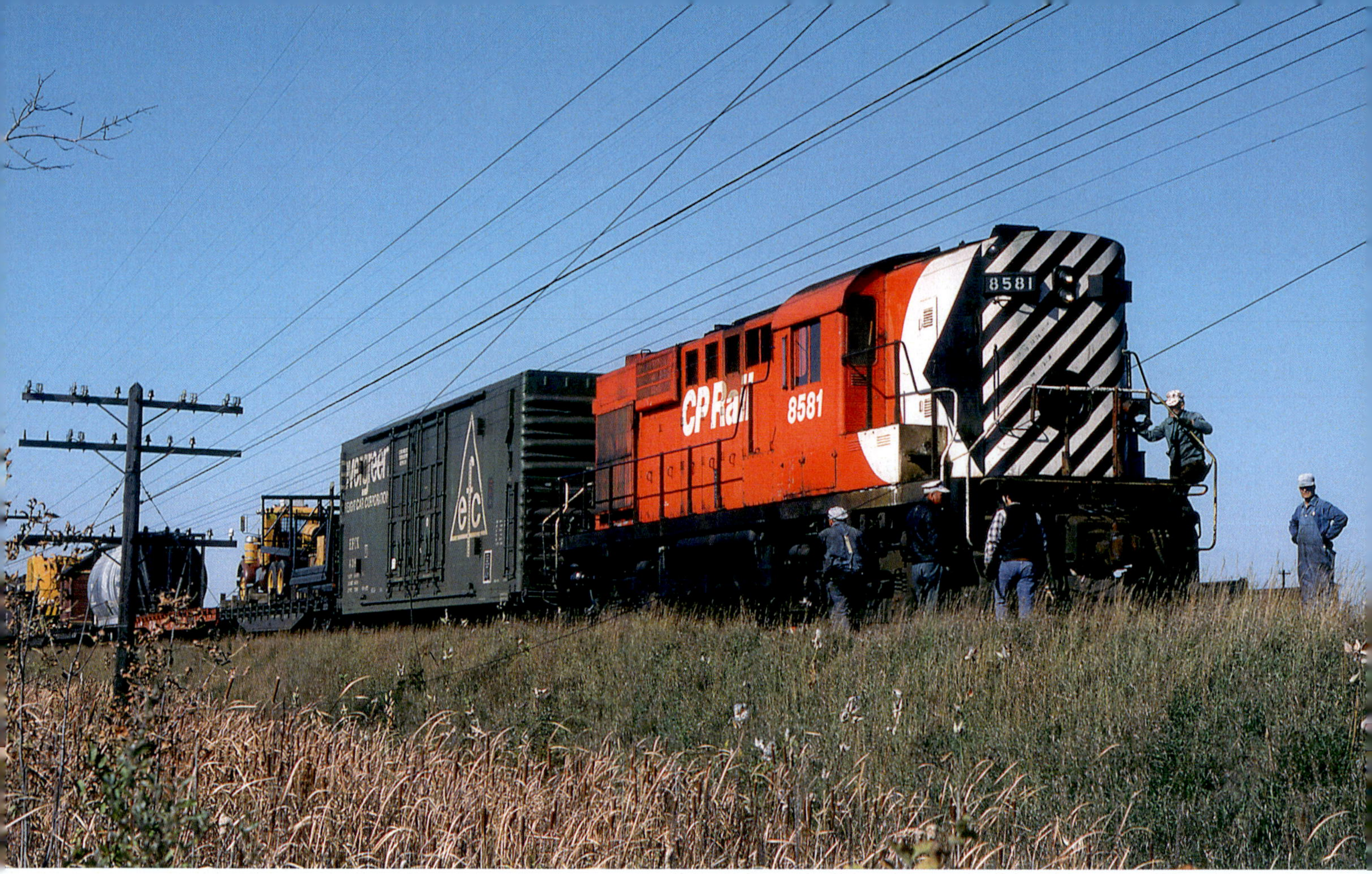

ABOVE: RS10 #8581 was switching the east side of the yard at Smiths Falls with a full crew in October 1975. The CPR's RS10s were set up to run long-end forward, hence the black and white striping on the short hood, denoting the rear end of the locomotive. *(JC)*

BELOW: By the autumn of 1975, it was a rare treat to get a C424 in its original paint scheme, even one as filthy as #4237 leading a westbound train past the control tower at Smiths Falls. Getting an RS3 as the second unit was almost as nice! *(JC)*

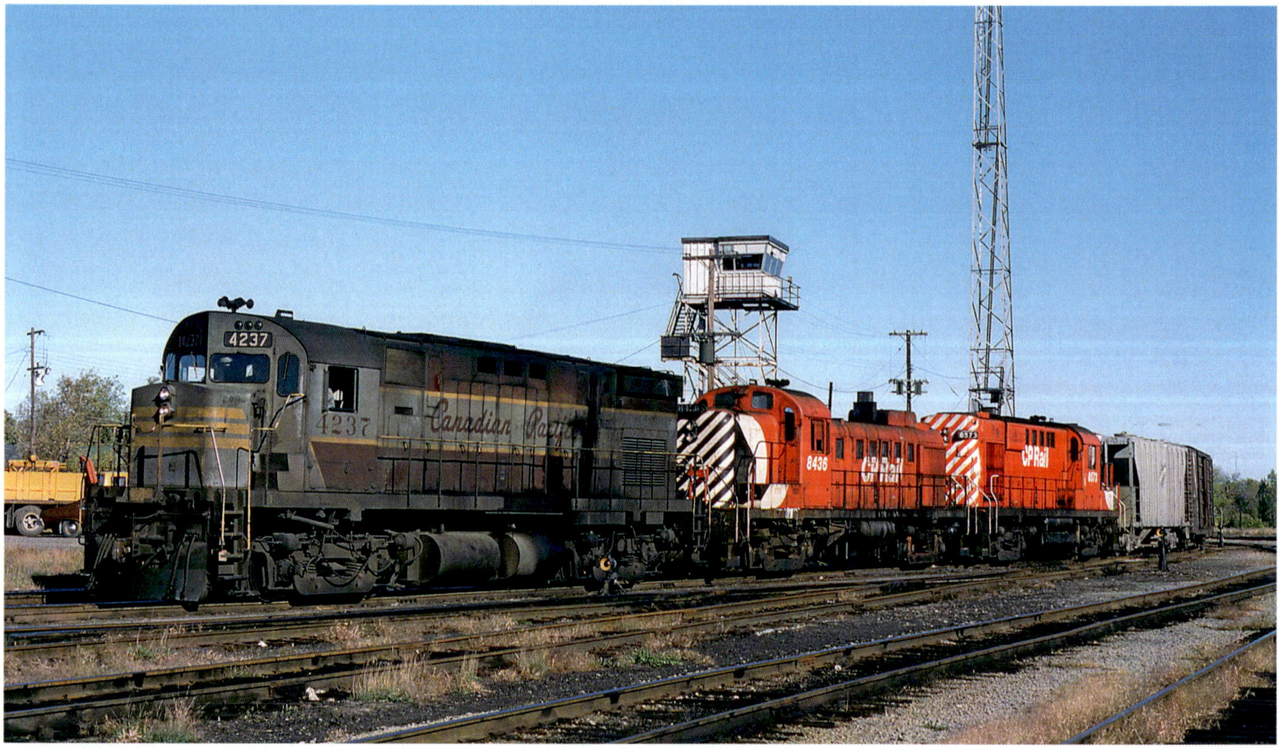

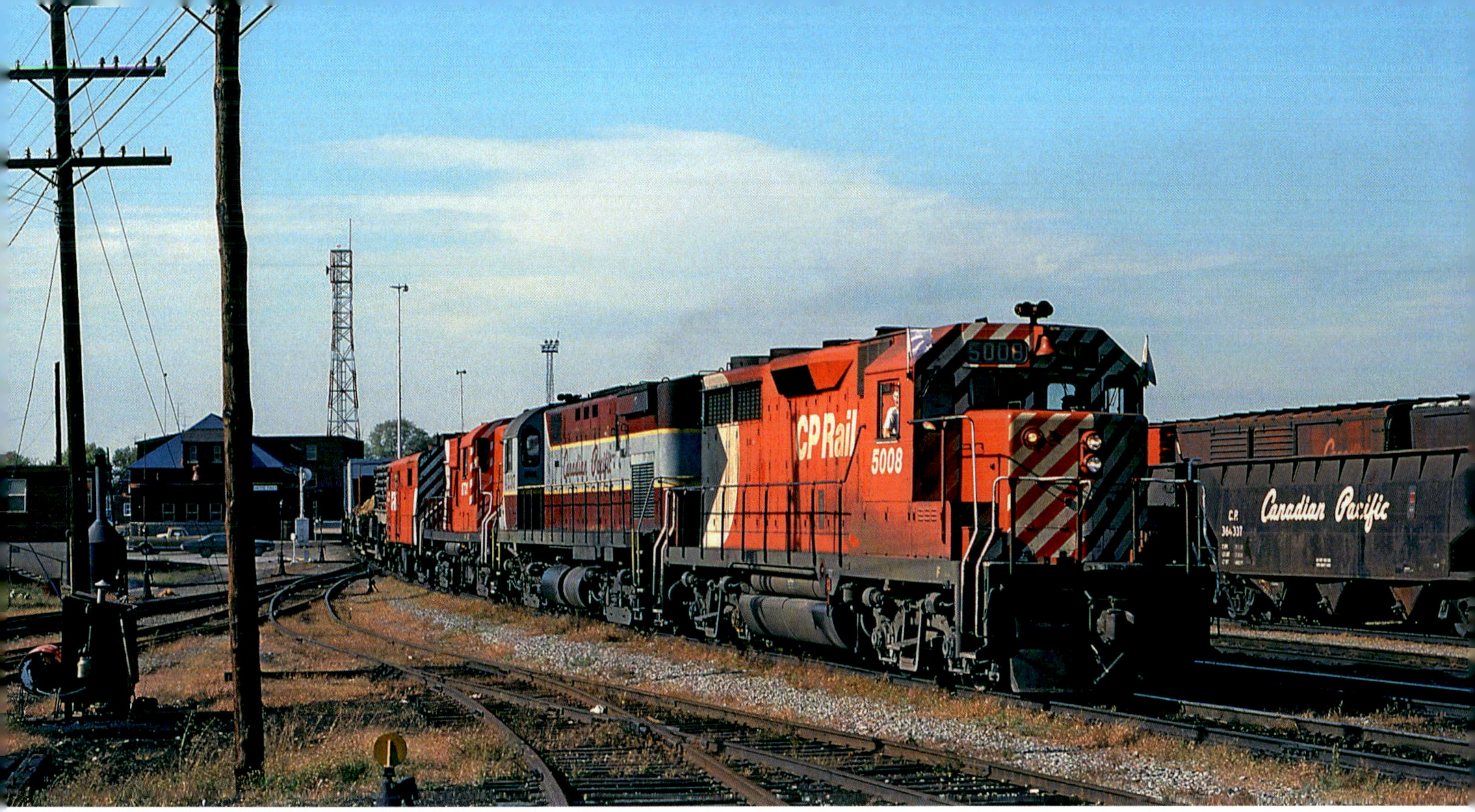

ABOVE: The CPR rostered 24 GMDD GP35s. By the mid-1970s they had been renumbered into the #5002 series and showed up frequently around the Smiths Falls area, confounding railfans who had come to see Smiths Falls as a good place to find MLW units. In October 1974, GP35 #5008 led a varied threesome of MLW units eastward after a crew change at the Smiths Falls station, visible in the left background. *(JC)*

BELOW: The GP35s seemed to be preferred lead power on CPR trains between Montreal and Smiths Falls in the mid-1970s. An example is this westbound freight entering the yard at Smiths Falls with GP35 #5020 leading an RS3 and RS18. *(JC)*

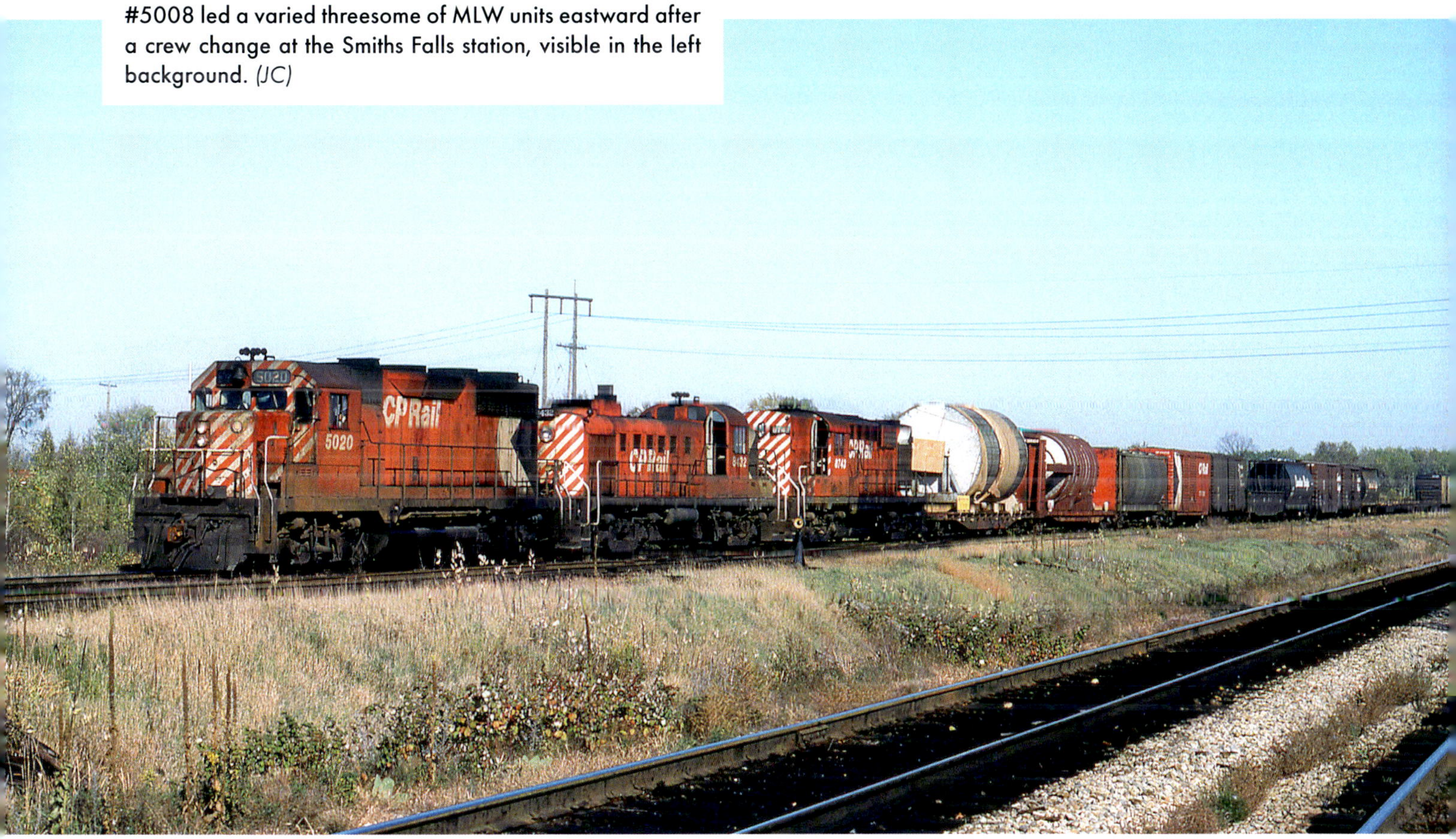

Canadian National at Smiths Falls

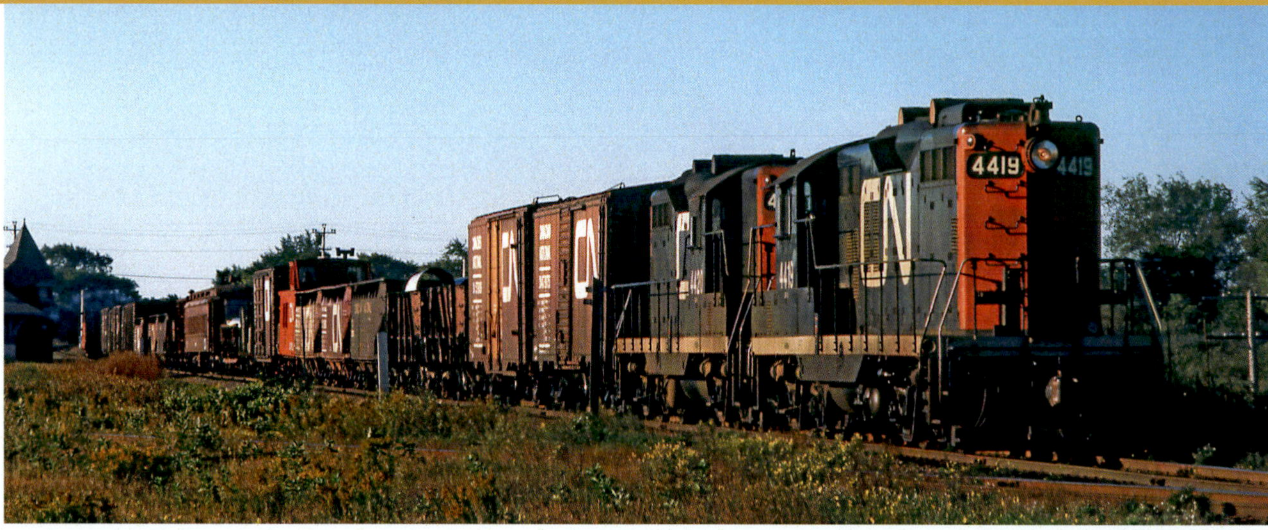

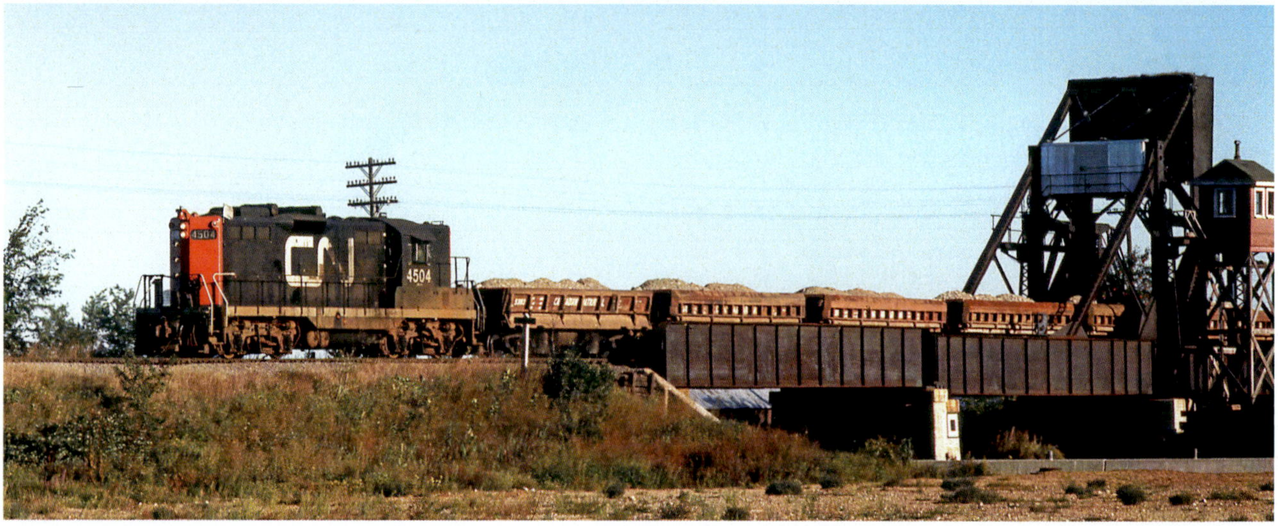

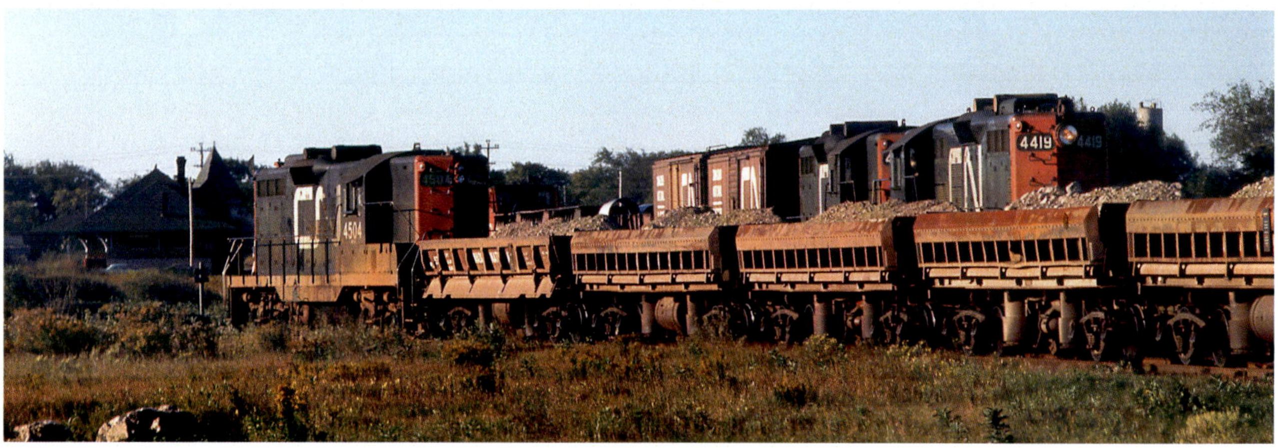

ALL, THIS PAGE: The CNR's secondary line from Napanee to Ottawa passed through Smiths Falls. On our first trip to Smiths Falls in September 1970 we were in the right place at the right time as a northbound train led by two GP9s stopped by the Smiths Falls CN station for a meet with a southbound work train led by GP9 #4504. The work train crossed the bascule bridge over the Rideau Canal and passed the waiting freight in the waning light of a late summer evening – magic! *(JFP)*

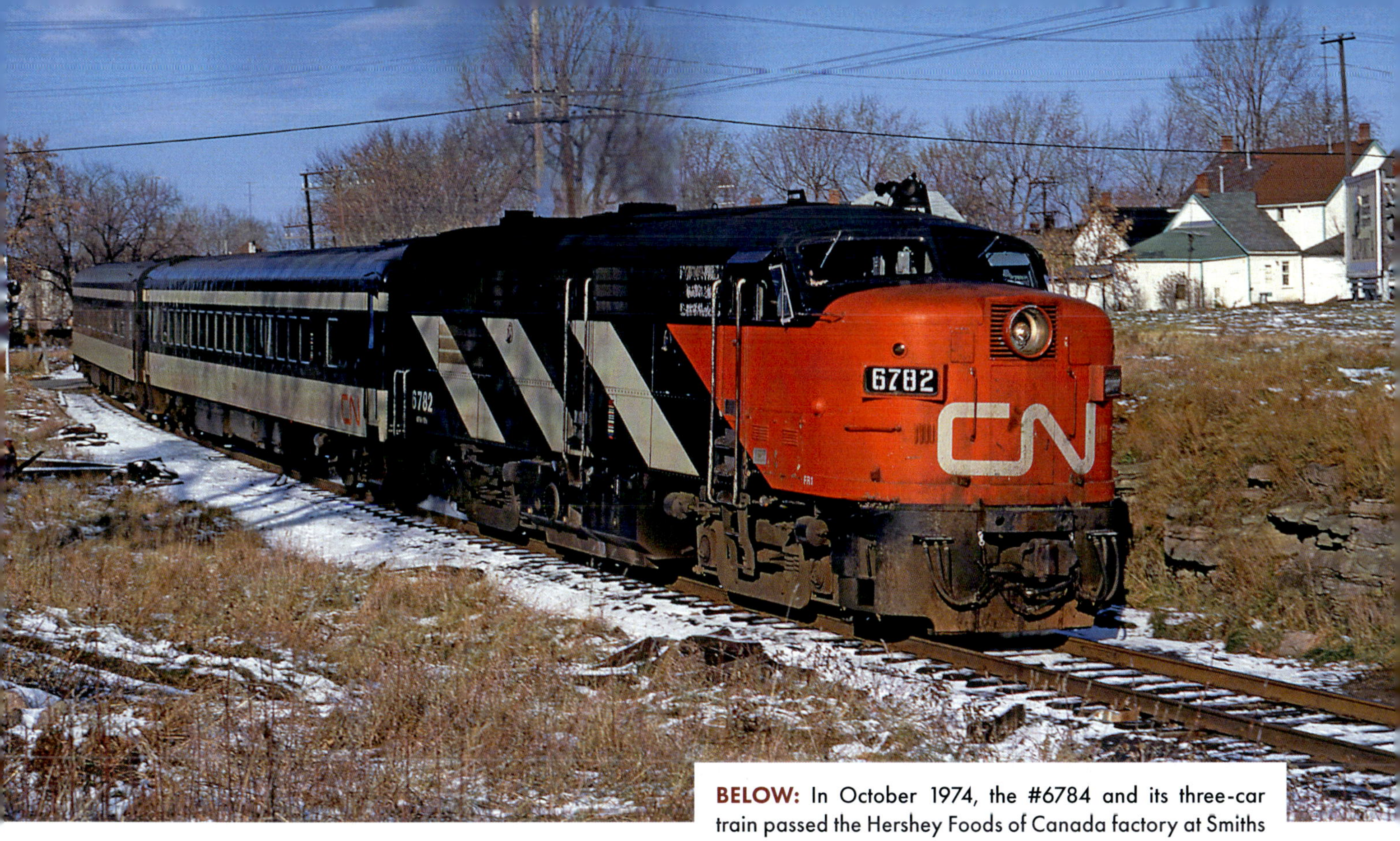

ABOVE: A dusting of snow covered the ground at Smiths Falls in late November 1973 as FPA-4 #6782 headed toward Brockville and the connection there for the continuation of the trip from Ottawa to Toronto. *(JGP)*

BELOW: In October 1974, the #6784 and its three-car train passed the Hershey Foods of Canada factory at Smiths Falls on its way down the CPR to Brockville. The stately elm tree seen above the FPA-4 was one of many in this part of Ontario; the blight that killed many elms in the eastern U.S. seemed to have spared many of their Canadian kinfolk. *(JC)*

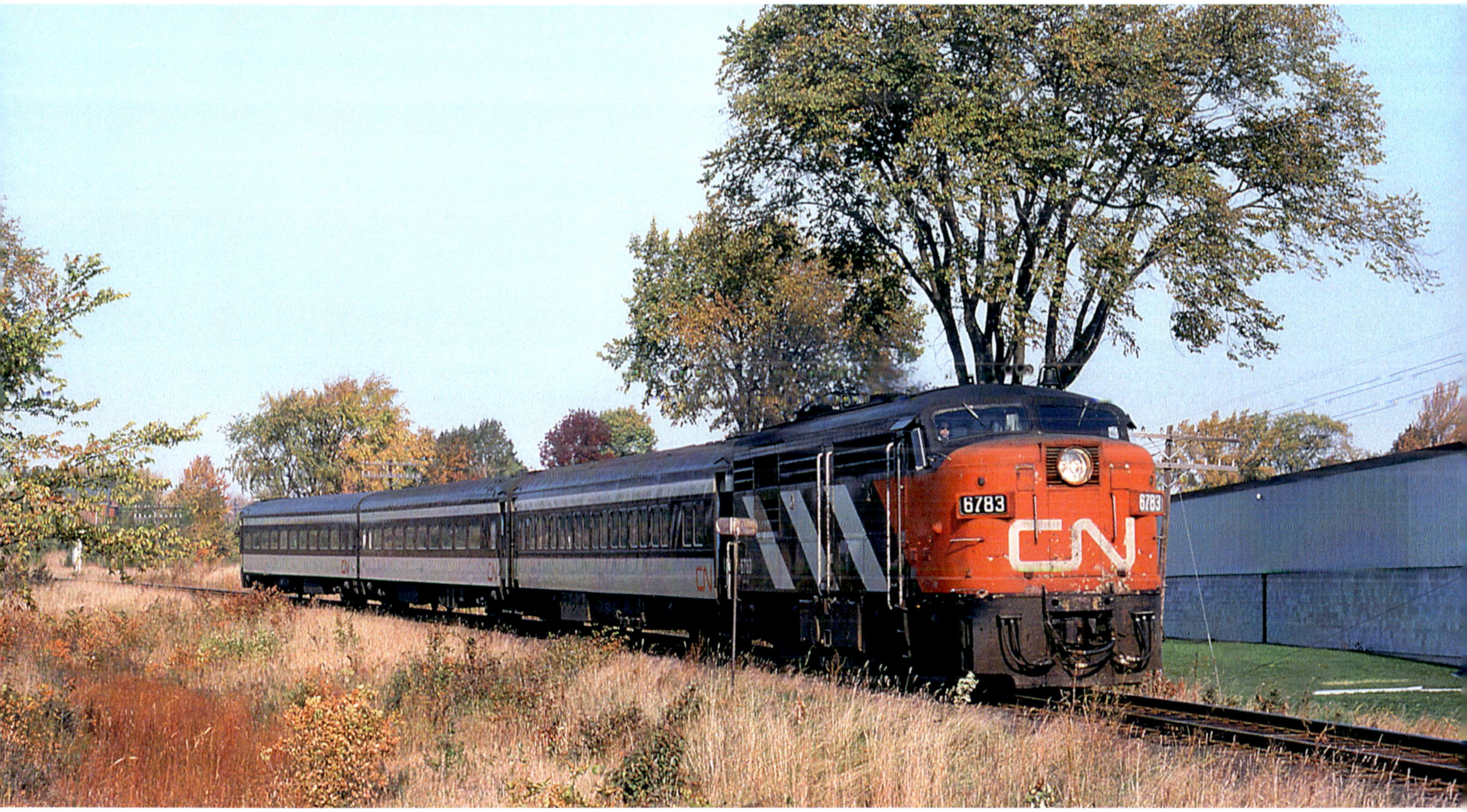

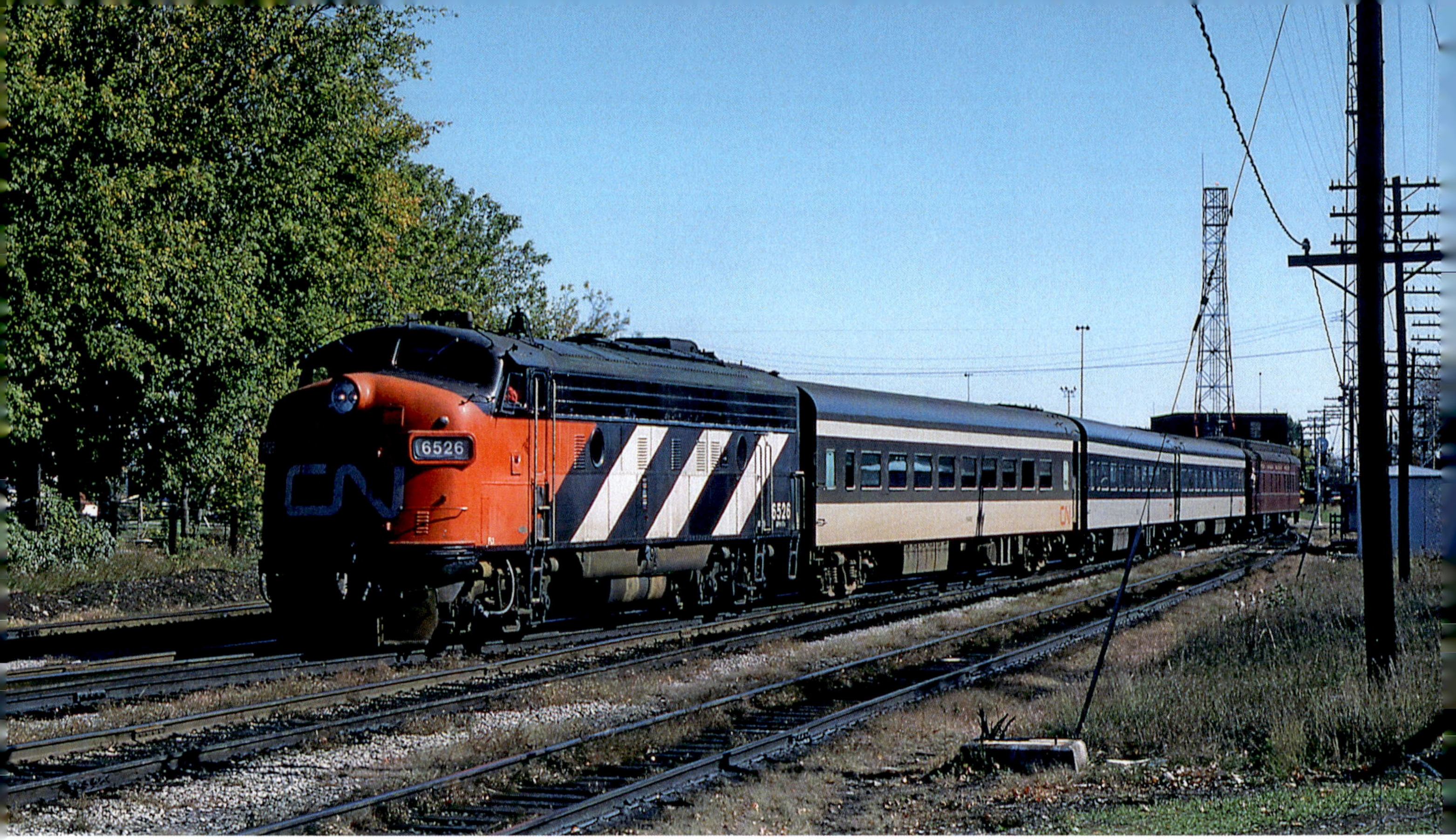

ABOVE AND BELOW: FP9 #6526 has passed the Smiths Falls station and was about to leave CPR tracks for those of CNR to Ottawa in October 1975. Trailing the usual three-car consist was Upper Canada Railway Society car #13. In the distance an eastbound CPR freight is waiting for clearance into the yard after the passenger train passes. *(JC)*

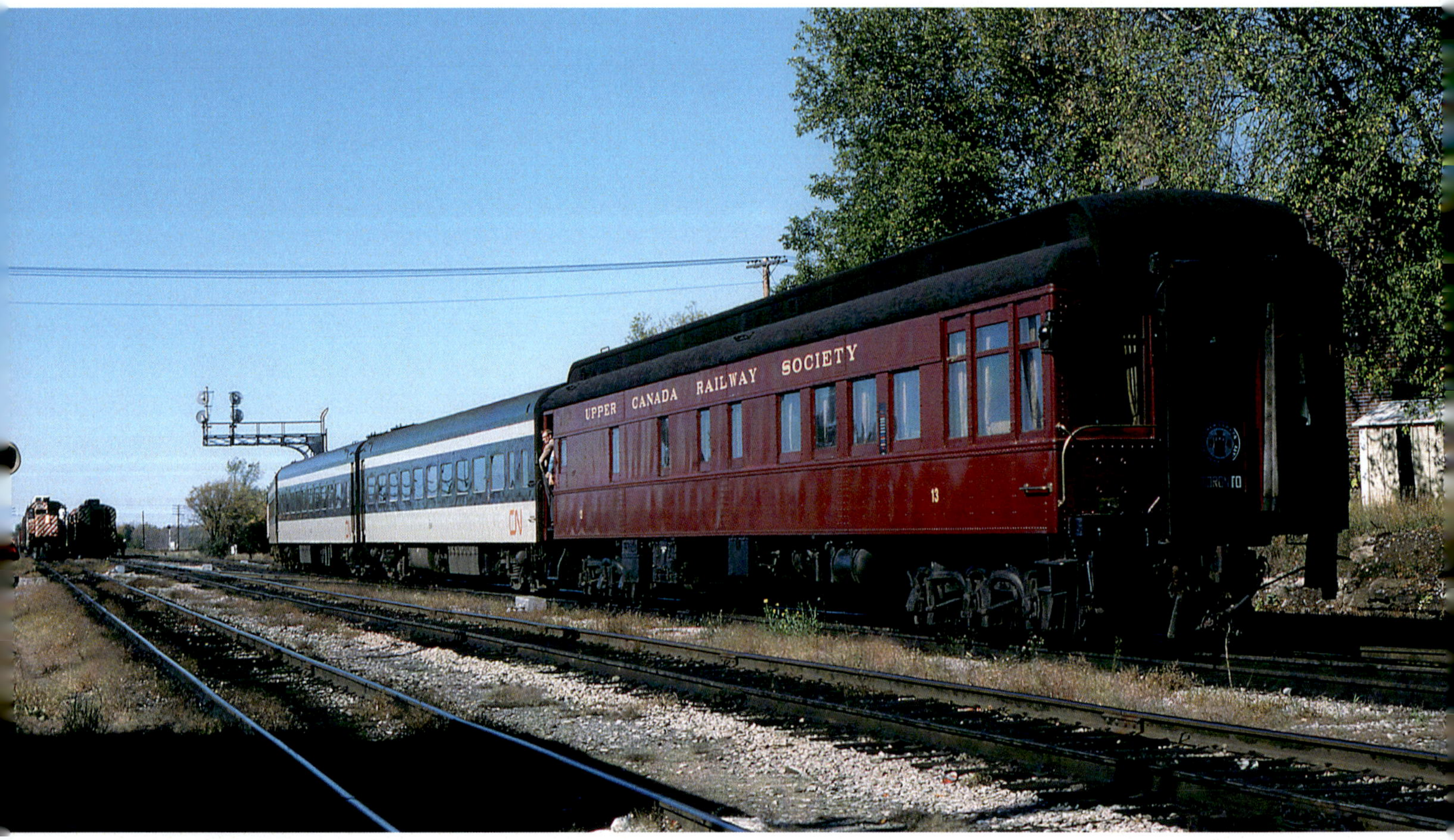

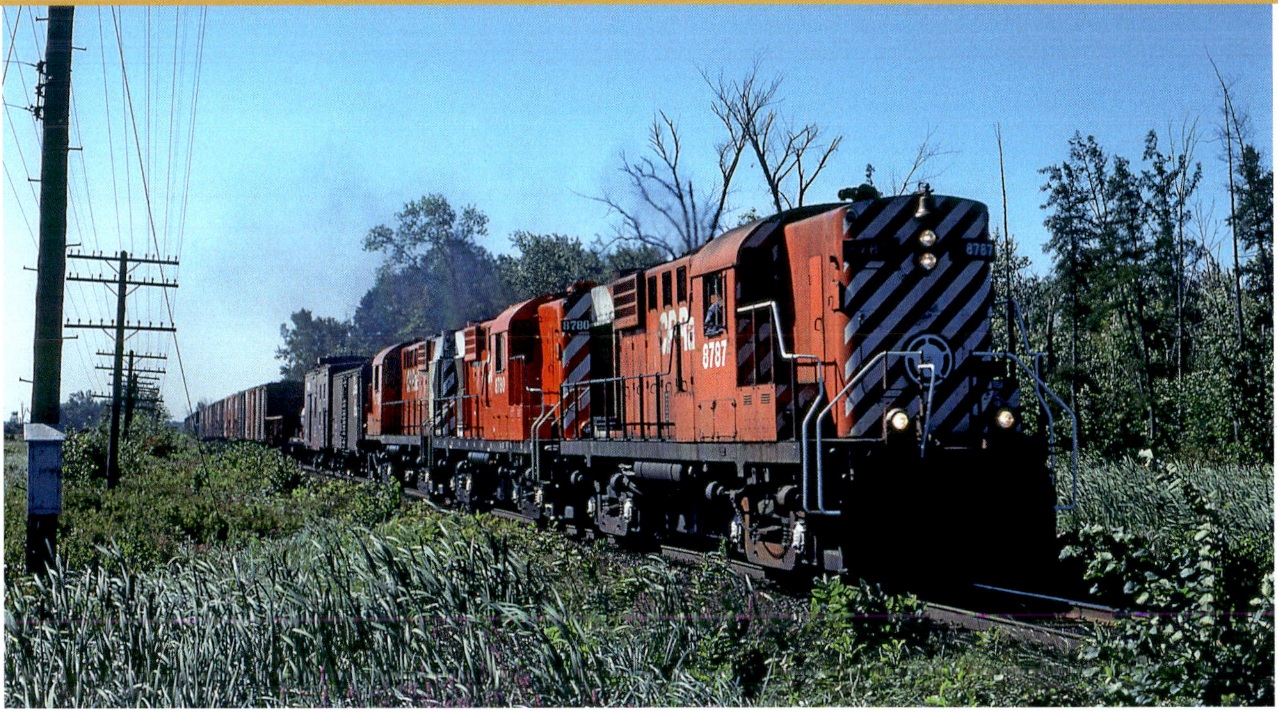

ABOVE: The Chalk River Sub of the CPR headed north and west from Smiths Falls to connect with the transcontinental main line from Montreal through Ottawa at Chalk River. A trio of RS18s headed north out of Smiths Falls on the Chalk River Subdivision on August 17, 1981. *(JFP)*

BELOW: GP9s were not that common on our trips to the eastern lines of the CPR in the 1970s. A pair powered this westbound freight a few miles west of Smiths Falls in October 1975. Even though the units are consecutively numbered, the size of the Multi-Mark emblem differs. *(JC)*

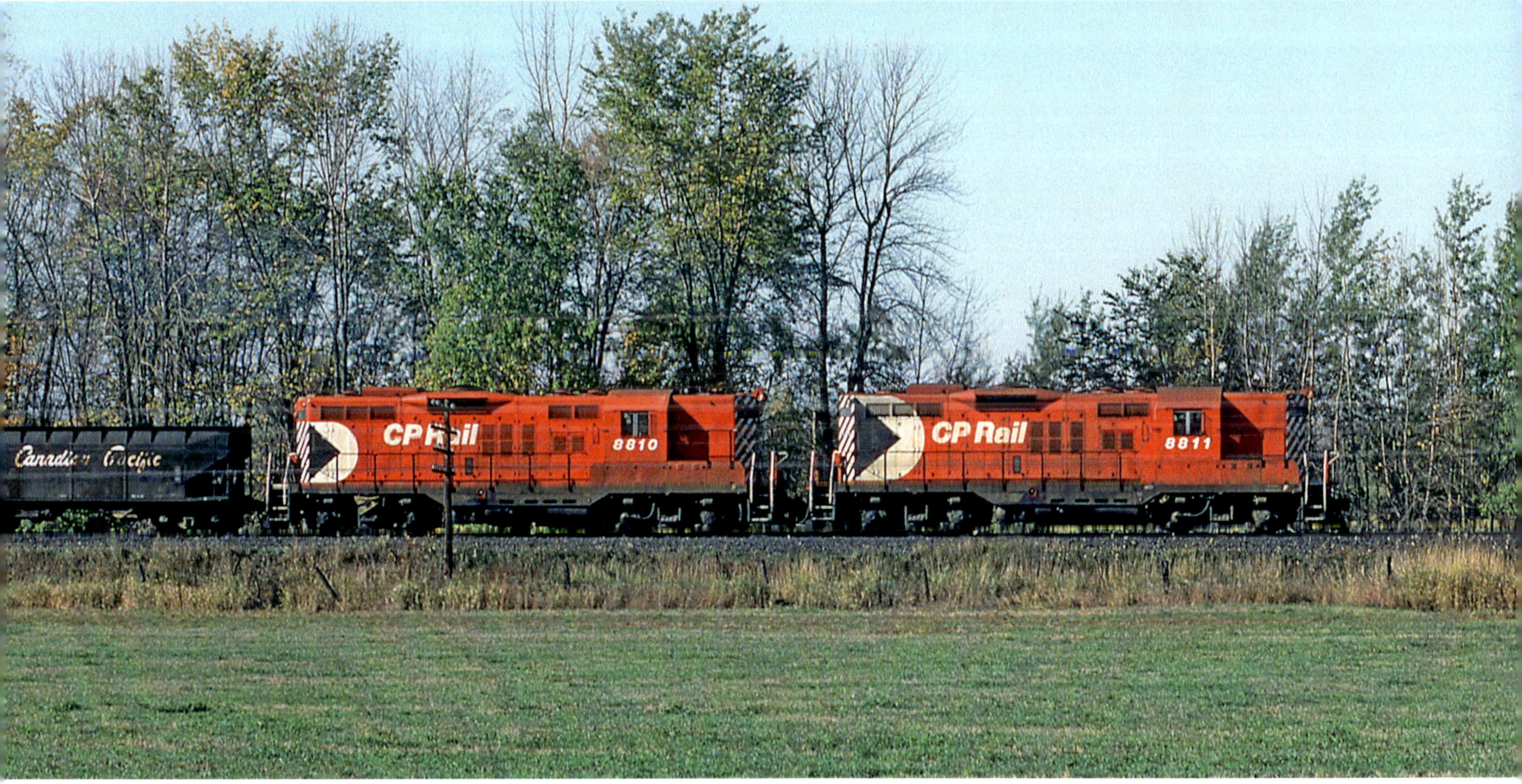

Belleville Subdivision

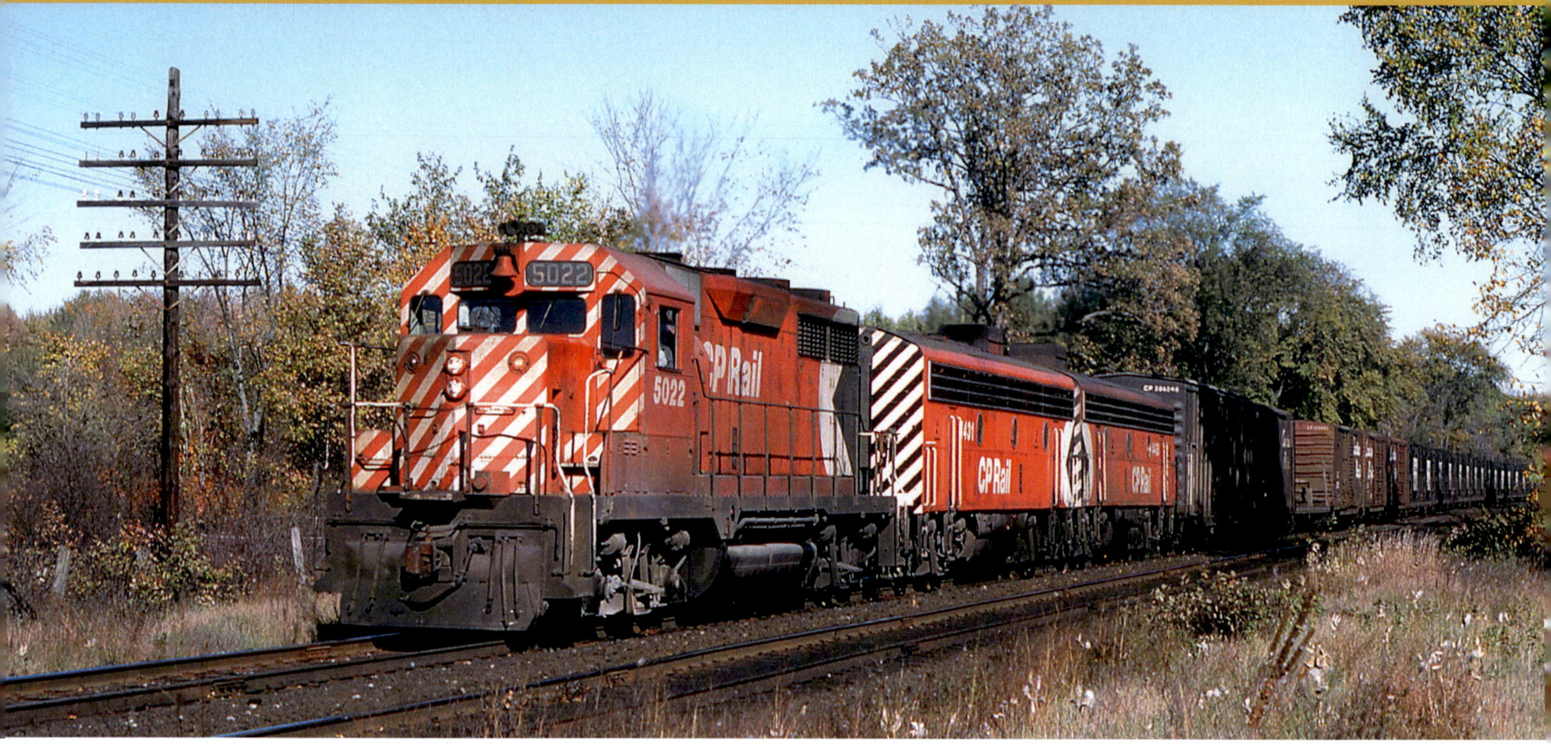

ABOVE: Heading southwest from Smiths Falls, the Belleville Sub was CPR's main line to Toronto. It hosted an all-GMDD power set as GP35 #5022 led a pair of F7Bs westward a few miles west of Smiths Falls at the Glenview Road crossing in October 1975. *(JC)*

BELOW: On a beautiful autumn afternoon in October 1975, a westbound freight led by a pair of M636s and an F7B was about to cross Glenview Road. This photogenic and relaxing location was a favorite spot to rest and perhaps have a picnic lunch while waiting for trains to appear. *(JC)*

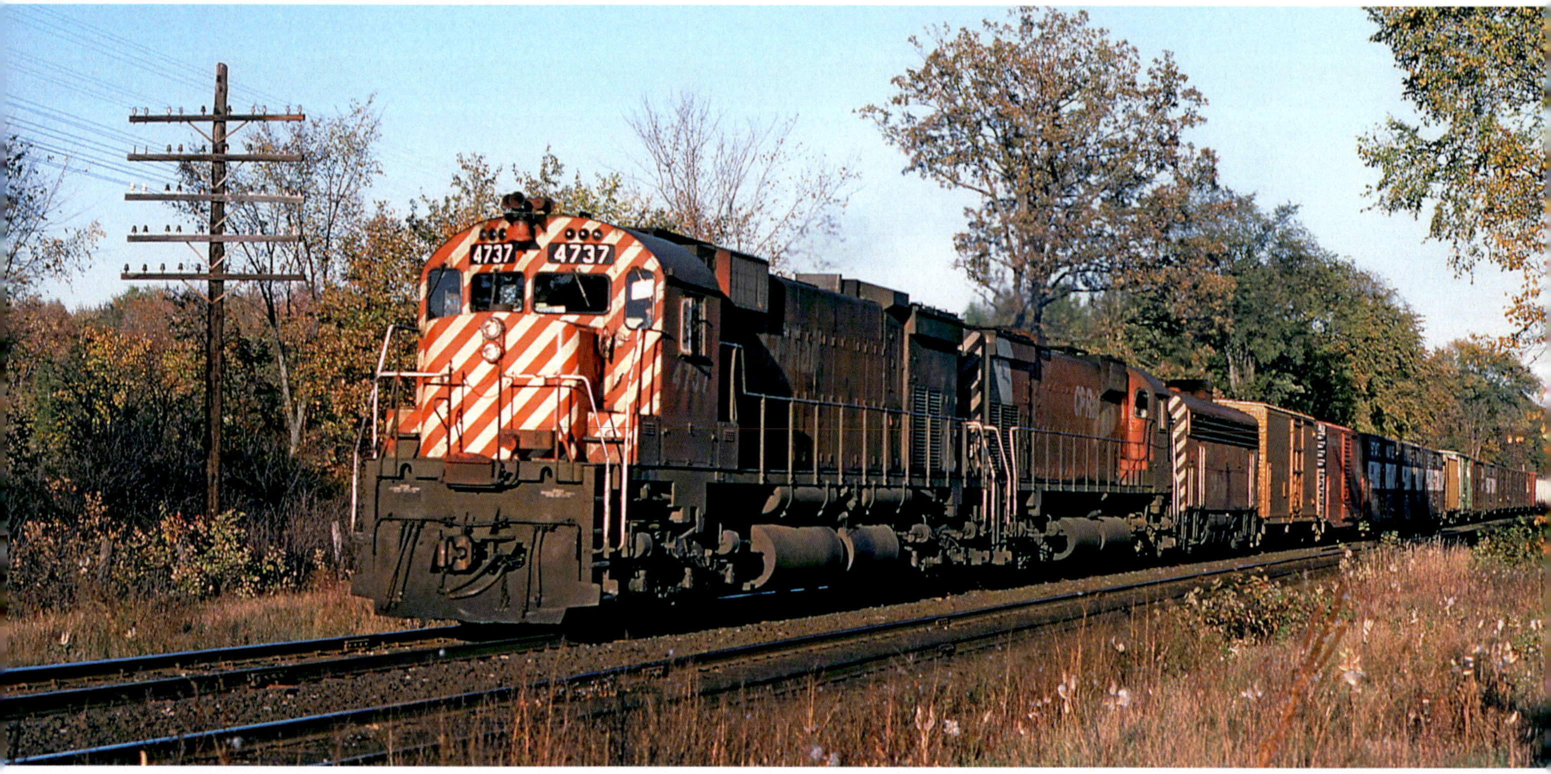

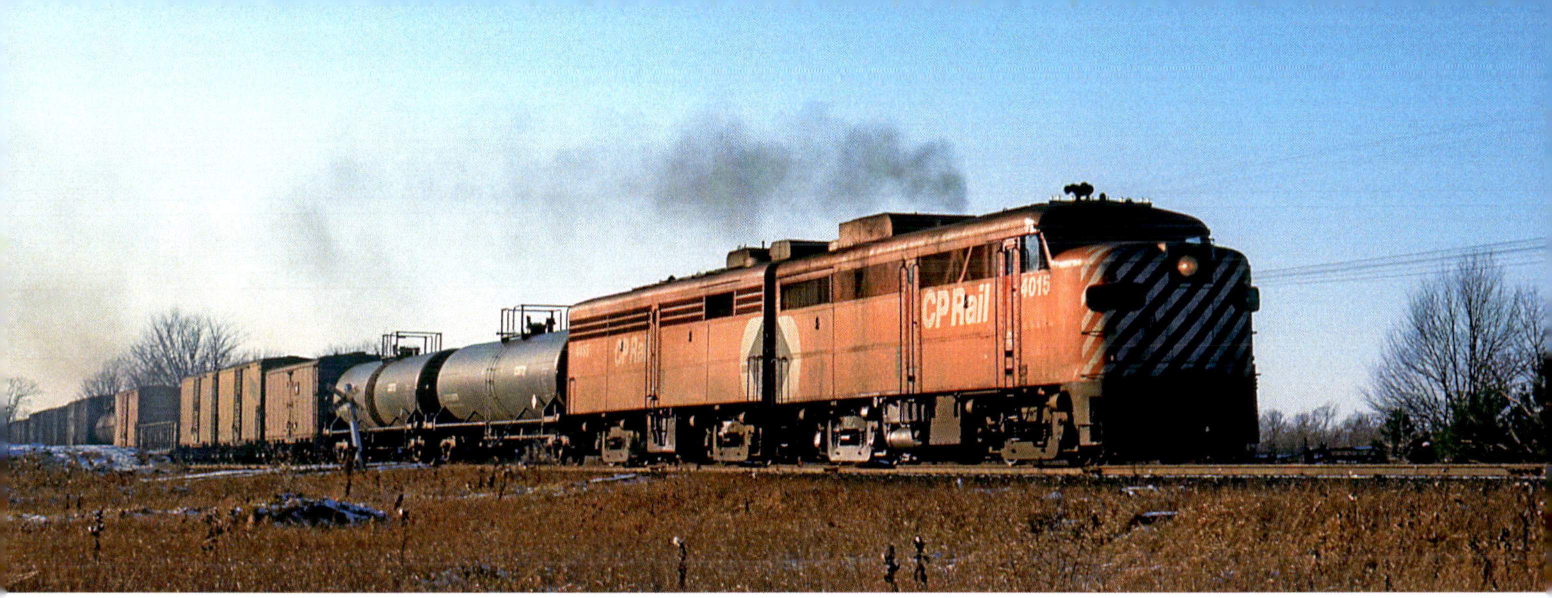

ABOVE: A rare find in November 1973 was FA-1 #4015 leading an FB-2 eastward at Glenview Road, the low sun highlighting the angular flanks of these Alco cab units. *(JGP)*

RIGHT: By 1975, the CPR's large roster of SD40s and SD40-2s was beginning to cut into the dominance of Alco power on the Belleville Sub. In October of that year #5511 led a westbound at Glenview Road ahead of M636 #4704, another SD40 and a deadheading Alco switcher. *(JC)*

BELOW: In the heavy mid-day light of July 19, 1991, five six-axle MLW units headed west with a hot container train at Glenview Road. *(JC)*

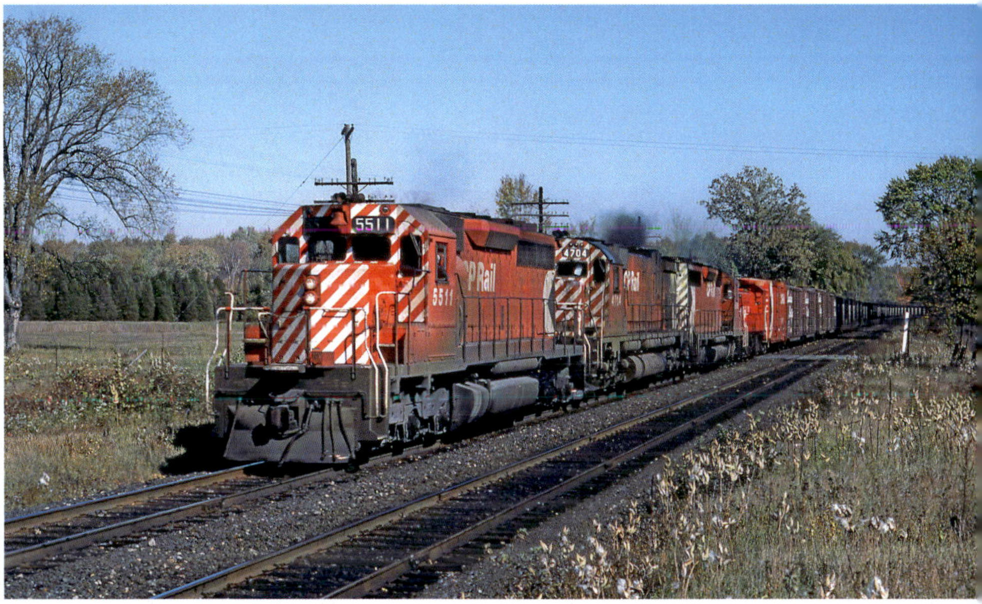

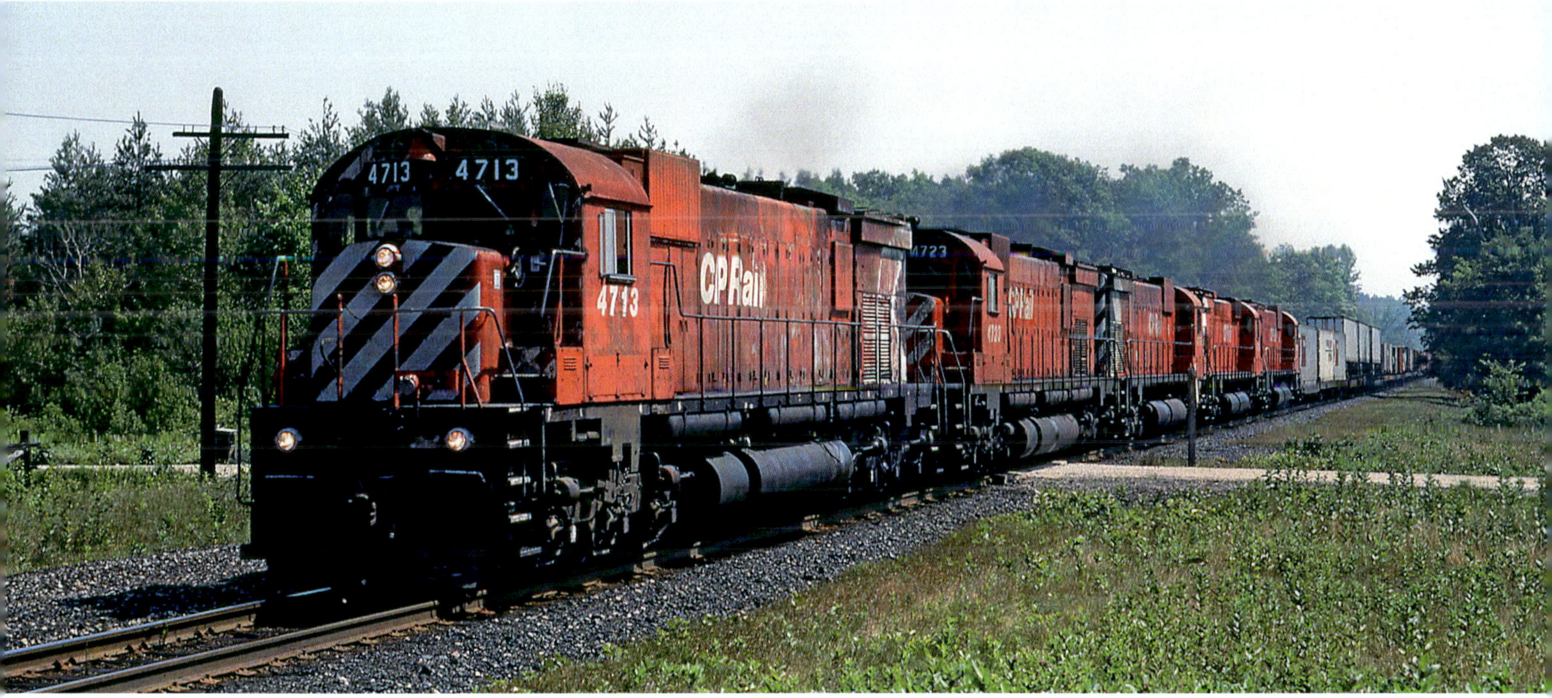

RIGHT: Bayview Junction outside the city of Hamilton was, and is, a favorite location for railfans. In September 1987 a pair of SW1200s headed west at Bayview. *(JGP)*

BELOW: Grand Trunk Western was an important subsidiary of Canadian National, providing access to the U.S. Midwest. A westbound freight was curving away from Bayview Junction in September 1987, heading for the border at Sarnia, ON and on into Michigan. *(JGP)*

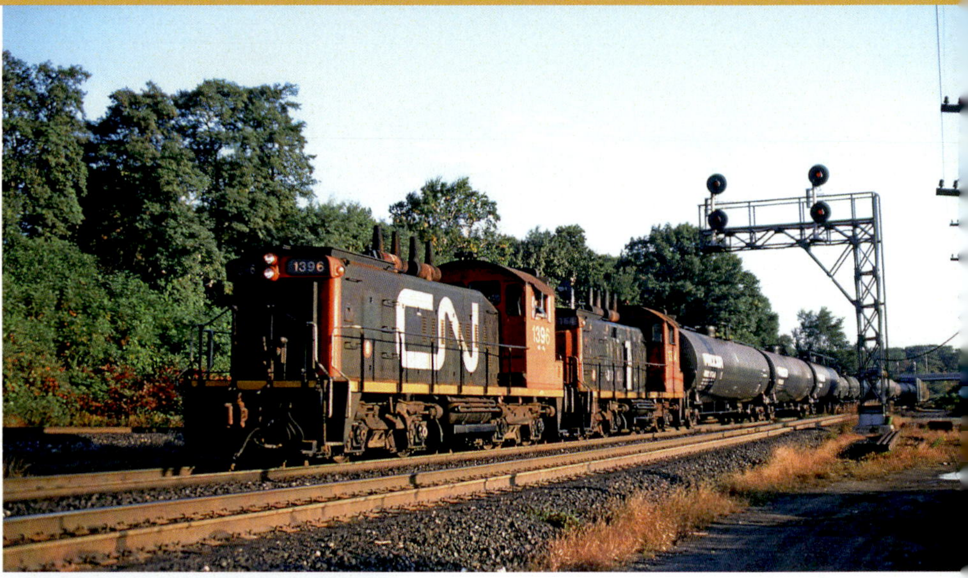

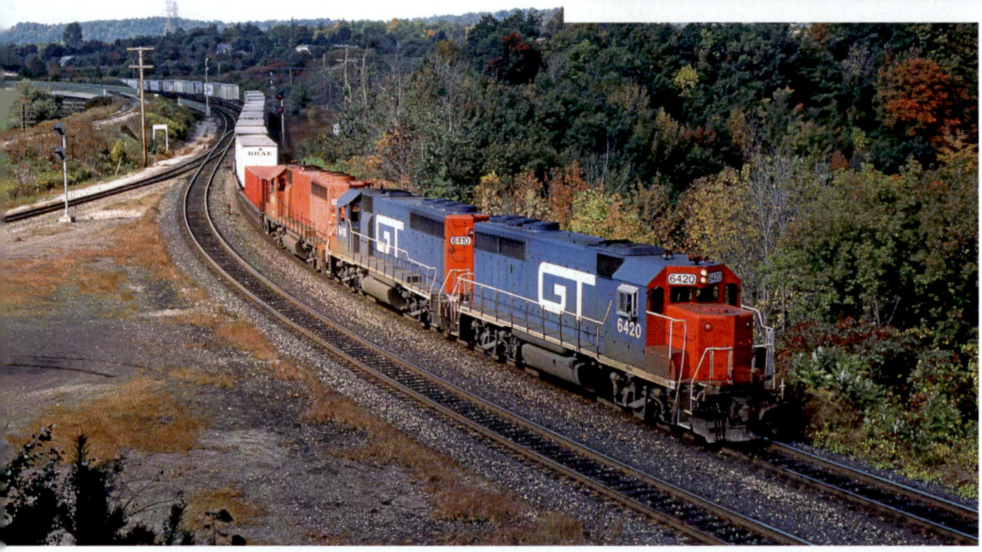

BELOW: A trio of Toronto, Hamilton & Buffalo Geeps, GP7s #73 and #75 bracketing GP9 #403 showed the effects of decades of hard work as they sat at the Hamilton engine terminal in September 1987. In 1988, they would be rebuilt by CPR at the Angus Shops in Montreal and join CPR's diesel fleet as GP7u and GP9u units. *(JGP)*

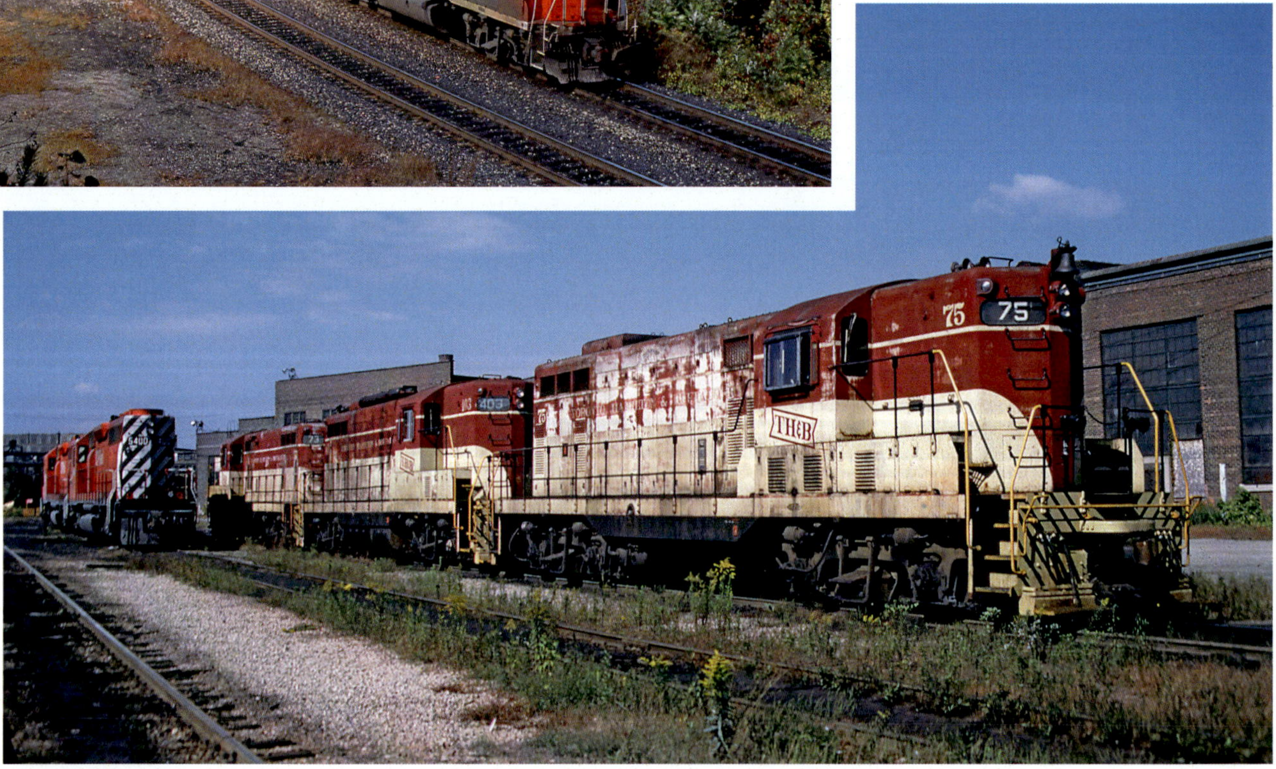

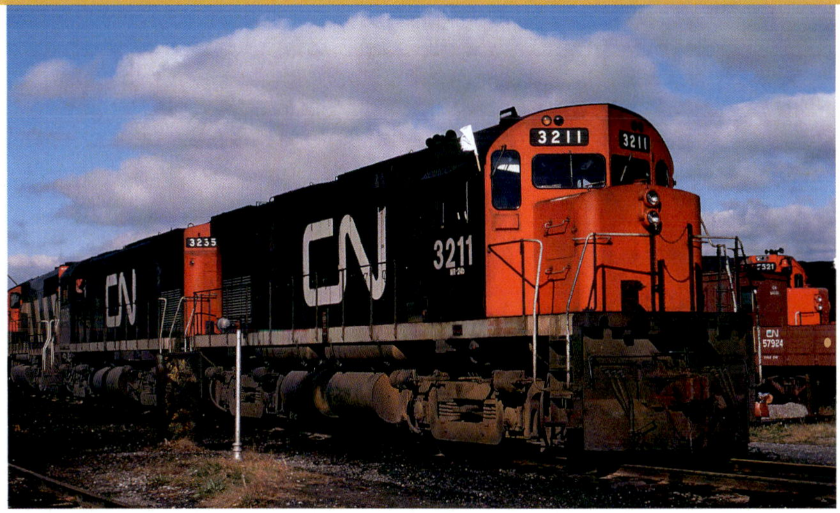

RIGHT: CNR C424 #3211 rested at Fort Erie, ON awaiting its next assignment in October 1974. The CNR acquired 41 of the type in 1964. *(JGP)*

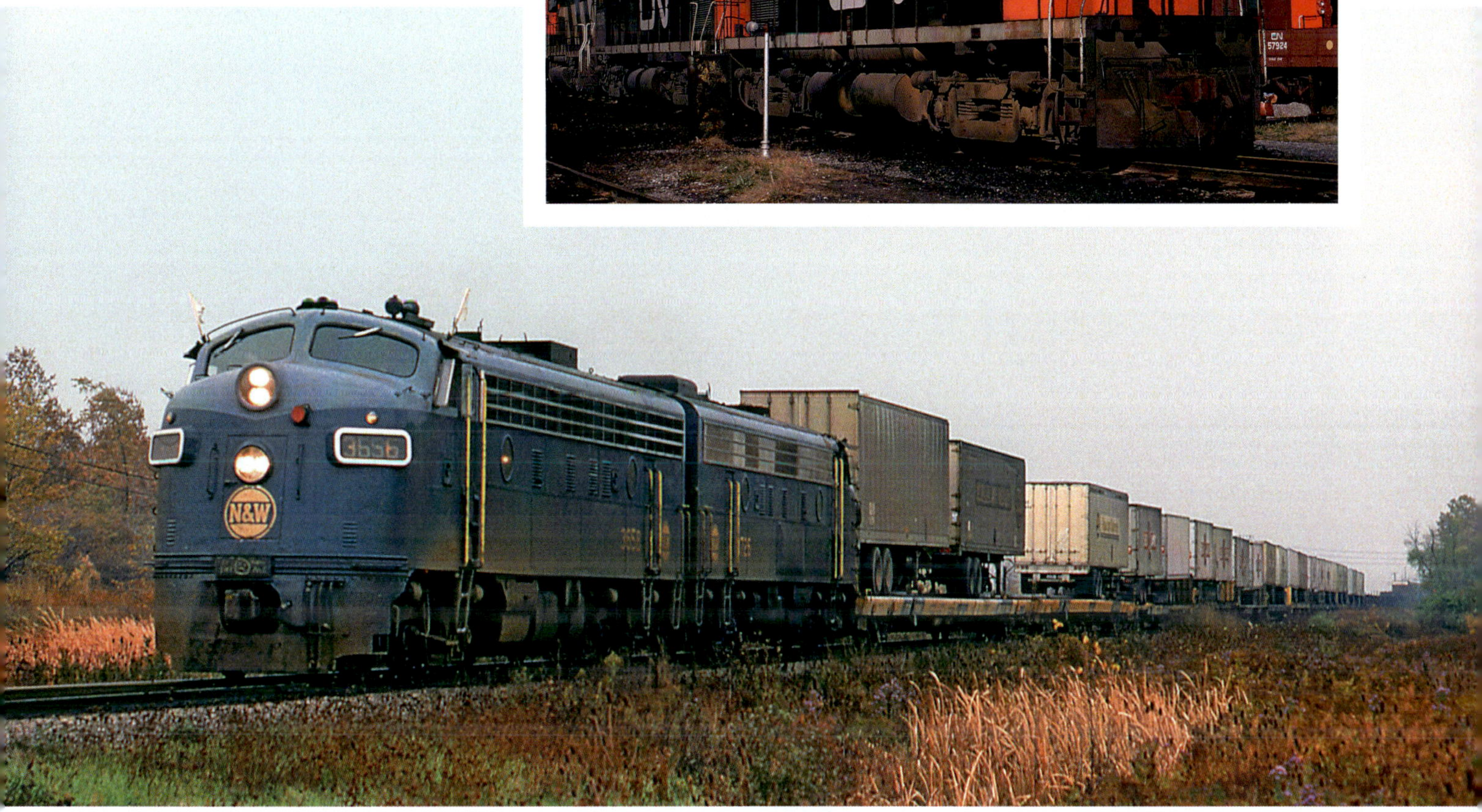

ABOVE: The Norfolk & Western operated into Fort Erie, ON over trackage rights on the CNR. The usual motive power in the 1970s was a set of former Wabash F-7s, such as this pair heading west a few miles out of Fort Erie in October 1974. *(JGP)*

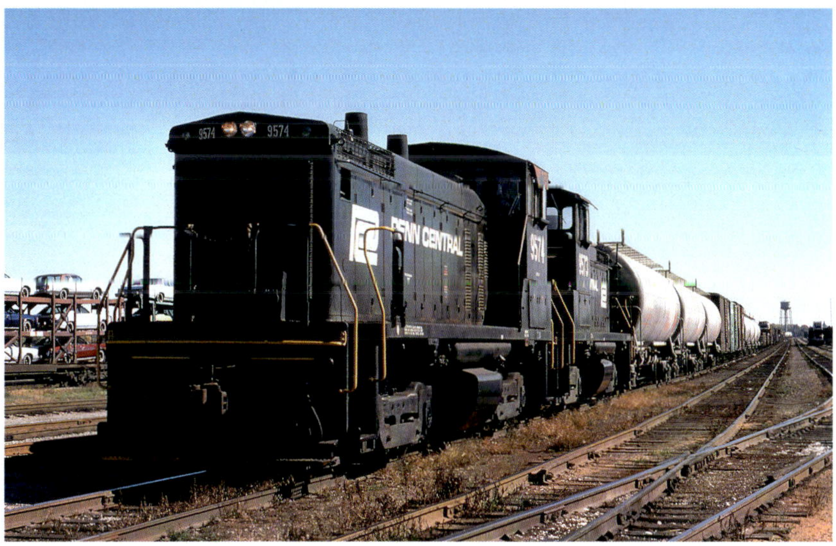

RIGHT: Consecutively numbered Penn Central SW1500s #9573 and #9574 brought a transfer freight from Buffalo into the CNR yard at Fort Erie in October 1974. *(JGP)*

Ontario Northland

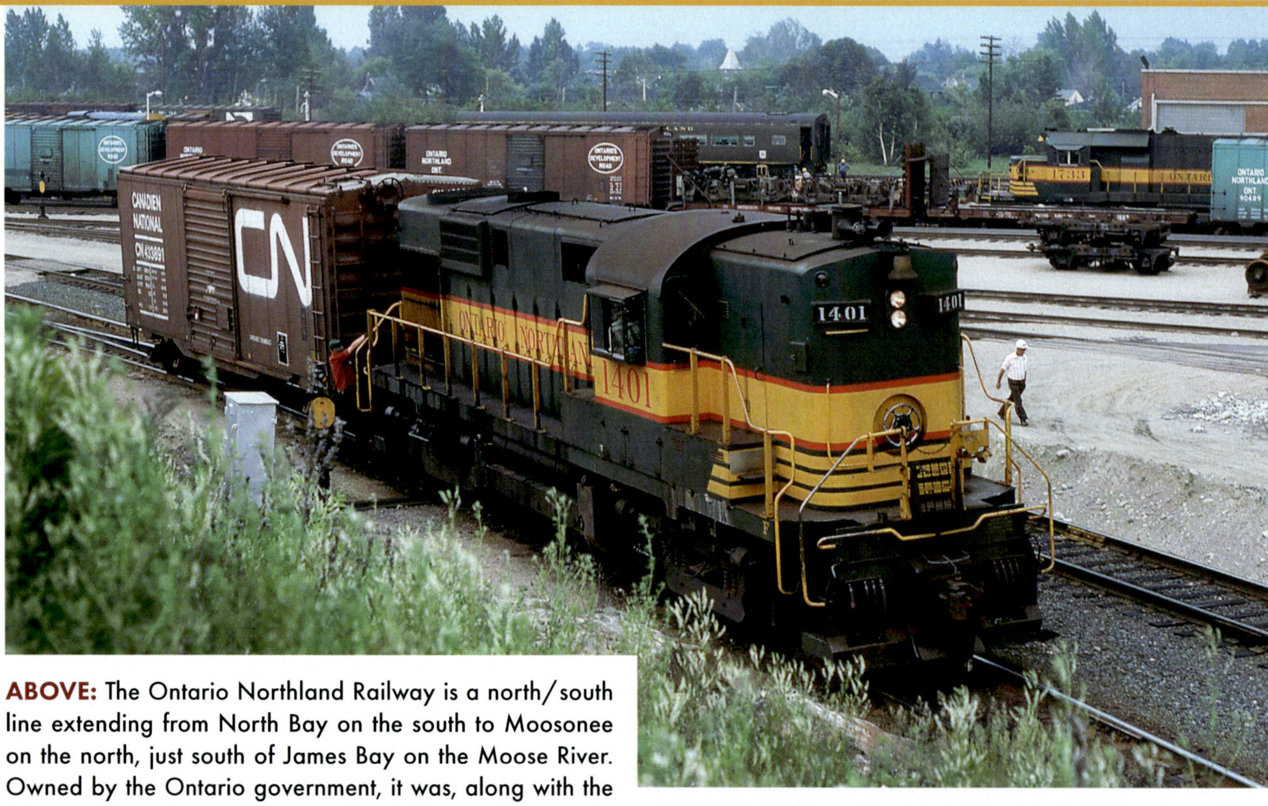

ABOVE: The Ontario Northland Railway is a north/south line extending from North Bay on the south to Moosonee on the north, just south of James Bay on the Moose River. Owned by the Ontario government, it was, along with the Algoma Central, a major target for Jeffrey and Jeremy in their trip to Ontario in June 1976. They received permission to photograph inside the ONR yard and engine terminal, where RS10 #1401 was switching the ONR yard at North Bay, ON in June 1976. The RS10 was a transitional MLW model, with the older 244 prime mover inside the body type of the later RS18. The ONR acquired four of this model in 1955. *(JC)*

BELOW: Well-weathered ONR RS3 #1306 was switching at North Bay in June 1976. The ONR rostered 12 of the type, plus four RS2s. *(JC)*

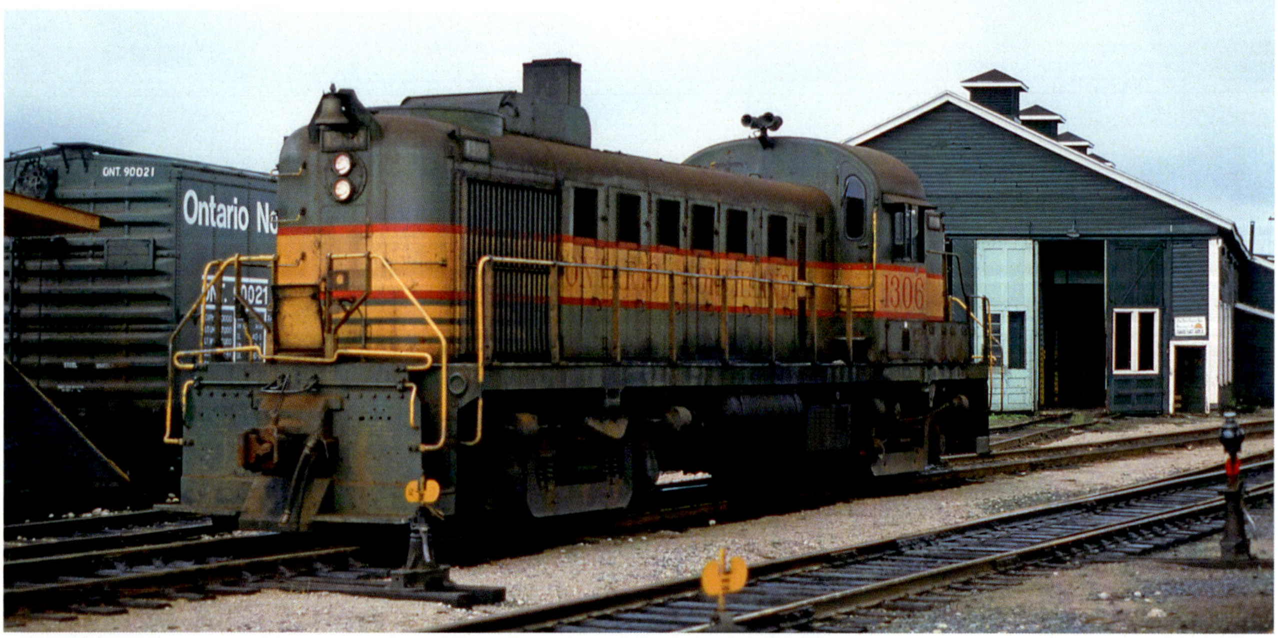

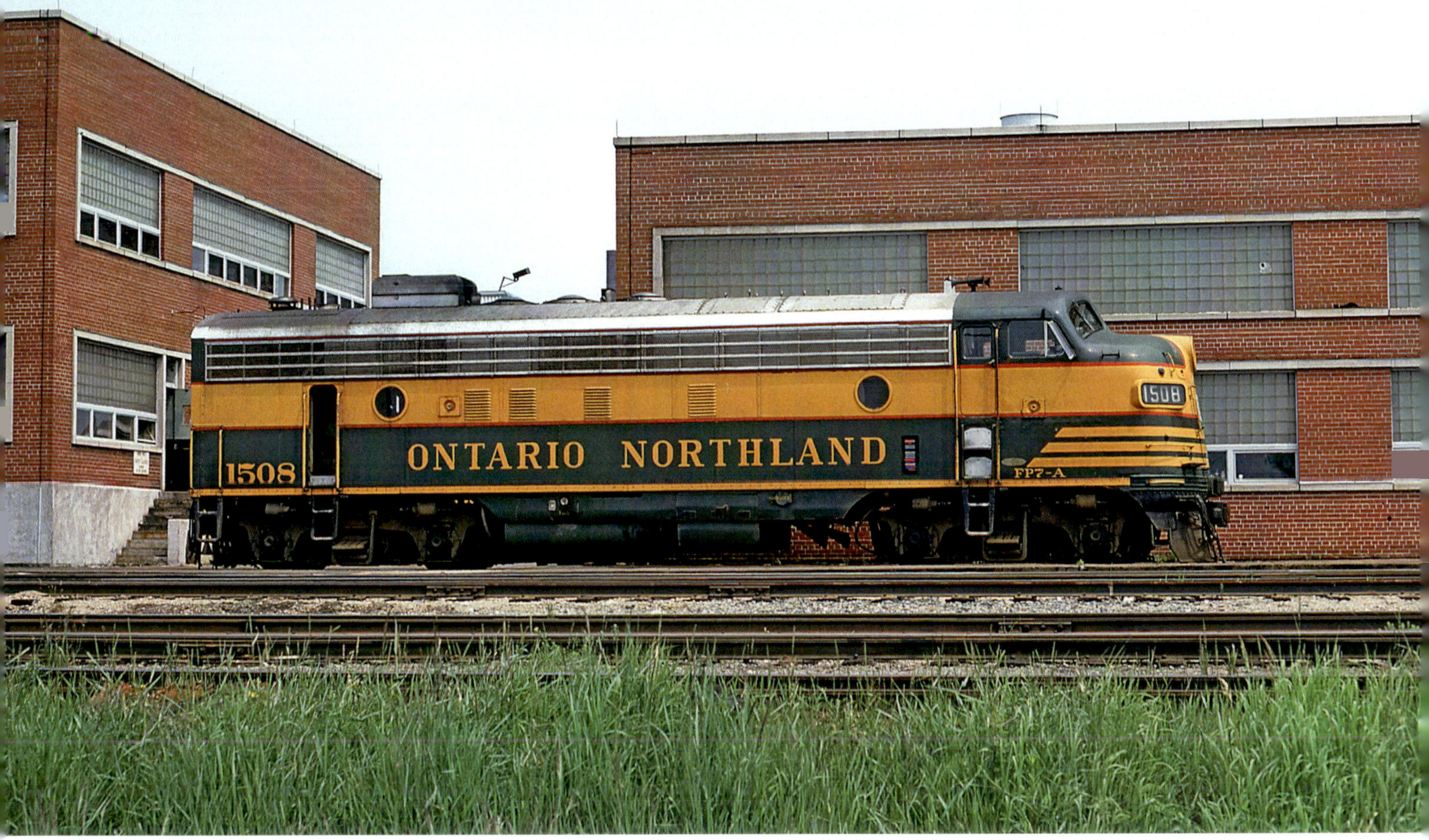

ABOVE: FP-7 #1508 posed near the extensive shop facility at North Bay in June 1976 in its original color scheme. The Ontario Northland used its fleet of 22 FP7s in both freight and passenger operations. *(JC)*

BELOW: The *Northlander* trainset was being serviced at North Bay in August 1988. The ONR had put the former Swiss-built Trans Europ train sets in service in 1977. By the time this photo was taken, the locomotives had been converted into unpowered passenger cars and the train was powered by an FP7. *(JGP)*

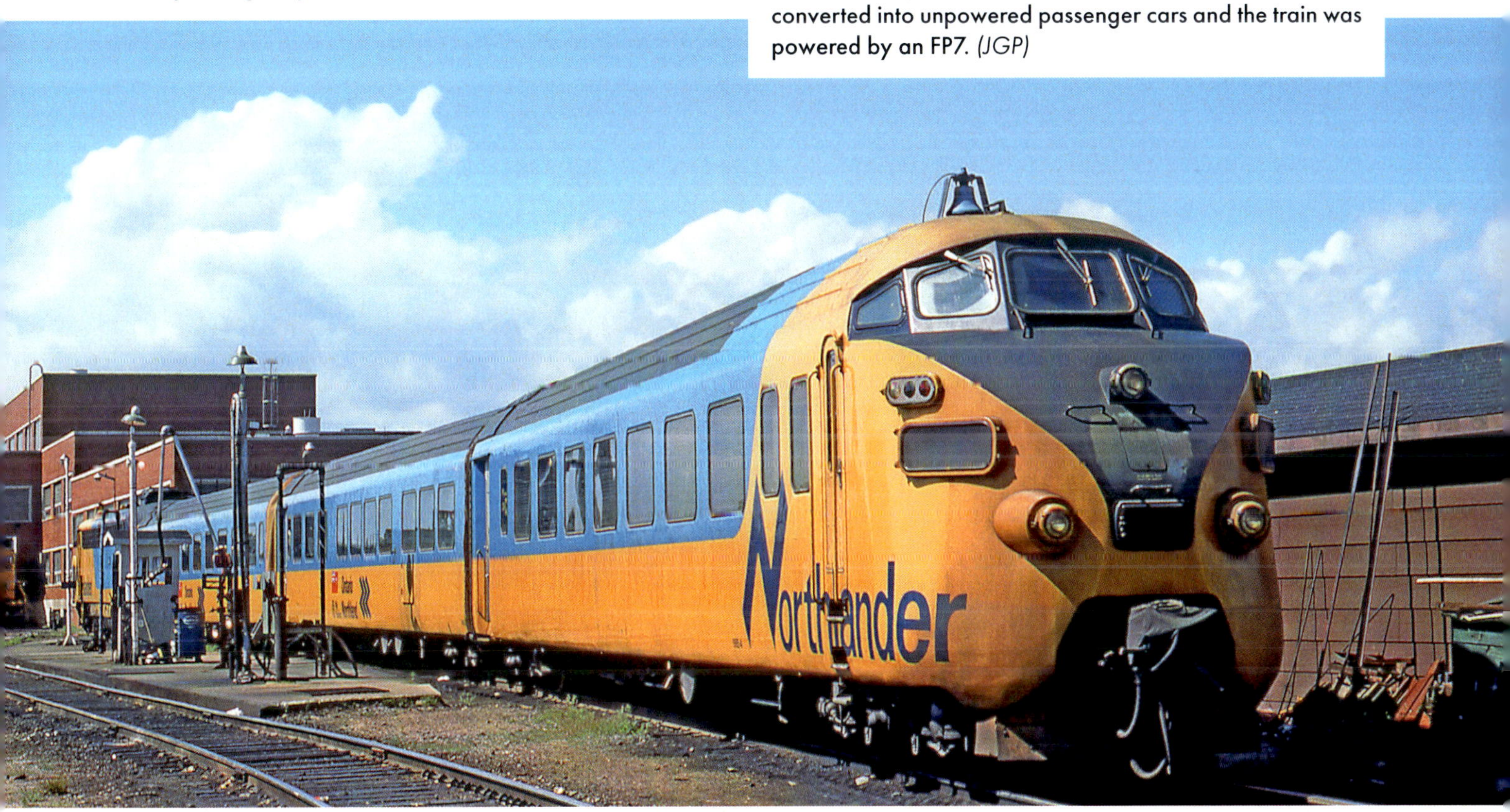

Temagami

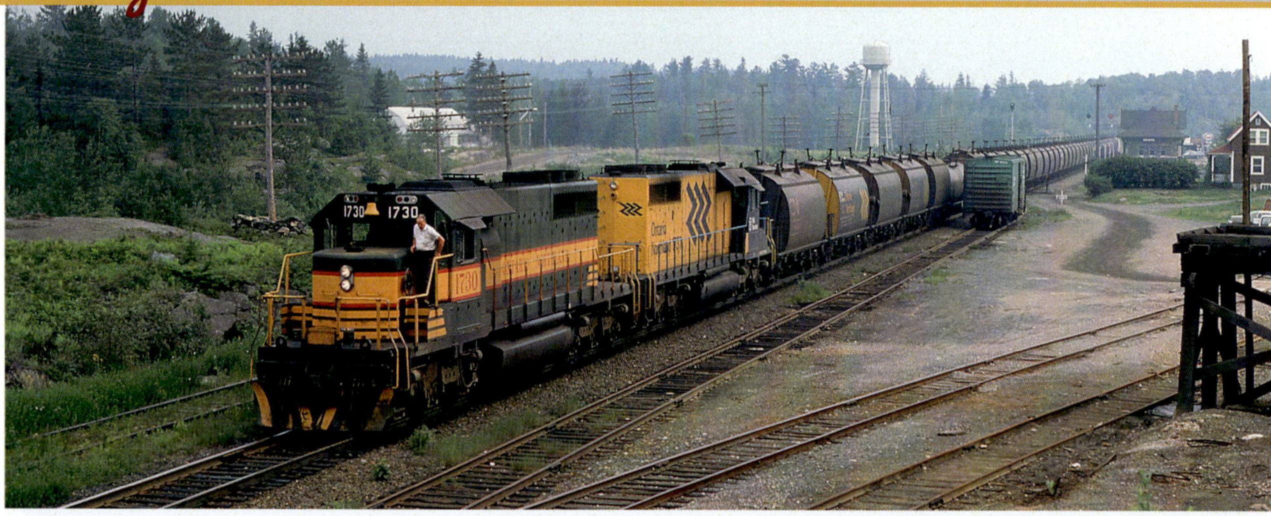

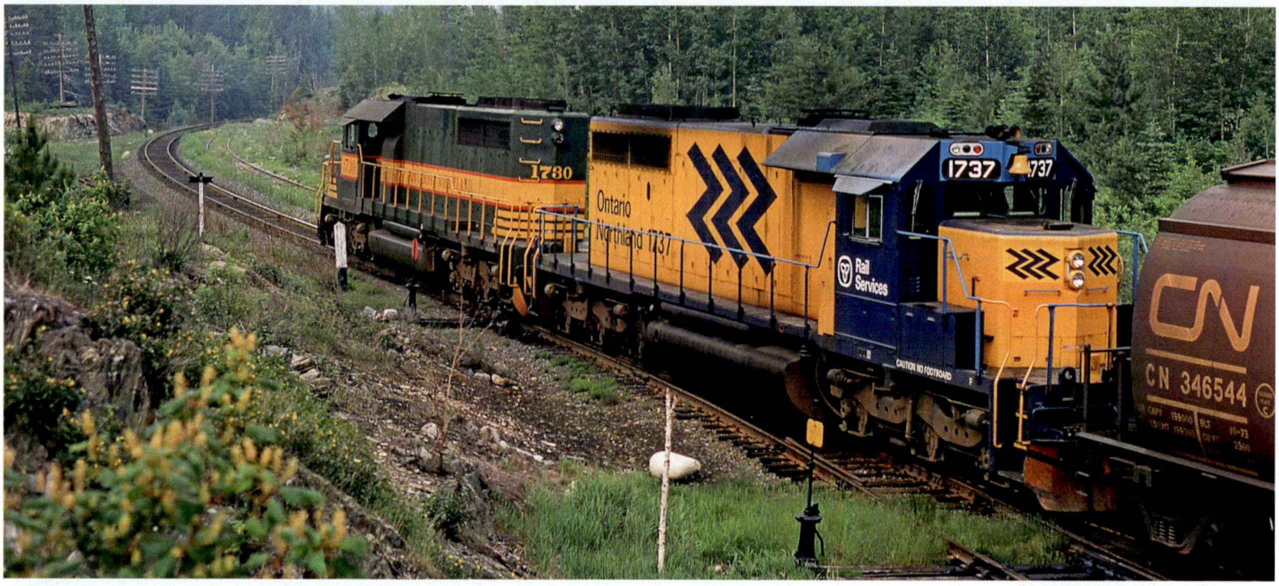

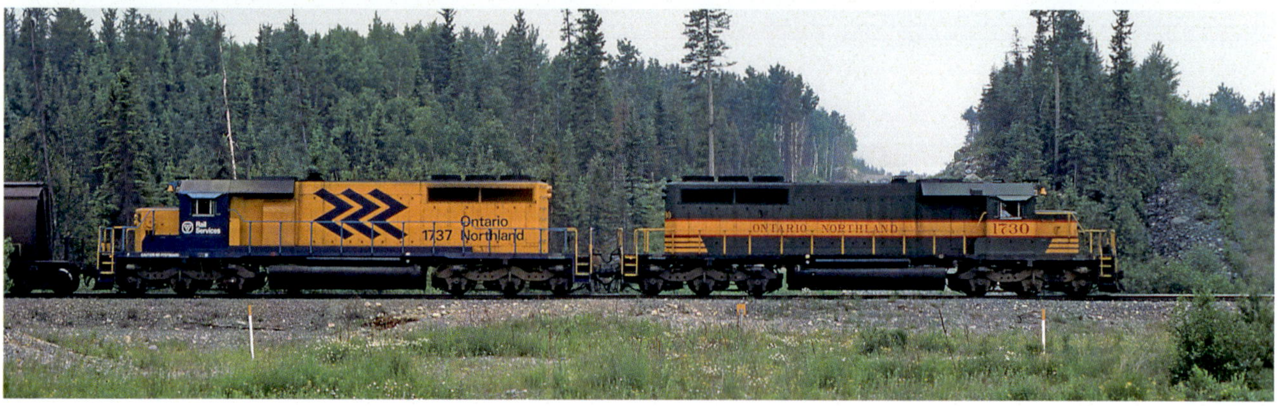

ALL, THIS PAGE: SD40-2 #1730 rolled to a stop just past the Temagami station on a warm and muggy night in June 1976. The train was bringing empty ore cars back to the Sherman Mine outside Temagami accessed by a short branch off the main line at Rock Junction. After entering the mine branch, the train headed down to the mine, the largest mine in Temagami, opened in 1968 and eventually closing in 1990. The ore was brought south to North Bay and interchanged with the CNR, which brought it to Hamilton, ON for steel production. *(JC)*

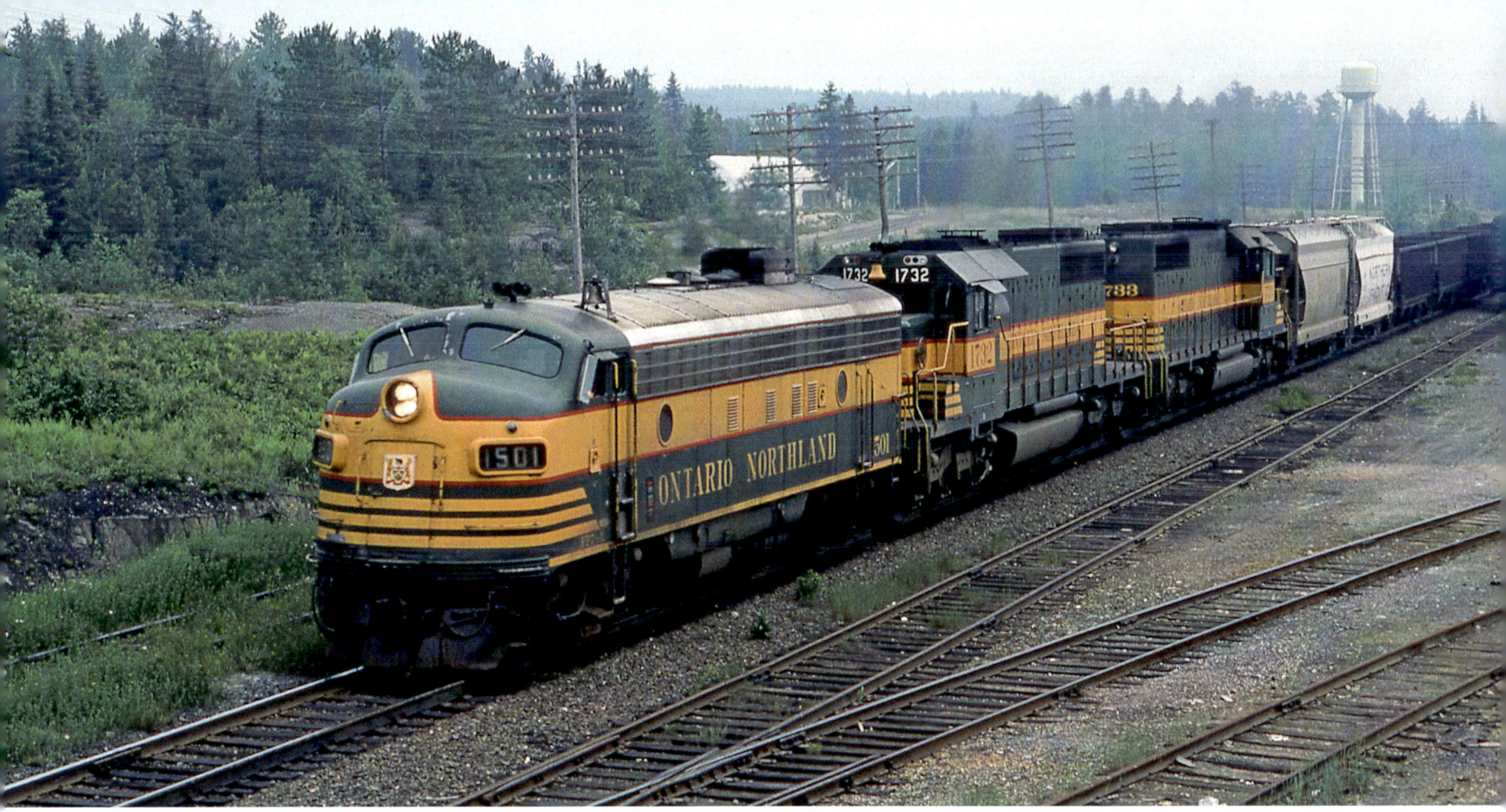

ABOVE AND BELOW: After the ore train cleared the main, a northbound freight sped through Temagami with FP7 #1501 leading a pair of SD40-2s, all still in the green and yellow paint scheme. A frantic chase ended with a second shot of the train in the evening mist near Cobalt, ON. *(JC)*

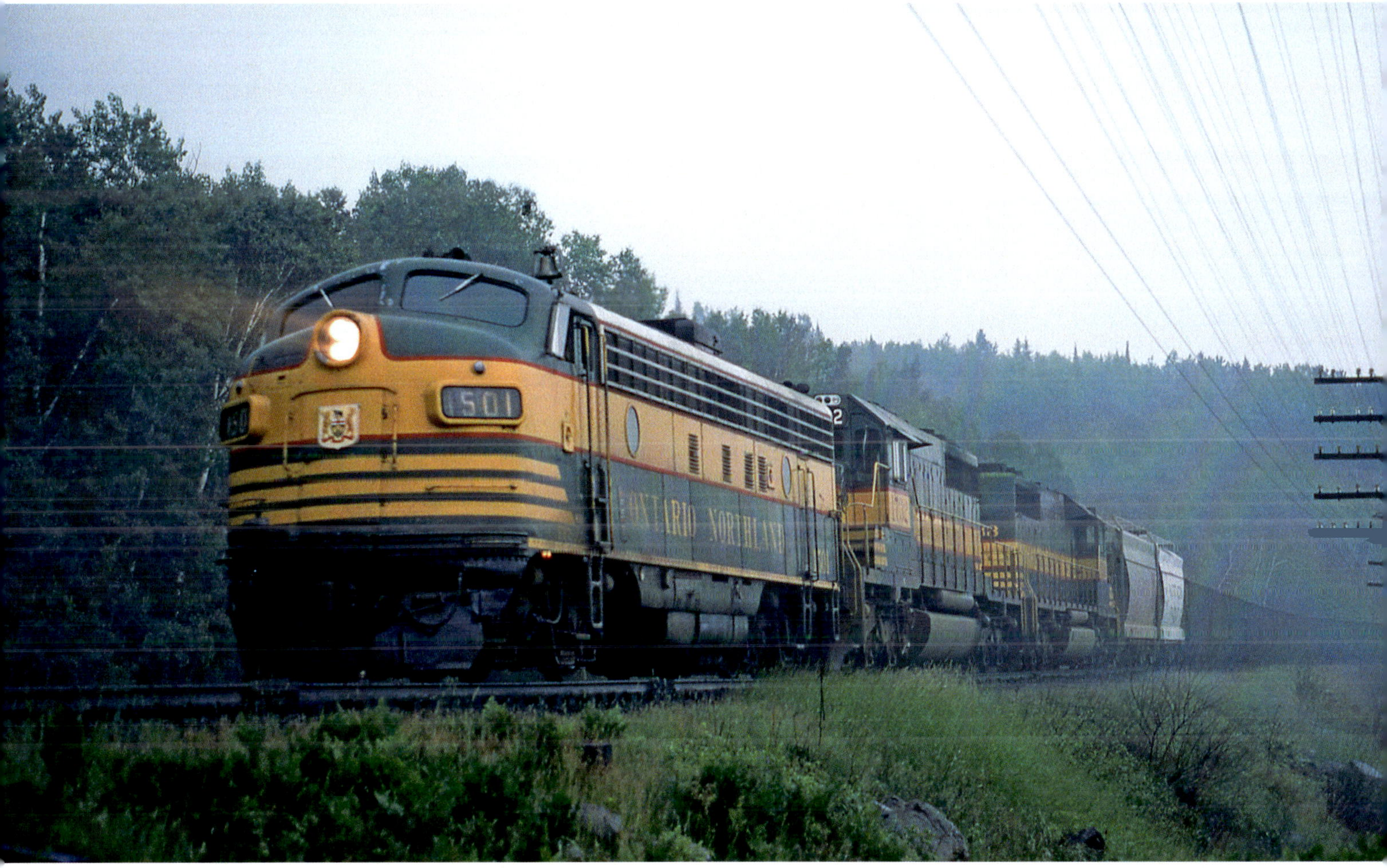

Northern Ontario

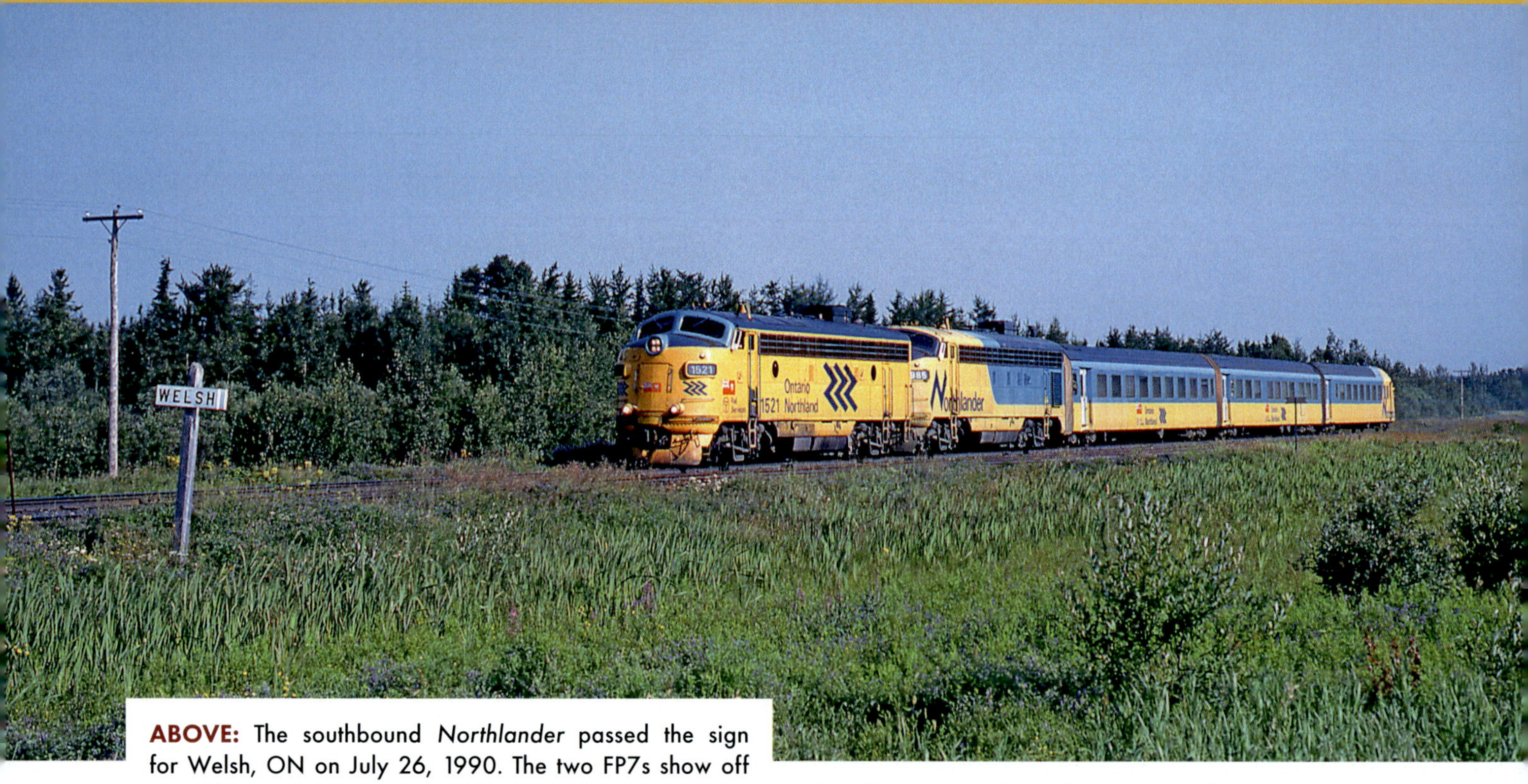

ABOVE: The southbound *Northlander* passed the sign for Welsh, ON on July 26, 1990. The two FP7s show off two different paint schemes, while the trailing car is a de-powered former Trans Europ Express car. Just ahead is Porquis Junction, where the line to Timmins joined the north/south mainline. *(JGP)*

BELOW: Train #307 was headed to Kidd as it left Porquis Junction on July 26, 1990, with GP38-2 #1801 leading SD40-2 #1730. *(JGP)*

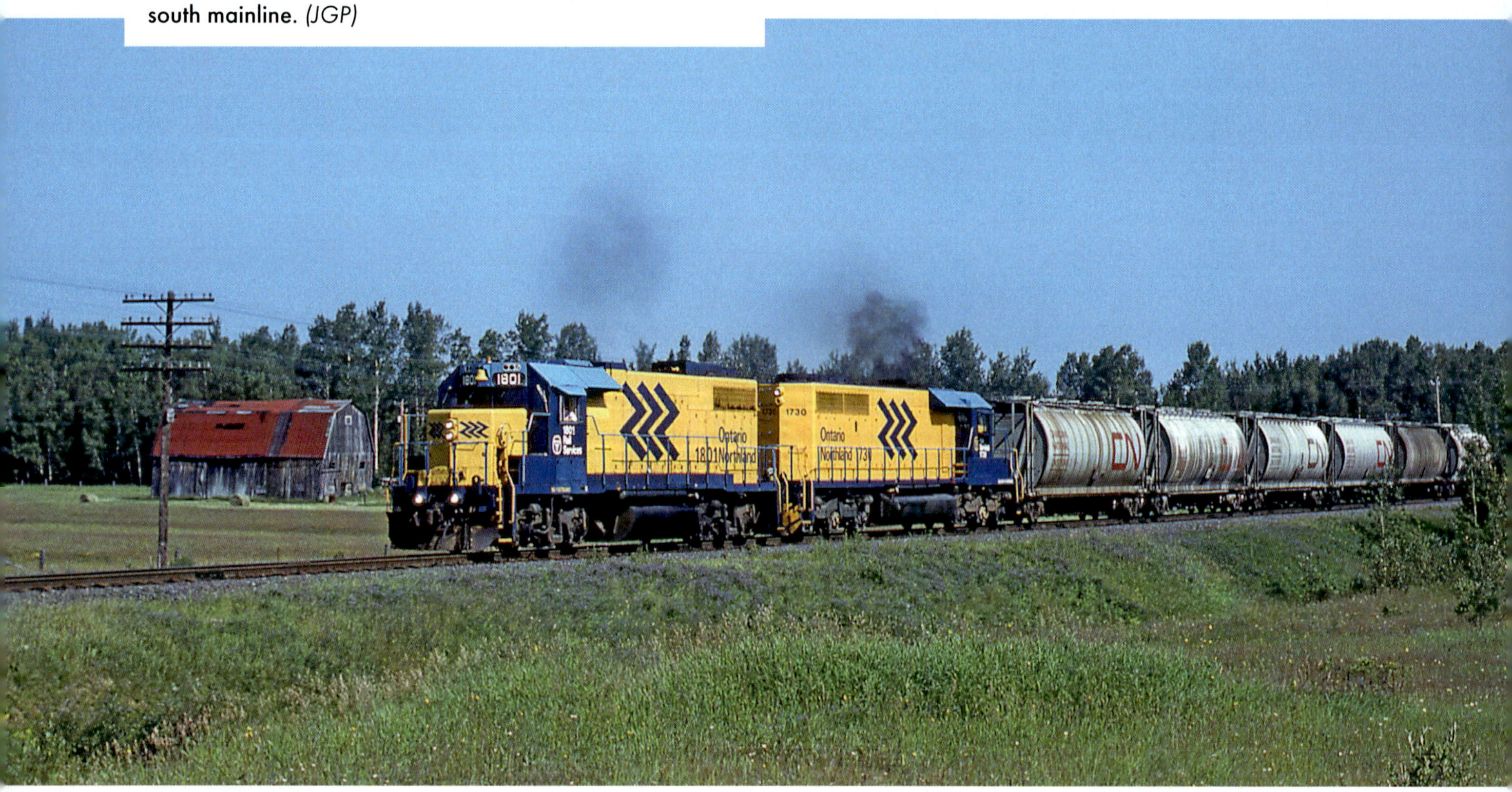

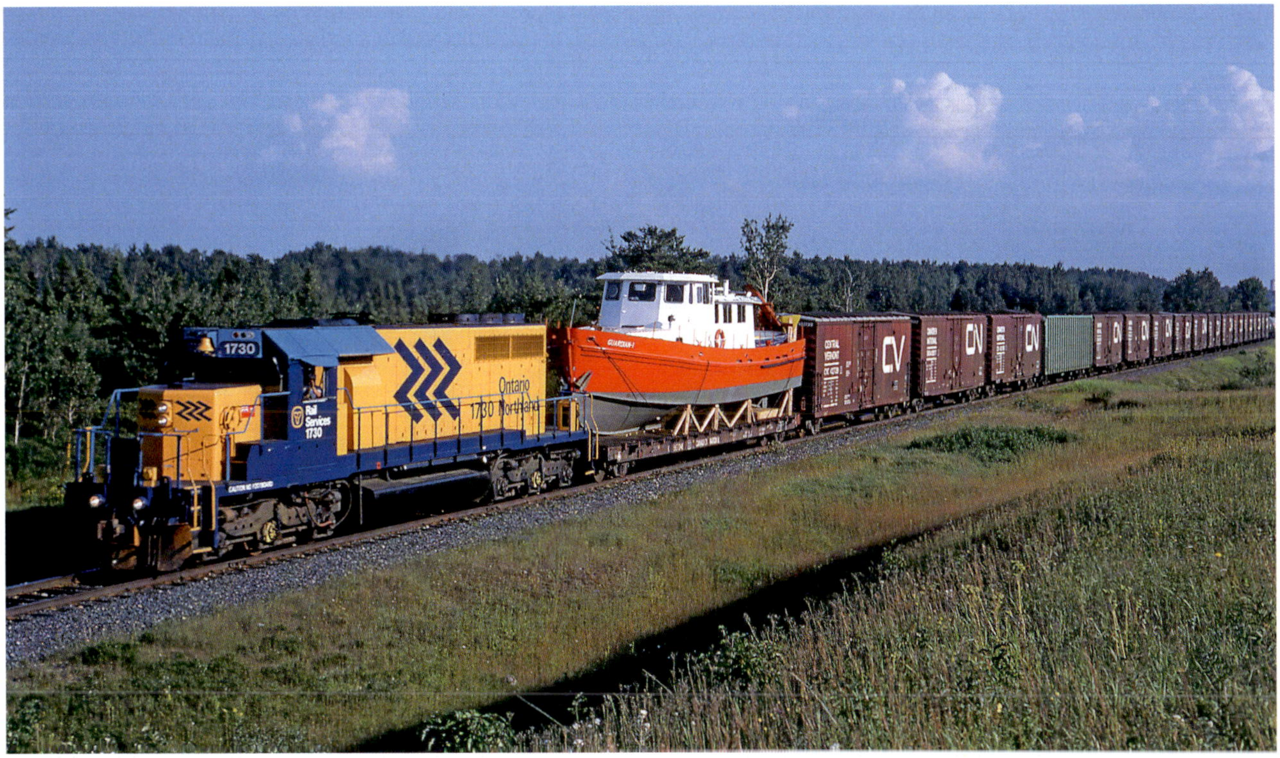

ABOVE: Northbound train #213 had boat *Guardian 1* ahead of a long string of CN boxcars heading north to Cochrane, ON for paper loading, north of Porquis on July 26, 1990. The boat is likely heading to the Moose River at Moosonee, ON. Not what you normally think of as intermodal freight! *(JGP)*

BELOW: Train #308 crossed the Frederick House River at Connaught, ON heading east from Timmins, ON on July 27, 1990. *(JGP)*

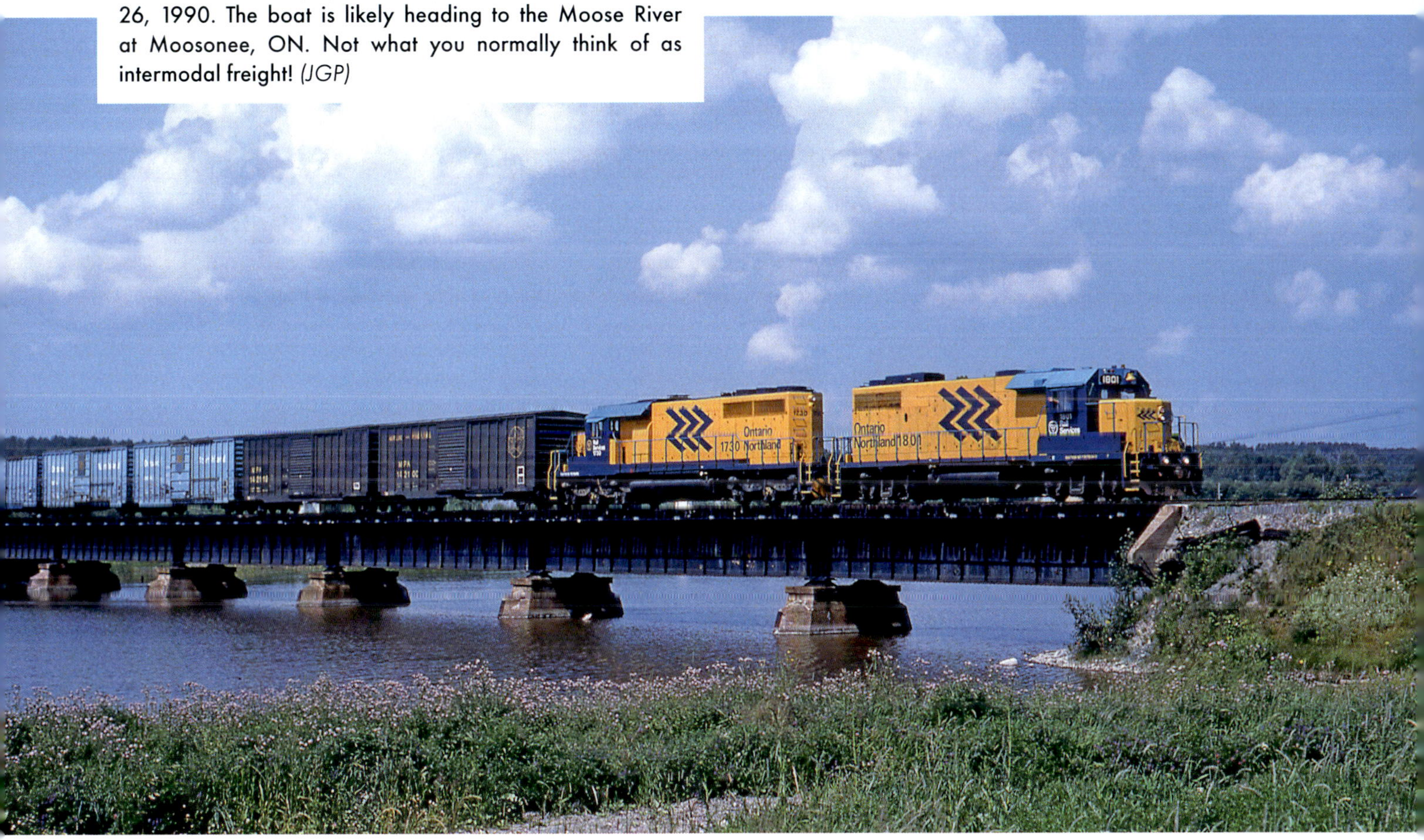

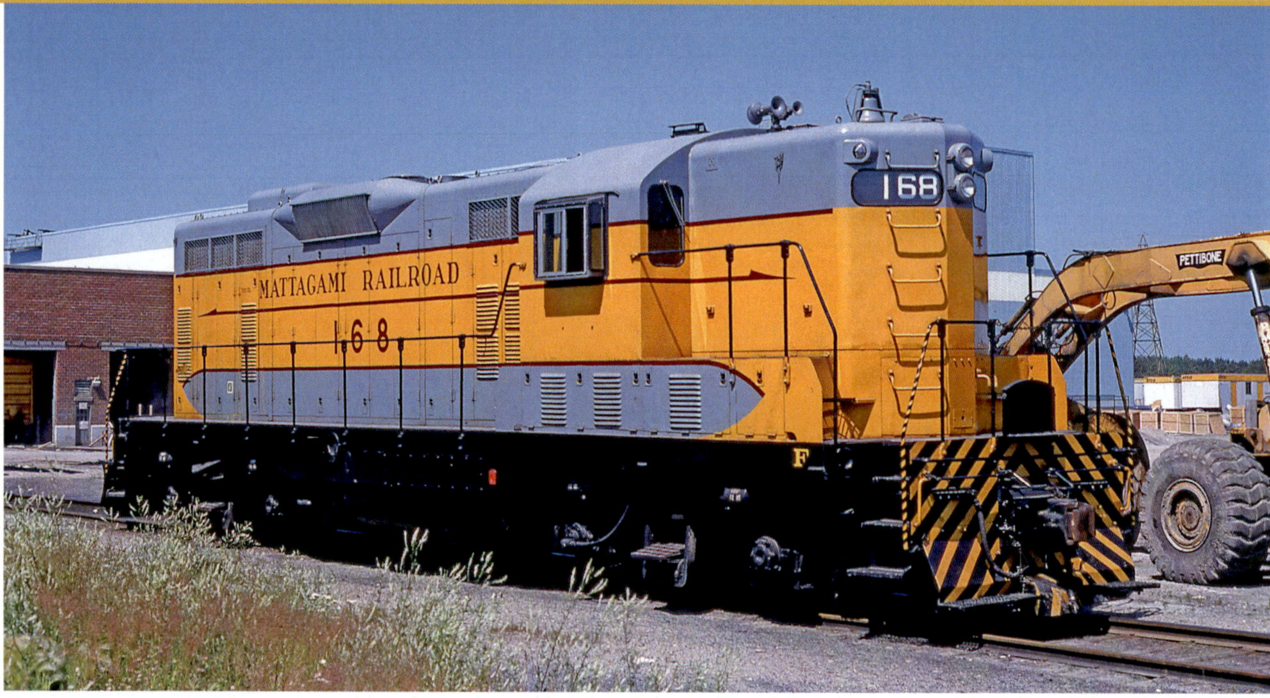

ABOVE: The Mattagami Railroad operated a short 3.3 mile stretch of track in Smooth Rock Falls, ON until it was acquired by the Ontario Northland. It serviced the Abitibi Fibre plant in Smooth Rock Falls. When Jeffrey and Glen Perry visited on July 26, 1990, the personnel at the engine house were kind and brought GP7 #168 out of the house so they could photograph it in full sunlight. *(JGP)*

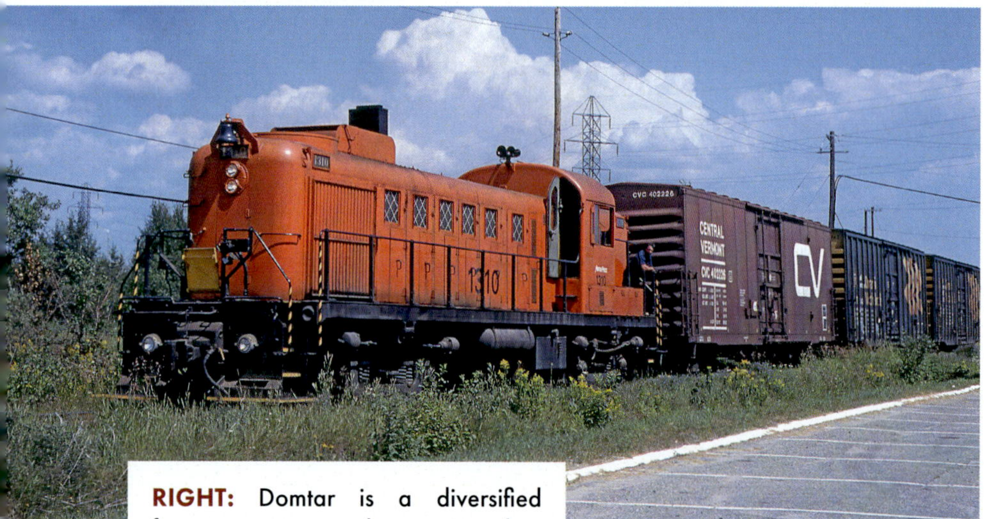

LEFT: Abitibi-Price RS3 #1310 switched the paper mill at Iroquois Falls, ON on July 26, 1990. The unit was formerly Ontario Northland #1310 and was acquired in May 1995. *(JGP)*

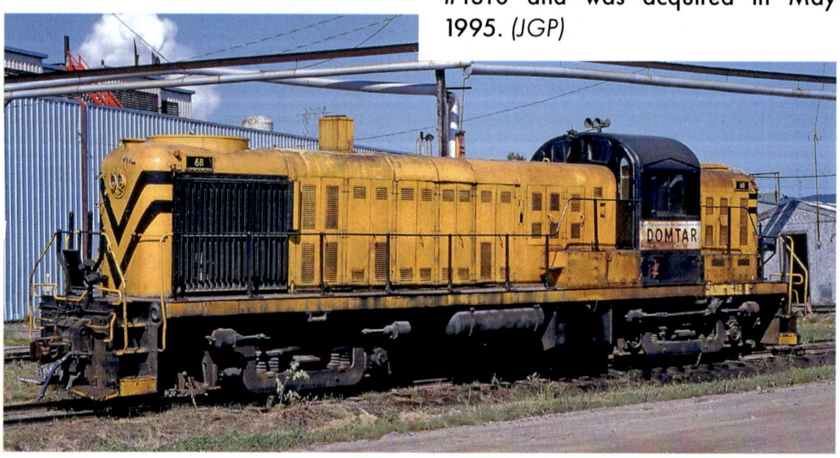

RIGHT: Domtar is a diversified forestry company that operated a pulp and paper mill in Red Rock, ON, northeast of Thunder Bay. It rostered a number of second-hand diesel locomotives, including RS3 #485, originally a Reading Company unit. It was acquired by United Railway Supply of Montreal and served on the Roberval & Saguenay before finding its way to Domtar. It was at Red Rock in August 1990. After it finished its Canadian service it was acquired by the Reading Company Technical & Historical Society and returned to Pennsylvania. *(JGP)*

Canadian Pacific: North Bay & Points West

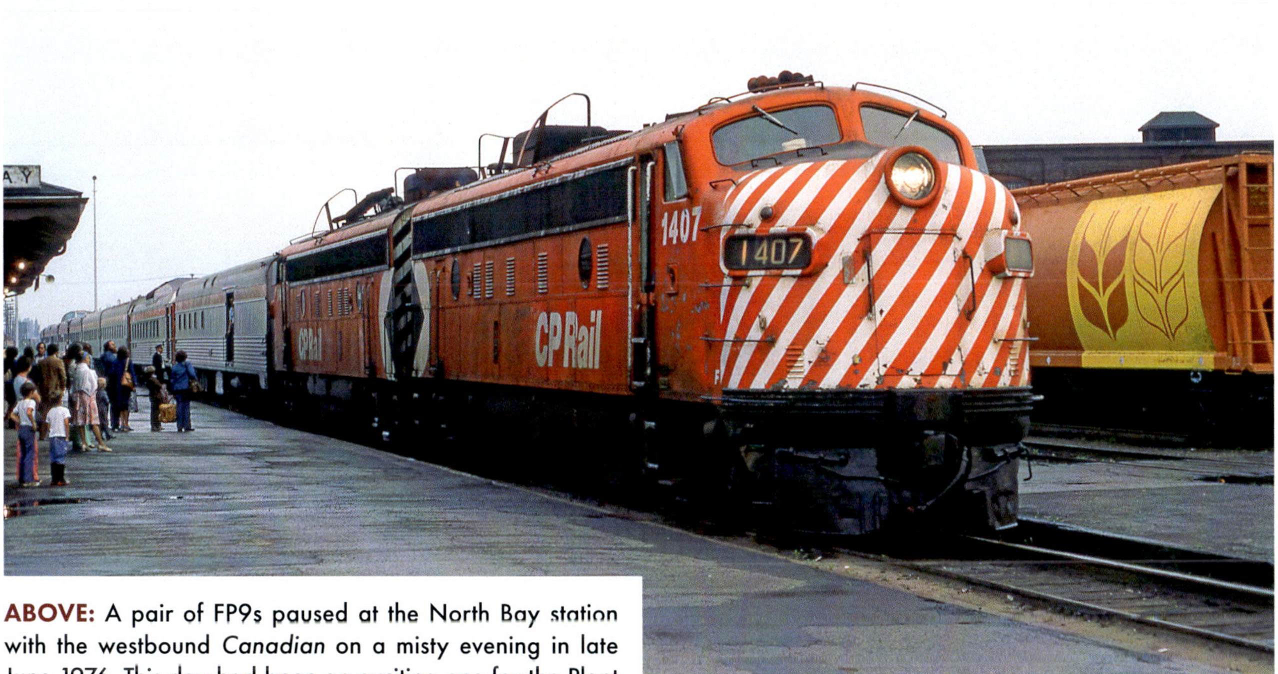

ABOVE: A pair of FP9s paused at the North Bay station with the westbound *Canadian* on a misty evening in late June 1976. This day had been an exciting one for the Plant brothers, with a tour of the Ontario Northland shops, a side trip to Temagami, and back to North Bay for the arrival of the *Canadian*. But the fun was about to continue as the annual shad fly invasion was about to begin, as millions of the short-lived insects poured out of Lake Nipissing and covered the lamps and streets of North Bay in a foul-smelling but harmless swarm. *(JC)*

BELOW: Freshly painted RS18 #8794 led an empty CPR grain train out of North Bay on a misty morning in June 1976. *(JC)*

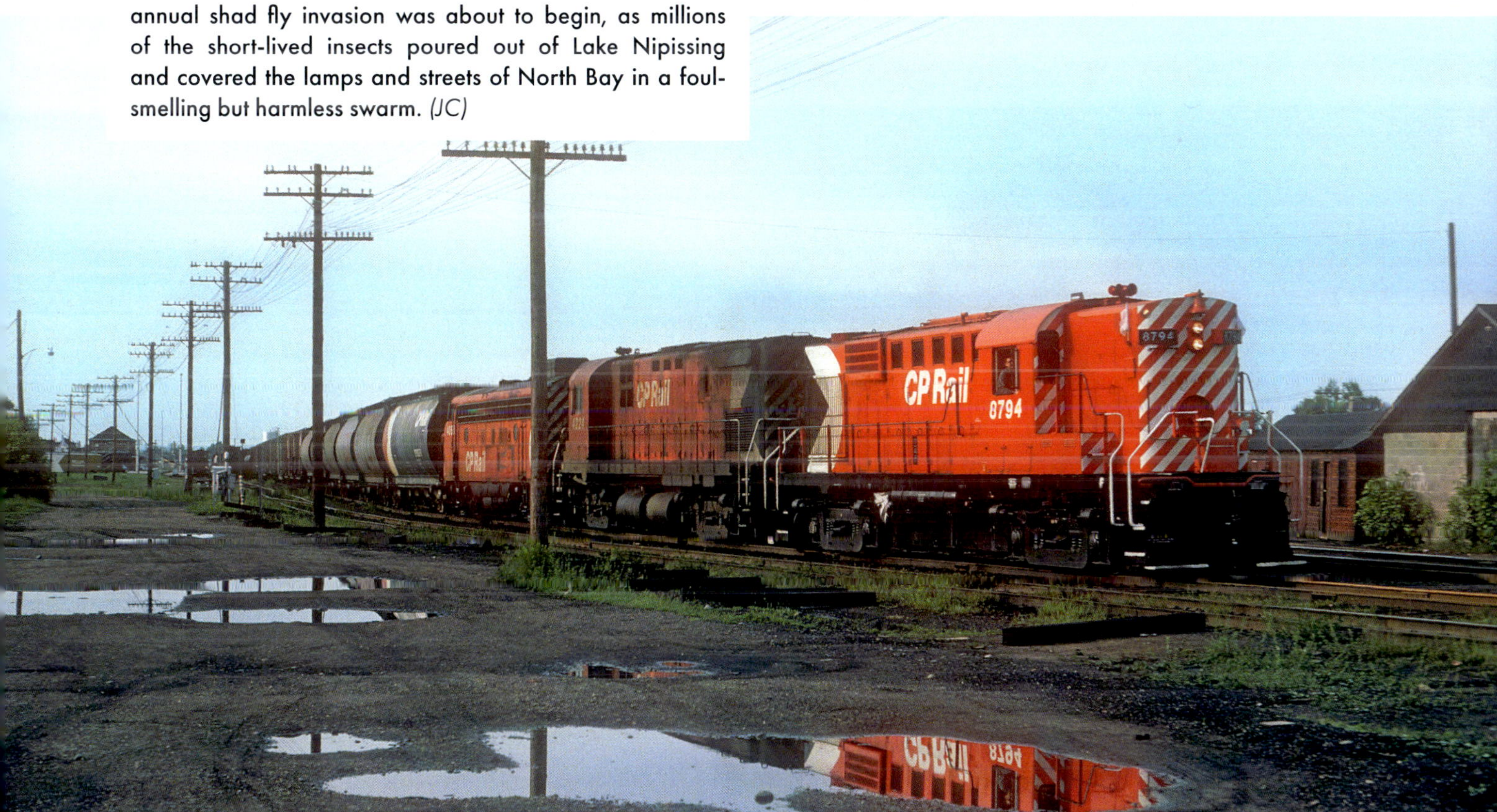

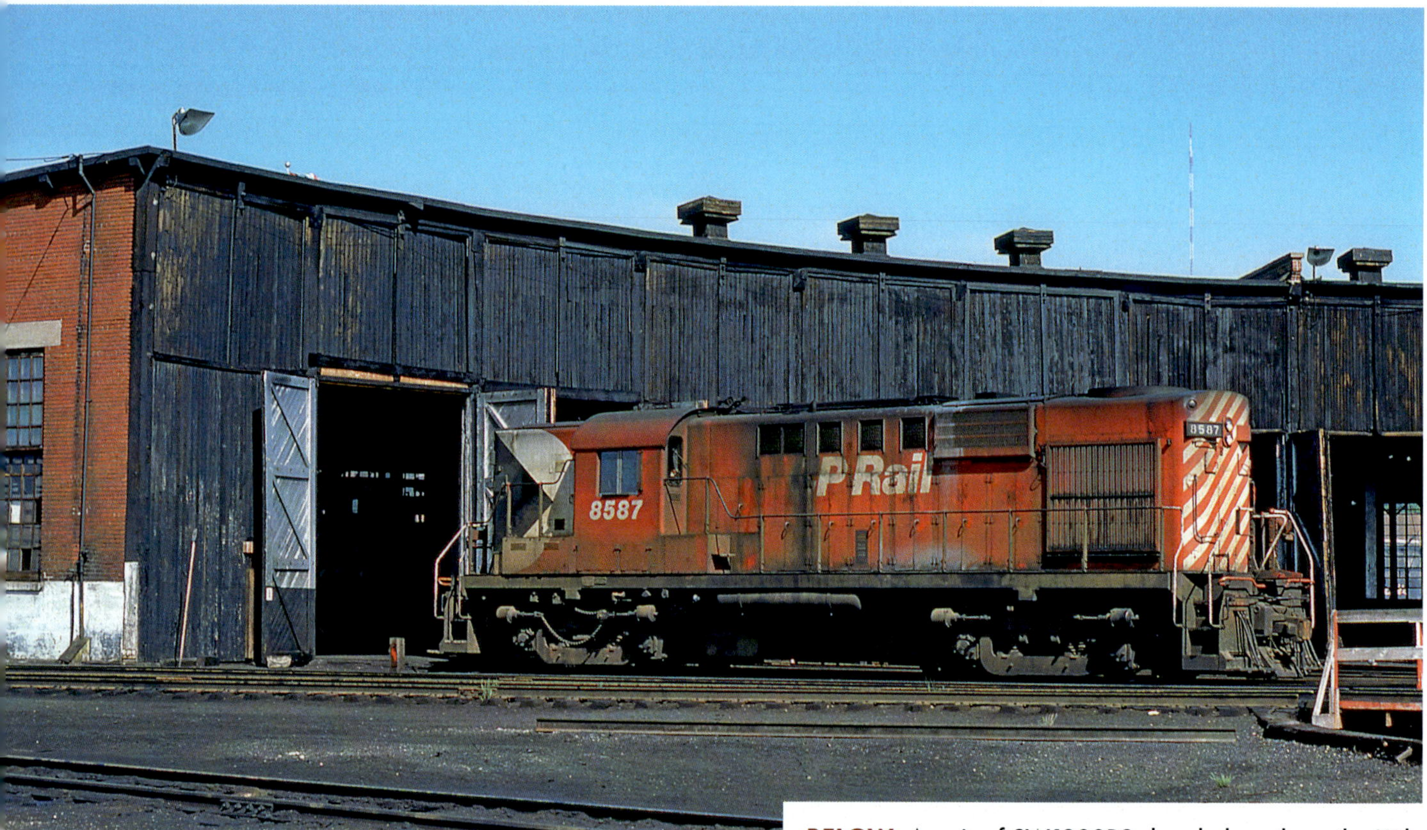

ABOVE: RS10 #8587 posed in front of the roundhouse at Sudbury, ON in June 1976. Structures like this helped provide indoor space for engines and people in the harsh winters of Canada. *(JC)*

BELOW: A pair of SW1200RSs headed south on the Little Current Sub at McKerron, ON in June 1976. These versatile units were the standard power on this line, operating in multiples as light road switchers. The CPR rostered 72 of the type, #8100-#8171. *(JC)*

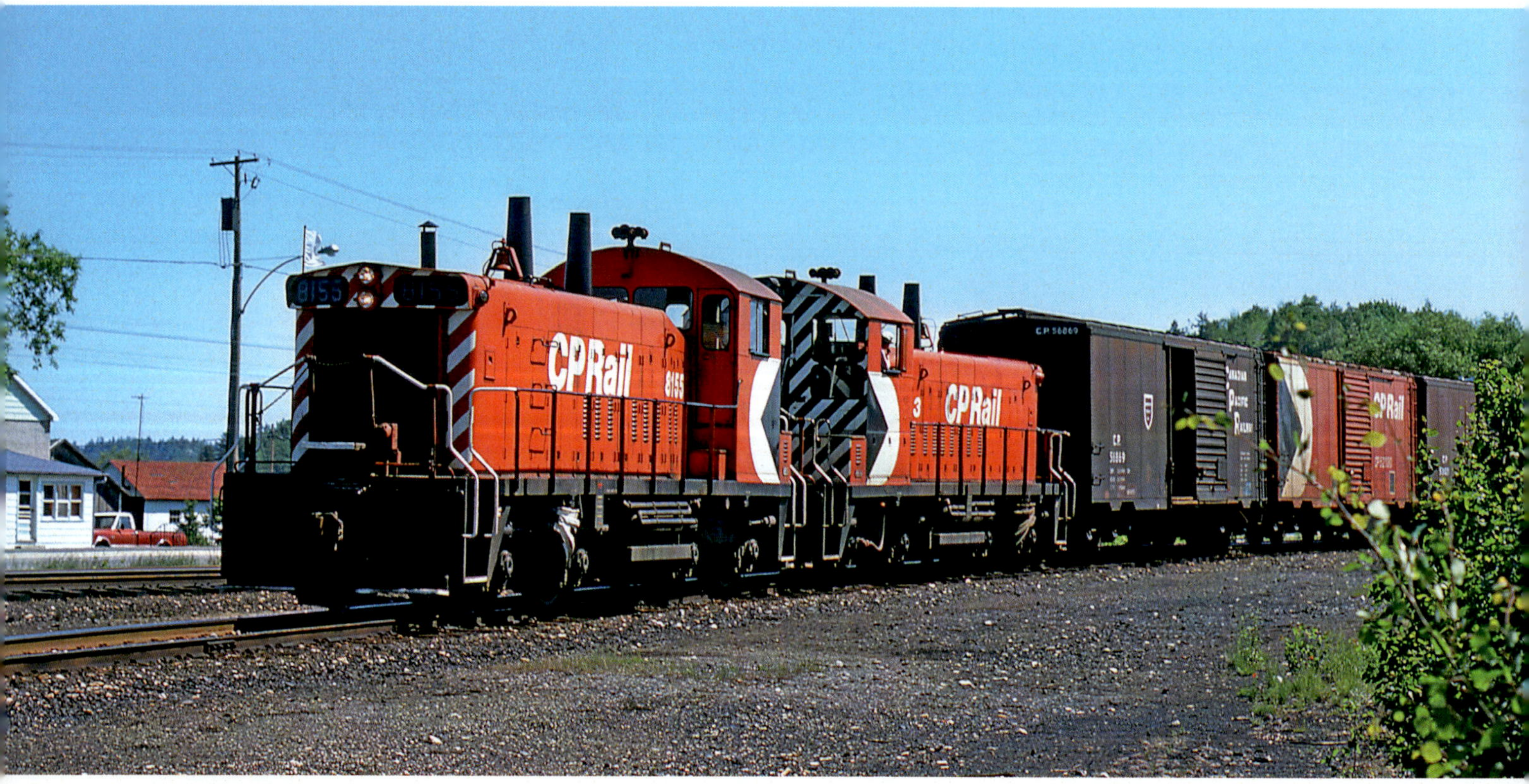

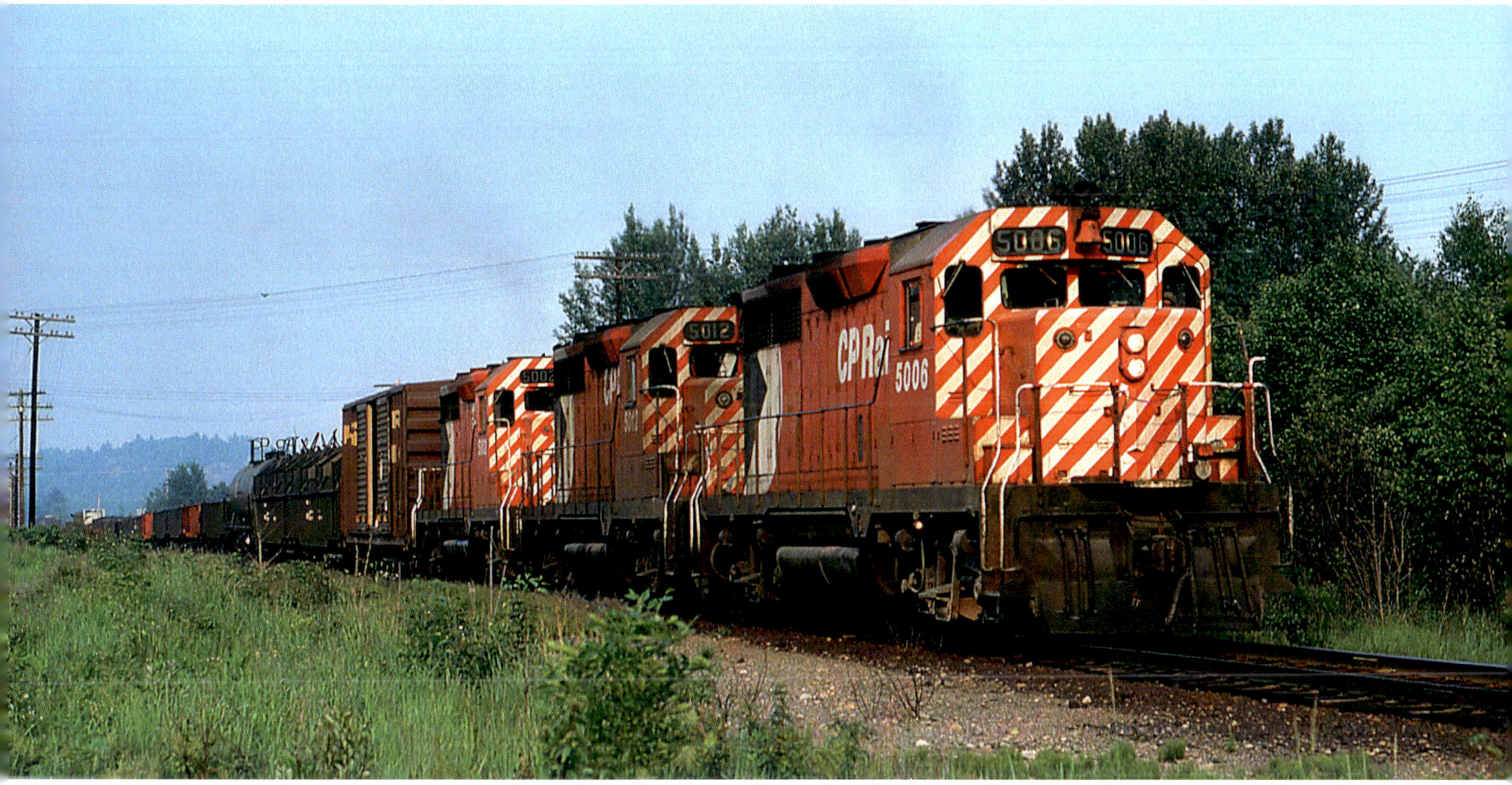

ABOVE: In June 1976, a trio of GP35s headed west at Spanish, ON on the Webbwood Sub headed for Sault Sainte Marie, ON. *(JC)*

BELOW: Three C424s brought in a train from Sudbury and were switching the yard at Sault Sainte Marie, ON on a June evening in 1976. *(JC)*

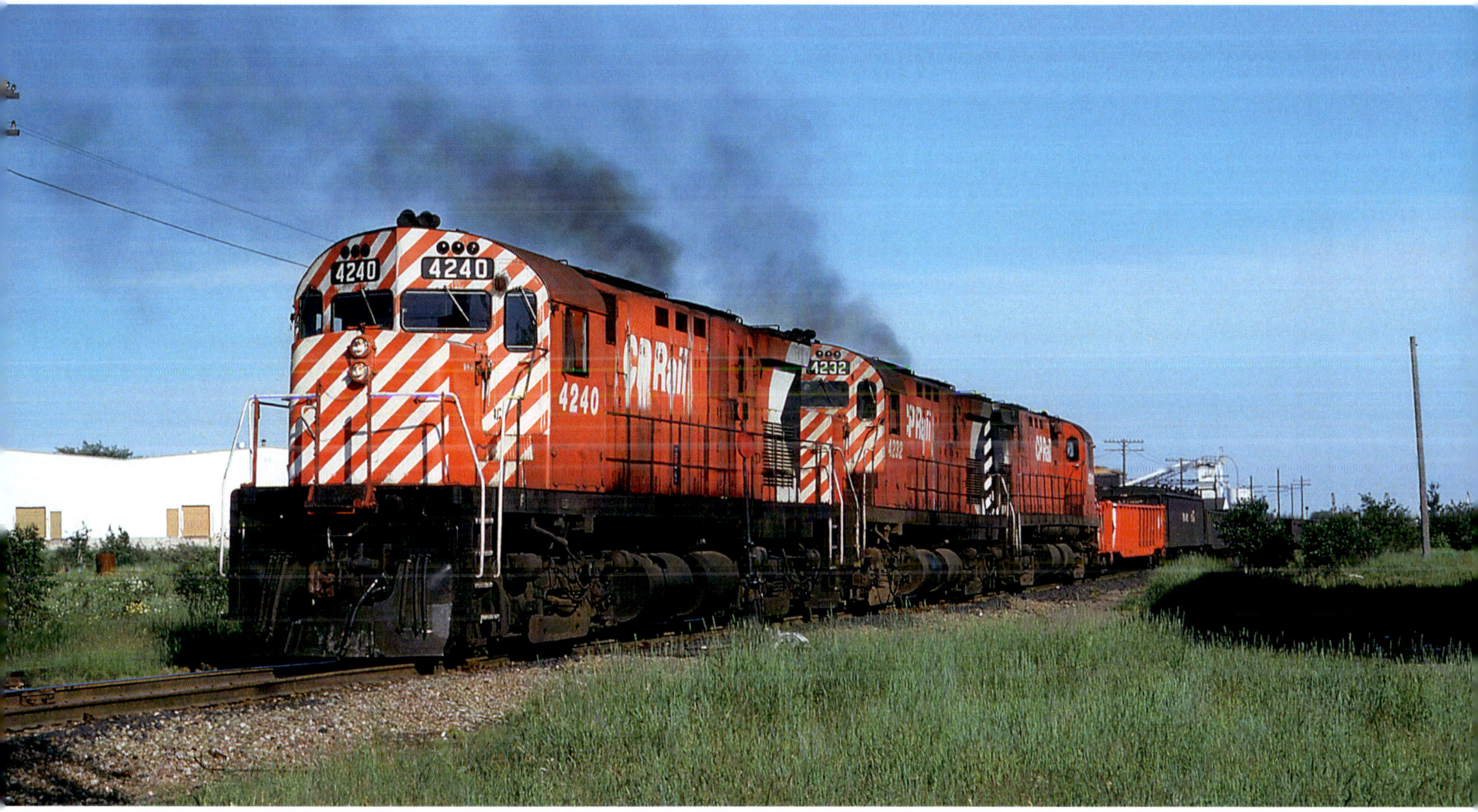

Algoma Central

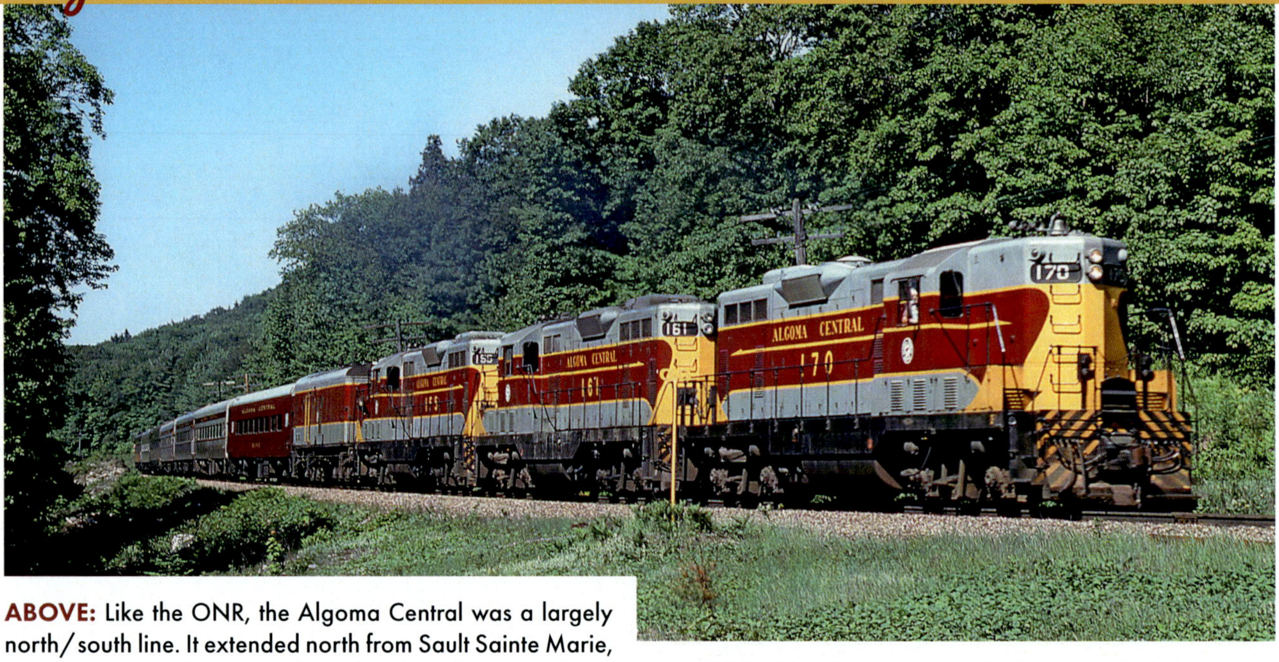

ABOVE: Like the ONR, the Algoma Central was a largely north/south line. It extended north from Sault Sainte Marie, ON to Hearst, ON. It ran through a largely unpopulated region, with a major purpose bringing iron ore from mines to the Algoma Steel mill at the Sault. It also had a robust passenger business. One of the most popular trains in Canada was Algoma Central's Agawa Canyon train. At Heyden, north of Sault Ste. Marie, the passenger train was returning in June 1976 to the Sault with three of the road's GP7s providing the power. The Algoma Central was the first Canadian railway to fully dieselize, in 1952, with GP7s such as these. For visitors from the U.S. Northeast, it was almost like seeing the Erie Lackawanna reborn, given the similarity of the paint schemes. *(JC)*

BELOW: The Algoma Central also provided passenger service along its entire line from Sault Ste. Marie to Hearst, ON, where it connected with the ONR and CNR. Heading south to the Soo in June 1976 was the "Hearst Train" behind two GP7s at Heyden, ON. *(JC)*

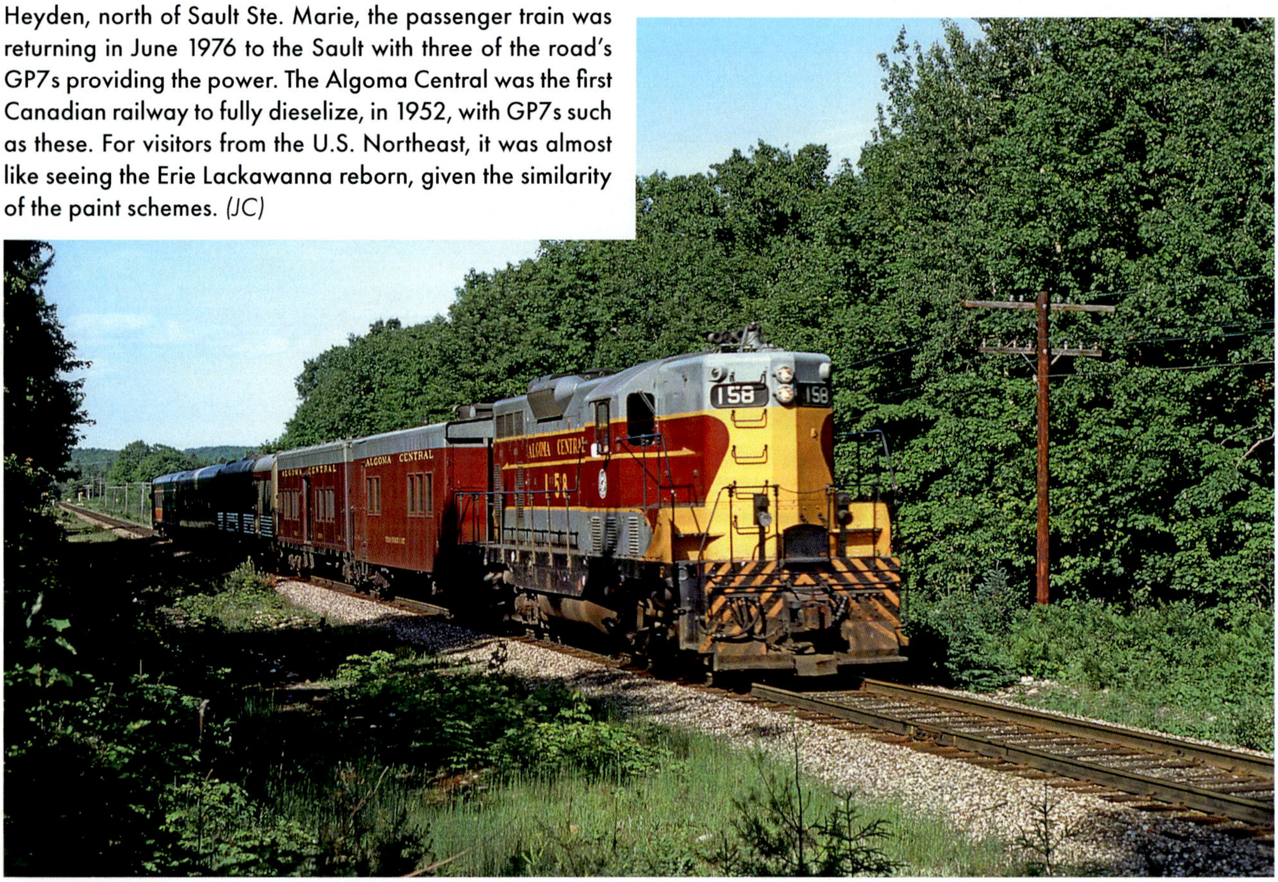

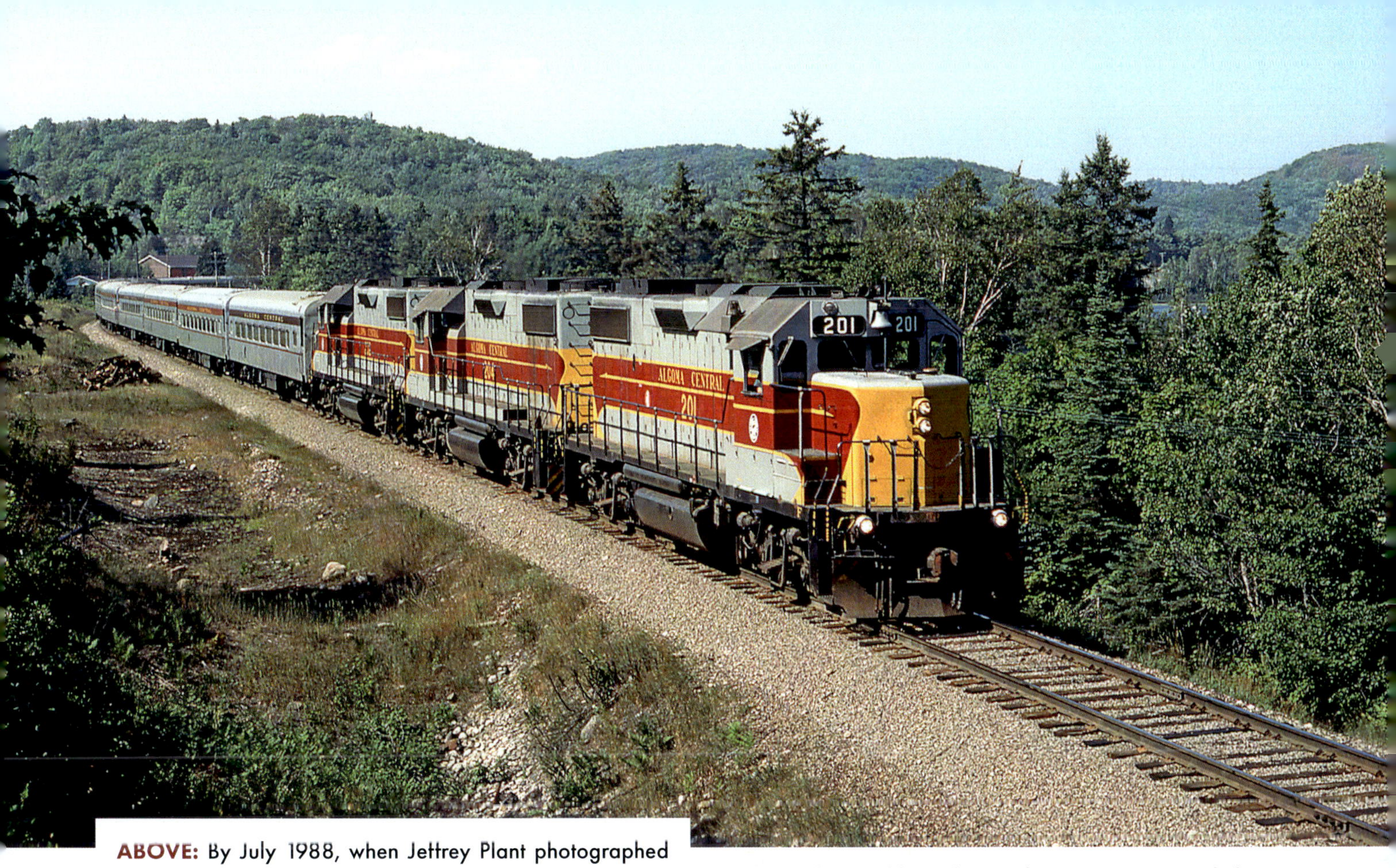

ABOVE: By July 1988, when Jeffrey Plant photographed the northbound Canyon train, the GP7s had been replaced by six GP38-2s, three of which powered the train on its trip north. *(JGP)*

BELOW: The southbound train from Hearst crossed the Bellevue Trestle a few miles north of Heyden, ON in July 1988. *(JGP)*

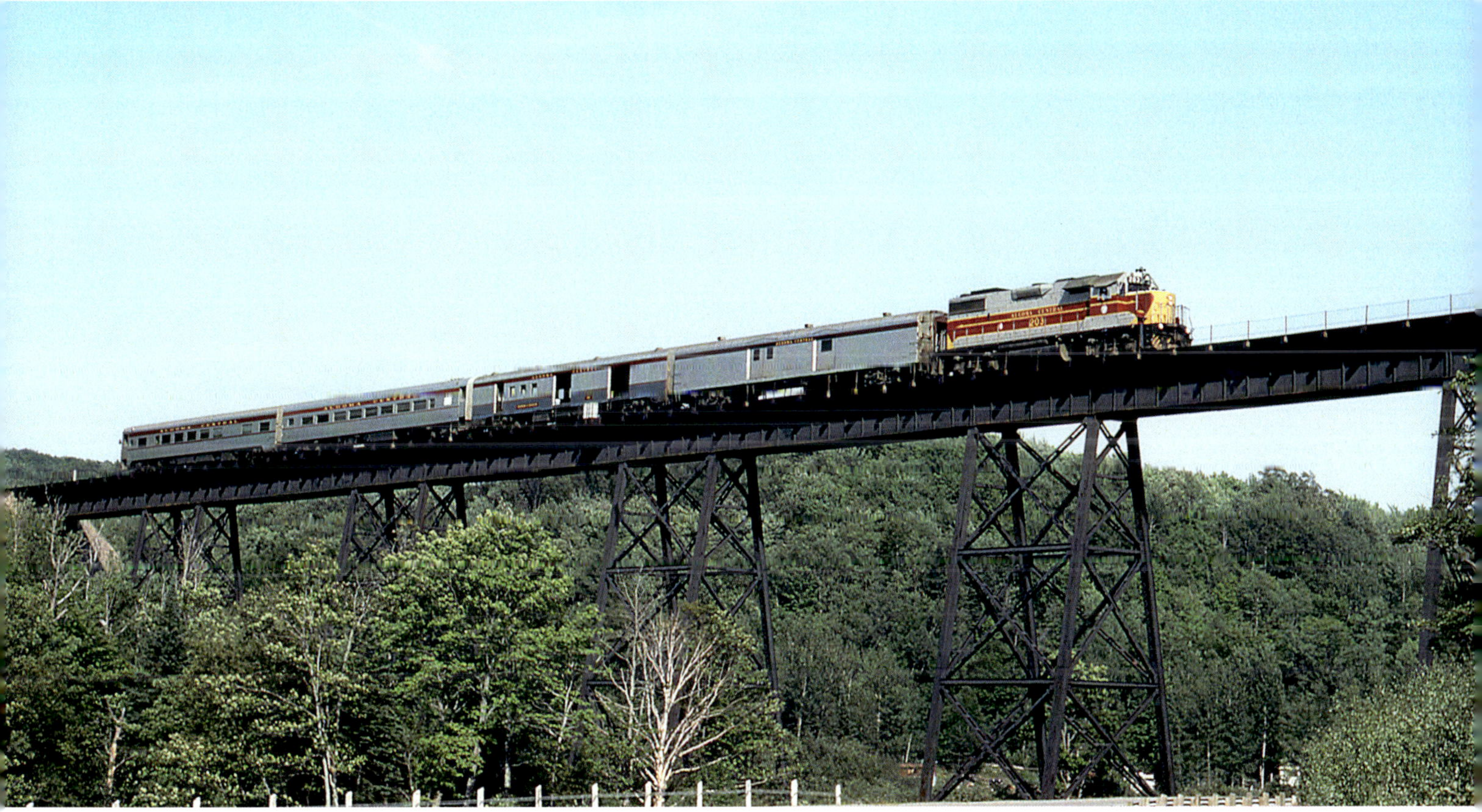

Riding the Algoma Central

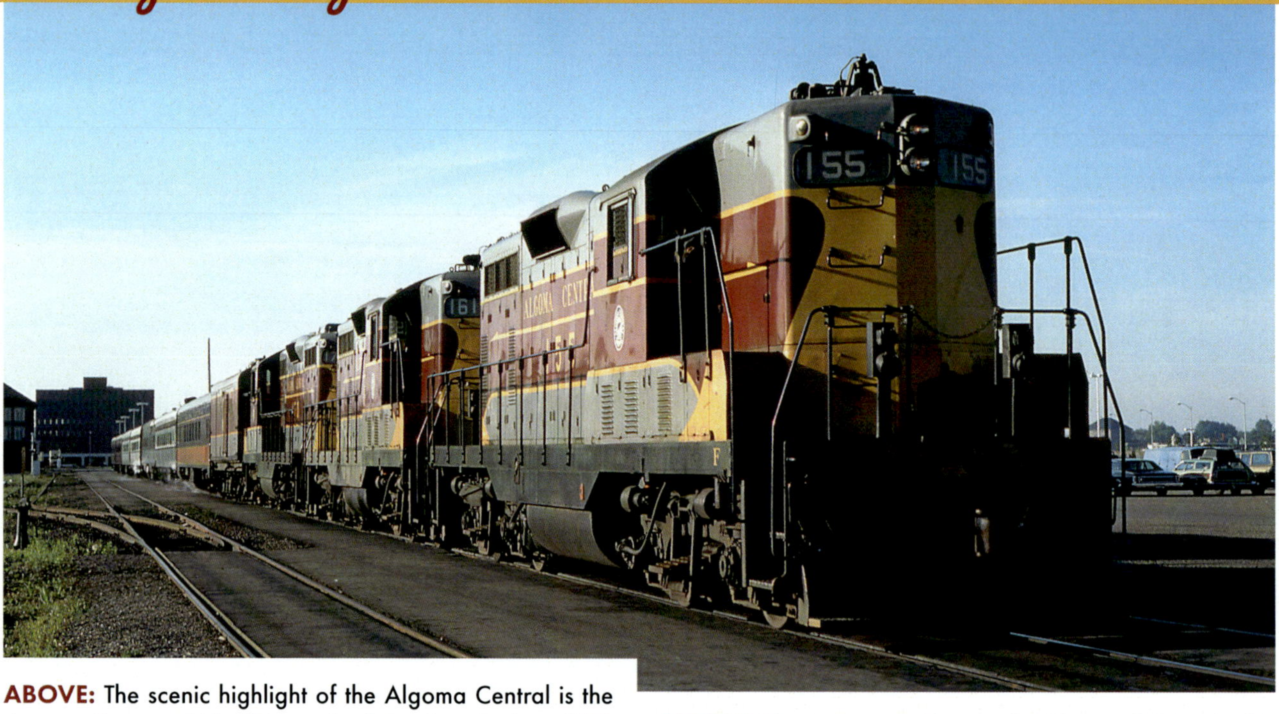

ABOVE: The scenic highlight of the Algoma Central is the Agawa Canyon, 114 miles north of the Soo. In June 1976 Jeffrey and Jeremy rode the train the 114 miles to the canyon. Prior to departure the long train waited for boarding at the station in Sault Sainte Marie, ON. *(JC)*

BELOW: The train passed over the Montreal River in this shot taken from the train. The train entered sparsely settled country soon after leaving the Sault. *(JC)*

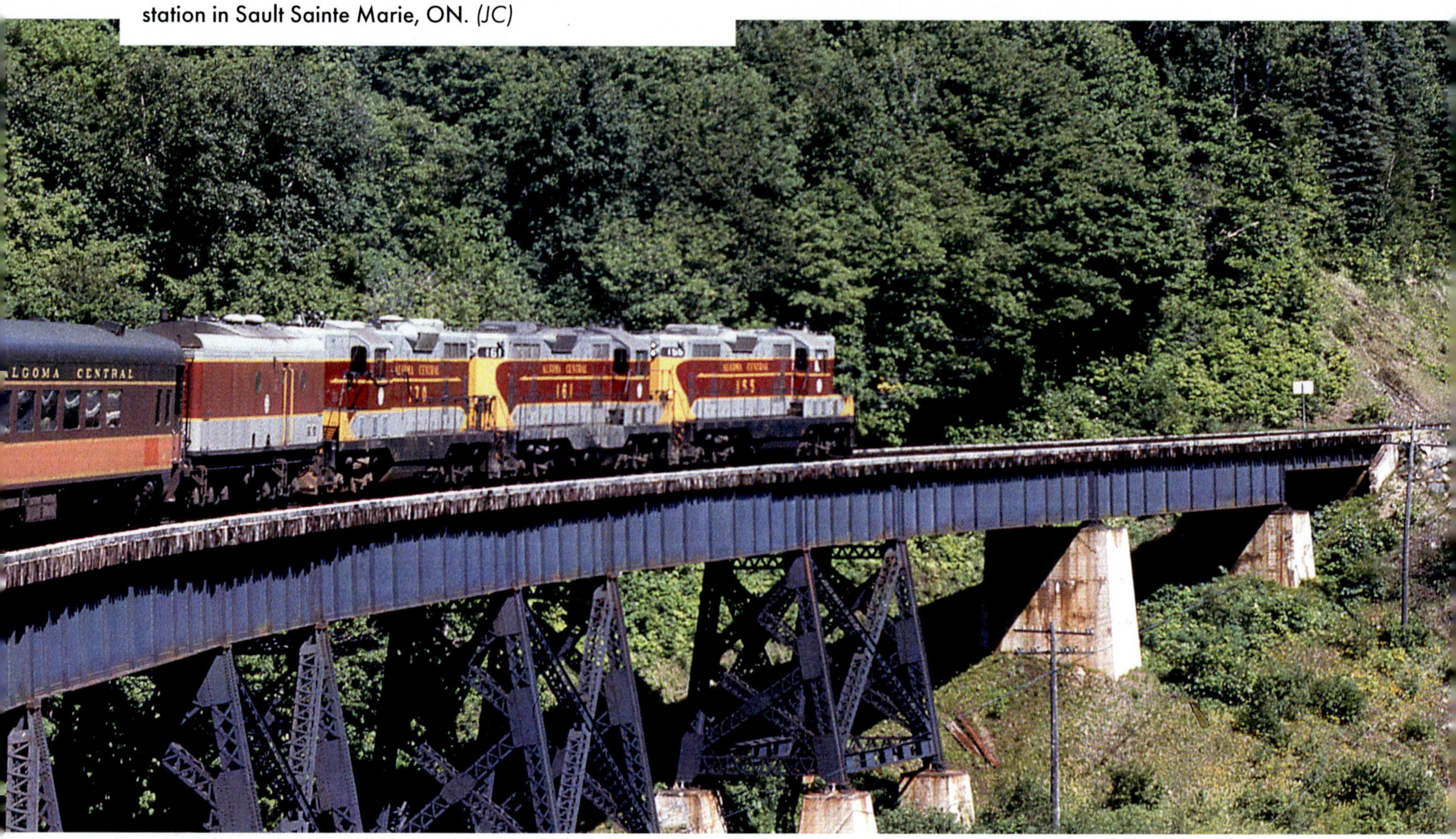

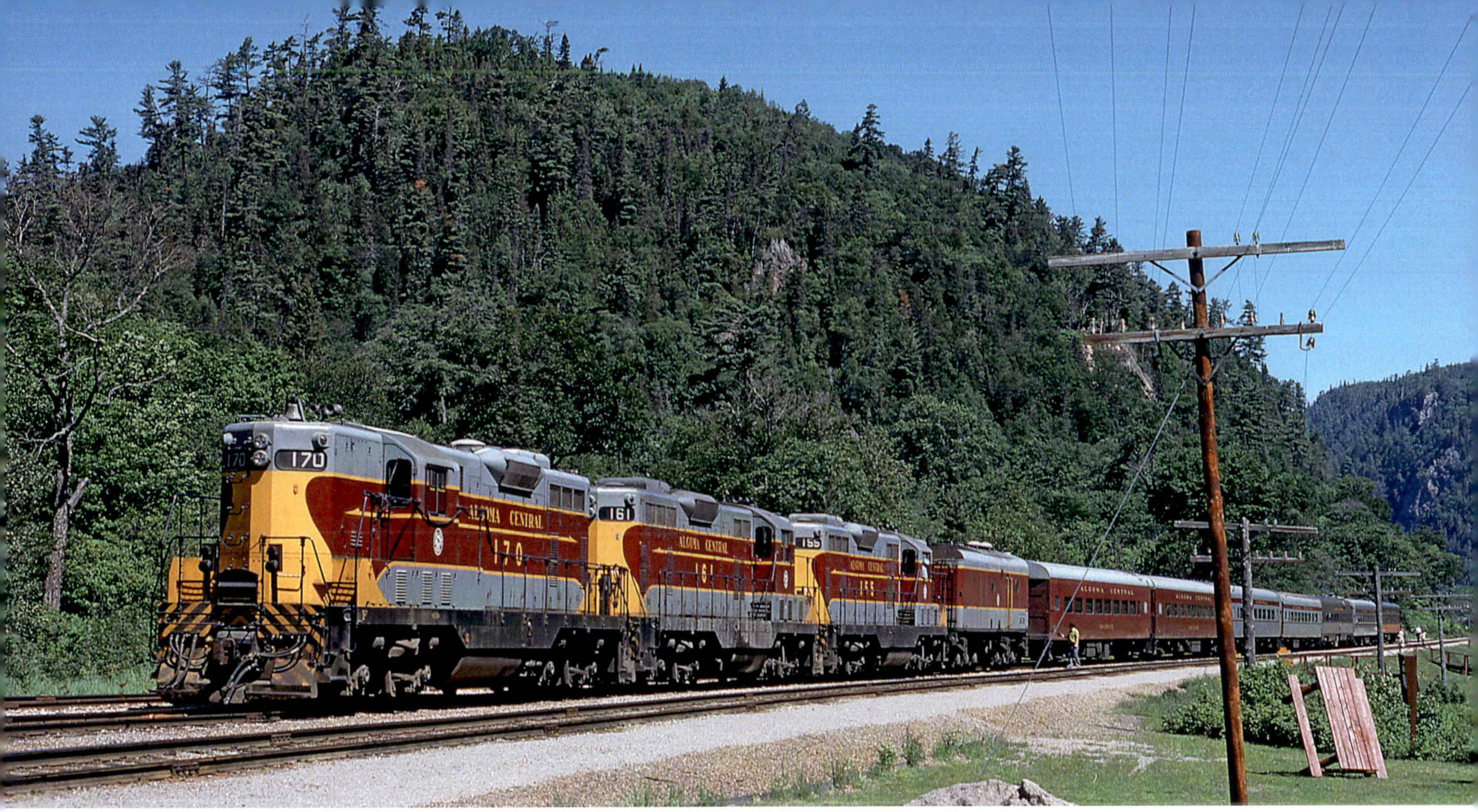

ABOVE: The train was parked at the canyon station to allow passengers to view the spectacular canyon of the Agawa River. We had hoped a freight might pass during the lengthy stay, but we were not in luck this day in June 1976. *(JC)*

RIGHT: Coming into Sault Sainte Marie the train passed the engine terminal of the Algoma, where three of the road's freight units were parked. The Algoma rostered three SD40s and six SD40-2s for freight service. *(JC)*

BELOW: Algoma Steel in Sault Sainte Marie, ON was switched by GE center cab switchers and a pair of Algoma Central SW8 switchers. Both types were working around Steelton Yard in June 1976. *(JC)*

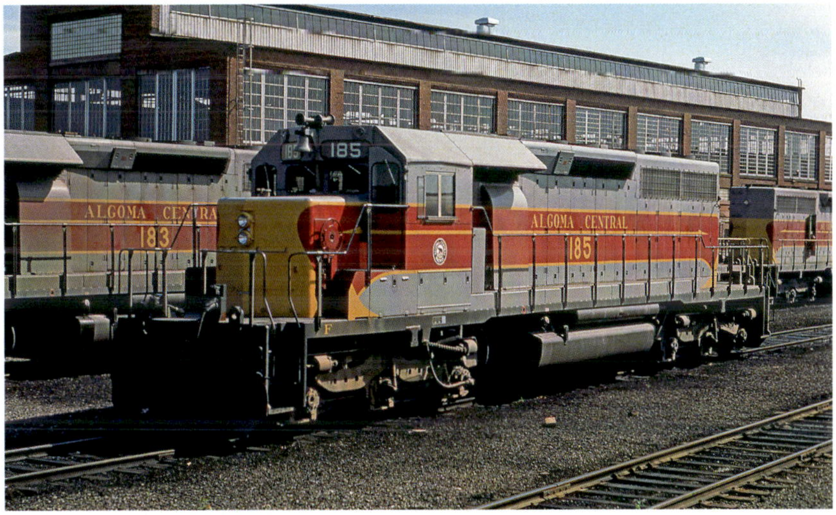

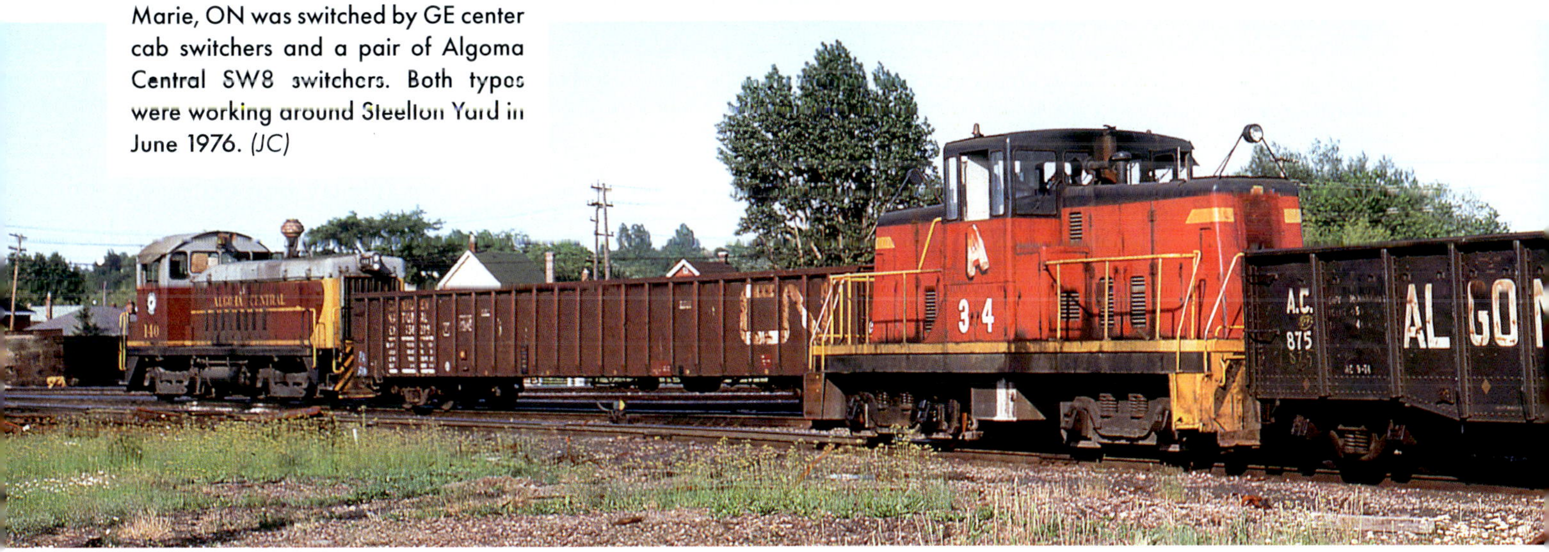

Northern End of the Algoma

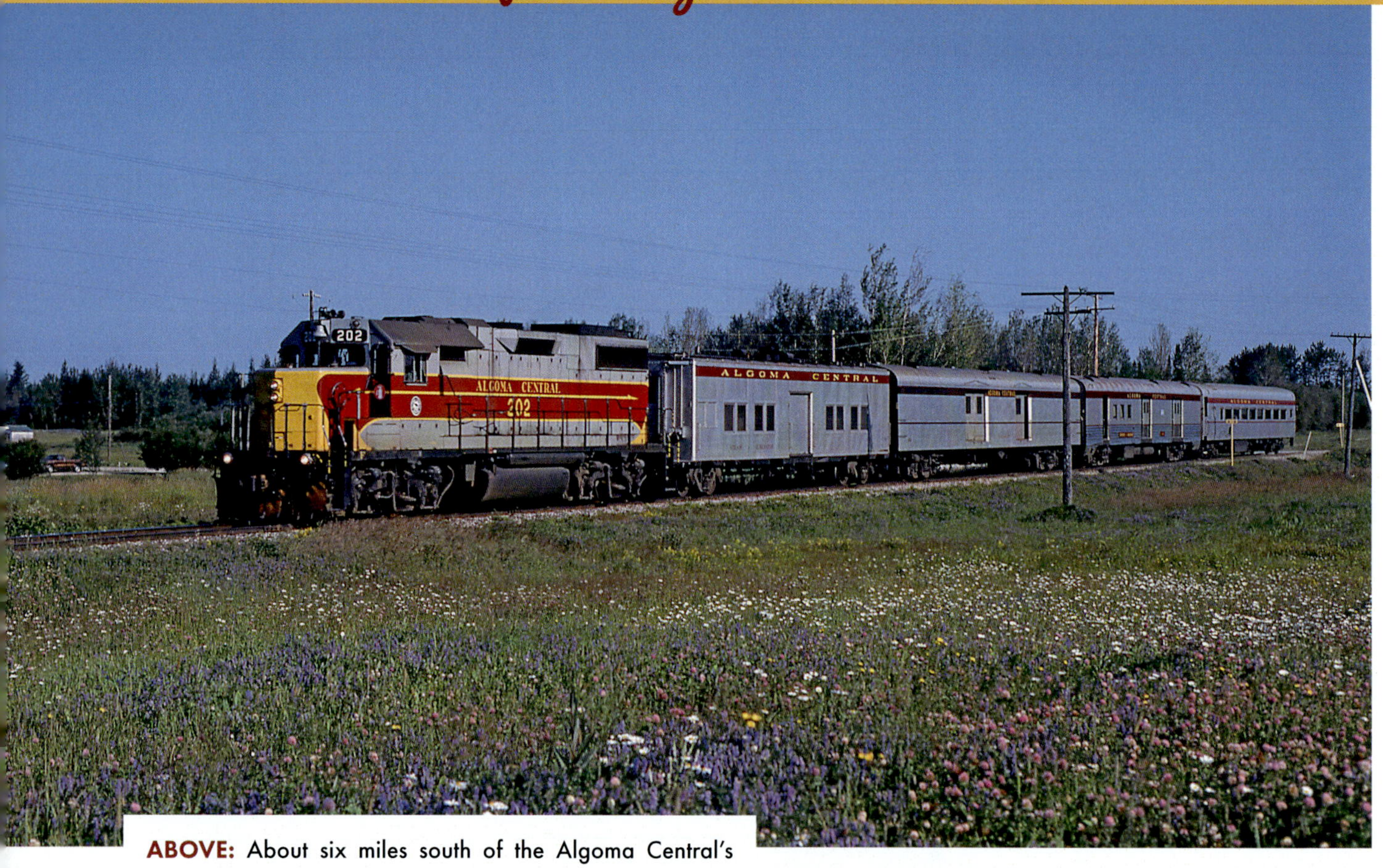

ABOVE: About six miles south of the Algoma Central's northern terminus of Hearst, the train from Hearst to the Sault was heading south past a spectacular display of wildflowers at Jogues, ON on July 26, 1990. Short as it may be, the northern summer in Ontario produces some fantastic flower displays such as this meadow in bloom. *(JGP)*

BELOW: Following the passenger train south, a short freight behind a pair of Geeps headed southward at Jogues on July 26, 1990. Thus ends our journey from the northern tip of Cape Breton Island to the vast Canadian Shield of northern Ontario. We hope you have enjoyed the trip! *(JGP)*

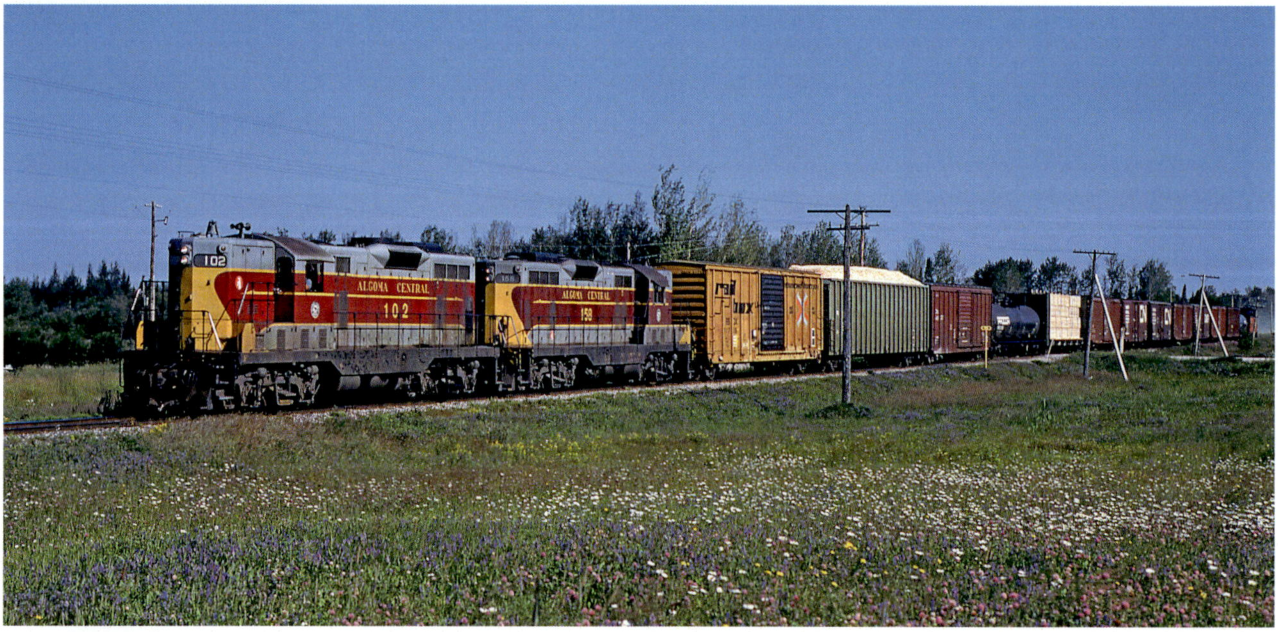